Ex Líbrís

Randy Manning

B212 © APCo

April '65

CONFEDERATE COVERT ACTION

IN THE AMERICAN CIVIL WAR

April '65

WILLIAM A. TIDWELL

THE KENT STATE UNIVERSITY PRESS

Kent, Ohio, & London, England

© 1995 by The Kent State University Press, Kent, Ohio 44242
ALL RIGHTS RESERVED
Library of Congress Catalog Card Number 94-33226
ISBN 0-87338-515-2
Manufactured in the United States of America

Library of Congress Cataloging-in-Publication Data

Tidwell, William A.
  April '65 : Confederate covert action in the American Civil War /
William A. Tidwell.
    p.   cm.
Includes bibliographical references and index.
ISBN 0-87338-515-2 (cloth : alk.) ∞
1. Southern States—History—Civil War, 1861–1865—Secret service.
2. United States—History—Civil War, 1861–1865—Secret service.
3. Lincoln, Abraham, 1809–1865—Assassination.   I. Title.
E608.T5   1995
973.7'86—dc20   94-33226
                                         CIP

British Library Cataloging-in-Publication data are available.

CONTENTS

PREFACE

In 1976 I bought a small piece of country property in Virginia in King George County, in the "Northern Neck" of Virginia between the Potomac and Rappahannock rivers. My sons and I discovered a very old log cabin on the property and decided to restore it. When we were fairly well along with our task, I told the local newspaper about our work, thinking that their readers might be interested in learning about this piece of local history. Indeed, the paper printed a nice story about the cabin, complete with pictures.

I later learned that in working on the story of the cabin the editor had gone to the County Clerk's office to find out who had owned the property. The ladies in the office reported that they had looked up the same property a short time before because "a couple of men were writing a book about John Wilkes Booth, and they said that he spent the night at that place."[1]

That got my attention. I knew that Booth had fled to Virginia after the assassination and that he had been killed in nearby Caroline County, but I knew almost nothing else about Booth or the assassination. My son, Robert, who at the time was working in his school library, brought home Stanley Kimmel's *The Mad Booths of Maryland* for me to read.[2] This book had a fairly detailed description of the main events of Booth's escape through southern Maryland and into Virginia, treating it as a picaresque journey from one adventure to another. To Kimmel, the escape was a series of unrelated coincidences; but to me,

having spent my entire adult life in association with the American intelligence community, it seemed clear that there were threads of
manipulation present. It appeared that Booth was being "handled" and
that there were players in the drama who did not appear on stage.

Determined to find out what really happened, I began to investigate
the literature bearing on Confederate secret service work and discovered that very little had been written on the subject. One of the
principal books was by John Bakeless, with whom I had served in G-2,
the Military Intelligence Division of the War Department General
Staff, during World War II.[3] I had long admired Bakeless for his discovery of Christopher Marlowe's association with the intelligence service
of Queen Elizabeth I, but I found that his book concentrated on the
more sensational exploits of pro-Confederate individuals who had been
caught during the war or who had written memoirs after the war.
Unfortunately, Bakeless did not try to analyze the concepts and organizations used by the Confederates in their secret service work. That
information is essential if one is to understand the objectives and the
strategy of a nation, but it is dry stuff to some readers, and Bakeless
may have been forced to write in a more sensational manner in order
to attract readers for a commercial publisher.

I concluded that there was very little available in the existing literature on clandestine activity in the Civil War and determined to work
instead with original source material. My first venture was to look into
the Records of the Governor of Virginia. I assumed that the records of
the Confederacy had already been worked over by other scholars but
that in all likelihood nobody would have thought to look for signs of
the Confederate secret service in the records of a state, even though it
would have been almost impossible to have conducted secret service
operations in Virginia without having some contact with the state
government. This inquiry turned out to be rewarding. There was
direct documentary evidence that at the beginning of the war Virginia
had secret service funds and was active in arranging for and organizing
clandestine courier services to bring information from Washington and
other points in the North across the Potomac. This clearly established
that leaders in the Confederacy were aware of secret service activity
and the body of lore accompanying it.

I located Virginia governor John Letcher's records of his dealings
with Richard Henry Thomas, also known as "Zarvona." Thomas, a

young gentleman from southern Maryland, was an admirer of the European republican revolutionaries and had served with Garibaldi in Italy. Early in the war, Thomas and a small group of daring souls took passage on a ship in the Chesapeake Bay. Once on the Bay, the group whipped out their pistols and commandeered the ship, taking it into Virginia waters. Thomas was captured in an attempt to repeat the maneuver on another ship, but his adventure focused my interest on the clandestine activities of southern Marylanders during the Civil War.[4]

Thomas had organized a unit known variously as the Maryland Guerrilla Zouaves, the Potomac Zouaves, or the Zarvona Zouaves and based it at Tappahannock on the Rappahannock River. What had happened to the unit after Zarvona's capture? Did it continue to act in clandestine crossborder operations? If it did continue to act in irregular warfare, might this give us another lead into the world of Confederate secret service?

The Zarvona Zouaves had been incorporated into the 47th Virginia Infantry Regiment and many of the men were later assigned to the Second Battalion of Arkansas Infantry, but I felt that there was a possibility that some had stayed with the 47th and decided to study that unit in greater detail.[5] Indeed, a most interesting pattern emerged from the National Archives records of the men of the 47th. A great many of them were captured at the Battle of Sayler's Creek on April 6, 1865, and only a few were left to take part in the general surrender at Appomattox three days later, which was more or less to be expected from what we knew of the unit's history. What was not expected was the large number of men of the 47th who were paroled at Ashland, Virginia, fifteen miles north of Richmond, between April 22 and May 3, 1865, long after the surrender of the Army of Northern Virginia. Furthermore, the soldiers came into Ashland in such numbers and during such a short period of time that they seemed to have been marched into the parole point in disciplined units.[6]

What could account for such a phenomenon? Here was the Army of Northern Virginia, hard-pressed for manpower and fighting with every available resource, yet this regiment went off on the Appomattox campaign without a large number of its men, including its commander and several other senior officers. There were stories of many desertions from the Army of Northern Virginia during its retreat from Richmond, but no reports of such a large proportion of any single unit to include its commander and senior officers. Allowing for a generous number of men to be at home on sick leave or recovering from wounds and for a number of deserters enroute to Appomattox, there were still too many men paroled at Ashland. What was the cause?

Perhaps there was something unique about the 47th Infantry. I decided to compare its records with those of other units recruited in the same area to see if they differed in any significant way. To my surprise, the records of the men of the 40th and 55th Virginia infantry regiments, also recruited in the Northern Neck of Virginia and along the Rappahannock, showed a similar pattern. In a comparison of the infantry regiment pattern with a cavalry regiment recruited in the same area, I discovered that the 9th Virginia Cavalry, although not involved at Sayler's Creek, had a similarly large number of men paroled at Ashland.

Further study showed that the infantry regiments belonged to Brig. Gen. Seth Maxwell Barton's brigade of Maj. Gen. George Washington Custis Lee's division, a recently organized unit made up of both regular and reserve units and assigned to a quiet sector of the Confederate defenses east of Richmond and north of the James River. Another regiment stationed nearby, the 30th Virginia, belonging to Brig. Gen. Montgomery Dent Corse's brigade, had been recruited in the Northern Neck as well and also had a large percentage of its men paroled at Ashland.

With sickness and desertion ruled out as reasonable explanations for the large number paroled at Ashland, the alternative was that the situation must have been created with Confederate official blessing. But why? What reason could be important enough to remove several hundred able-bodied soldiers and their officers from combat units when the Confederacy needed every man who could carry a weapon?

From the mass of information collected about the history of the regiments during the final months of the war, it appeared that these units were involved in a special operation with a secret mission. For some reason, the Confederacy wanted to deploy trained soldiers in the Northern Neck without the Union learning of the operation. The units could not be taken out of the line because Union intelligence would detect the change in the Confederate order of battle, but some of the men could be sent home on leave. Their homes would provide quarters and rations, and the soldiers could be organized into local units to provide increased security in the area. Thus the Confederacy could improve the defenses in the Northern Neck without changing the apparent condition of the defenses around Richmond.

I knew of no precedent for such a maneuver but found supporting evidence for it in the diary of Lt. Cornelius Hart Carlton of the 24th Virginia Cavalry. Carlton's unit, like Barton's brigade, was stationed north of the James River. On January 30, 1865, the unit was informed that half of the men were to be sent home on leave for twenty days, and then upon their return the other half would take leave. Carlton's home was south of the Rappahannock, but otherwise his situation was identical to that of the men from the infantry regiments.[7] Once at home, Carlton received orders from a headquarters at Taylorsville, just north of Ashland, to organize patrols along the Rappahannock. The patrols continued through February and March with no further orders to return to their unit and nothing said about leave for the other half of the regiment. Finally, at the end of March, the men received orders to return to their regiment.

I made a chronology of events on the battlefields around Richmond and Petersburg, the organization of Custis Lee's division and the history of its units, and the activities of John Wilkes Booth and his associates. I found no parallel activity in military operations to associate with the events involving the 47th Virginia and the other units of Barton's brigade, but there were very interesting parallels in the activities of Booth and his associates.

Booth was recruiting his team to capture President Lincoln at the same time that the Confederate War Department was sending a team to Washington to observe Lincoln's movements and the same time that Custis Lee was being promoted to major general. After Booth returned from conferring with Confederate agents in Canada, and after the team had reported on their observations of Lincoln, Custis Lee was ordered to form his division. While Booth was organizing the escape route for his action party with a captive Lincoln, the units of Lee's division were being moved into what was now a quiet sector of the Richmond defenses. While Booth was looking for an opportunity to capture Lincoln, the men from Barton's brigade and other units from the area north of Richmond were being sent home on leave. After Booth's attempt to capture Lincoln on March 17, 1865, had failed, the men on leave were ordered to return to their regiments, but the evacuation of Richmond on April 2–3, 1865, occurred before most of the men could return.

The more that activities in Virginia during the last six or seven months of the war were examined, the more they appeared to parallel activity by Booth and his associates. Particularly striking was unusual activity on the part of Col. John Singleton Mosby and his partisans in northern Virginia. On April 10, 1865, the day after Lee's surrender, a force of Mosby's partisans fought a skirmish with Union cavalry near Burke Station, Virginia, only fifteen miles outside Washington. In the course of the skirmish, four Confederates were captured. One of them was Thomas F. Harney, a former lieutenant in a Missouri regiment. Harney told his captors that he was from the Engineer Bureau and had just arrived to deliver "ordnance" to Mosby. In the aftermath of Lee's surrender, nobody paid much attention to Harney and his companions, and they disappeared in the general flow of Confederate prisoners. Nobody thought of Harney and the Mosby raid as having a possible connection to the assassination of Lincoln.

Several postwar memoirs, however, Union and Confederate, put a different appearance on Harney and his mission. From the memoirs of some of Mosby's partisans, it became clear that Harney was currently a sergeant in the Torpedo Bureau in Richmond, the organization charged with developing and employing explosives either as antipersonnel mines or as sabotage devices behind enemy lines. One veteran pointed out that Harney was essential to the mission of the Mosby unit and that his loss was "irreplaceable."[8]

General Edward H. Ripley, commander of a brigade of the Third Division of the Twenty-fourth Corps of the Union army and in charge of occupying Richmond, wrote that shortly after the occupation of Richmond, he had been warned by a soldier of the Confederate Torpedo Bureau that a party had been dispatched a few days earlier to attack the "head of government" in Washington.[9] It was clear from the description of Harney and his background that his mission was a highly unusual one. Mosby had been ordered a few days previously to move his operations south to the area west of Orange, Virginia; Harney's mission must have been of great importance to cause Mosby to send a special unit with an explosives expert so far out of his assigned territory and so close to superior Union forces near Washington.

The situation of the Confederacy at the end of March 1865 supported my conjecture. Booth had failed to capture Lincoln on March 17, and there was no assurance that another attempt would be any more successful than the first. The Confederate high command had plans to leave Richmond about the middle of April. Since Lee would be maneuvering between Grant in Virginia and Sherman in the Carolinas, anything that would disrupt coordination between Grant and Sherman would be of help to the Confederacy—blowing up the White House or the neighboring War Department would provide that disruption.[10]

Conjecture became more like a probability, however, when Joan Chaconas, a member of the Surratt Society of Clinton, Maryland, discovered the lost report of an interrogation of George Atzerodt, one of Booth's associates. In the interrogation, Atzerodt talked about alternatives to the abduction of Lincoln that Booth's group had discussed. In his rambling remarks, Atzerodt said that one of the alternatives was that of blowing up the White House. Earlier, Booth's groups had scouted the area between the White House and the War Department, and they knew the terrain and the environment. Black powder was plentiful in Washington, but what they lacked were fuses, detonators, and the expertise to set off a bomb. These were all things that Harney could provide.[11]

Accumulated evidence showed that the Confederacy had an active secret service and that it used this network to attack important targets in the enemy rear—not only bridges and warehouses, but people as well.

In the Kilpatrick/Dahlgren raid on Richmond in February and March 1864, Col. Ulric Dahlgren was killed; papers found on his body indicated the Union intention to kill or capture Confederate leaders and burn Richmond. The revelation of these papers caused a sensation and led many Confederates to urge retaliation in kind.[12] The Dahlgren papers could justify making Lincoln a target for clandestine action, and his capture also would have provided the Confederates with important political leverage. No official record that the Confederate government decided to exploit this course of action has been found, but there is considerable circumstantial evidence that they did just that.[13]

John Wilkes Booth clearly had the motivation and the ability to undertake a clandestine mission on behalf of the Confederacy. There is considerable testimony and other evidence that Booth organized a team for the specific purpose of capturing Lincoln and that he was in touch with known Confederate agents during that time. Aside from his political convictions, the only way that Booth could have benefited personally from such an activity would have been for him to receive the monetary reward that the Confederacy was offering to those who undertook destructive missions in the enemy rear.

Booth did actually try to capture Lincoln on March 17, 1865. After that failure, there was sound military reason not to try to organize another attempt. From the standpoint of the Confederacy's plans for the campaign of 1865, there was too little time left before the Confederate army would have to take to the field. There is ample evidence that the Confederates planned to evacuate Richmond about the middle of April, and once that happened it would be difficult to get Lincoln into safe Confederate territory, and there would not be time to exploit his capture in negotiations.

But after Booth's failed attempt at capture, the South had rational, tactical reasons to disrupt command and coordination in Washington. A Confederate explosives team was sent to Washington to blow up the White House, or a comparable target. It is clear that Booth decided to shoot Lincoln *after* the explosives team had been captured, and his plan to attack several government officials at the same hour is also well documented. The plan appears to have been designed to cause damage comparable to an explosion by attacking simultaneously the individuals that would have been caught by a successful attack on the White House.

In escaping Washington after the assassination, Booth took advantage of the arrangements previously made to help the Confederate operators escape after either the abduction of Lincoln or after the demolition of the White House. The well-documented activities of some of Colonel Mosby's partisans support that view.

ACKNOWLEDGMENTS

THIS BOOK has benefited from the ideas and assistance of many people. Family, friends, librarians, audiences, researchers, and the casual acquaintance have all made their contributions. Several people, however, have made unique contributions that deserve explicit reference.

James O. Hall pulled the first thread that unraveled the mystery of Confederate secret service gold: he discovered the forms signed by Jefferson Davis requesting secret service money from the Confederate treasury. In addition, he has been most generous in sharing material from his voluminous files and his prodigous memory. Michael P. Muzik of the National Archives pointed me to new information on personnel of the Confederate Torpedo Bureau and introduced me to the documents of B. J. Sage.

William Hanchett gave me excellent advice on the tone and organization of the manuscript and provided hard-to-find information on the Copperhead movement. John T. Hubbell demonstrated unusual editorial skills in helping to make the text tighter and better expressed, while at the same time keeping the author in good spirits. Virgil Carrington Jones and Erasmus Kloman of the Stuart-Mosby Society kindly reviewed the chapter on Colonel Mosby and gave me their comments. Harry Cummins drew the maps.

My son, Alan Caperton Tidwell, assisted me with essential research at the Library of Congress; Stephen D. Calhoun alerted me to the role played by his relative, Col. John H. Sothron, in St. Mary's County, Maryland; John Stanton provided unique information from the Northern Neck of Virginia; and John Brennan of the Surratt Society reviewed the manuscript in great detail to keep my facts in order and my language clear.

I thank them all.

Introduction

COME RETRIBUTION
REVISITED

W<small>HEN</small> John Wilkes Booth shot President Abraham Lincoln at Ford's Theater on April 14, 1865, the surrender of the main Confederate army under Gen. Robert E. Lee had taken place a full five days earlier. To most people the Civil War appeared to be at an end. In the euphoria of victory, the death of the president seemed pointless and therefore doubly tragic.

Nearly everybody, North or South, had lost friends or relatives in the war. And now Lincoln had become the final and greatest victim. For a population raised on sermons based on Old Testament parables, the situation reeked of mystical religious significance. There was an almost frantic need to explain the act in a way that could be accepted by people who believed in the triumph of righteousness. If Lincoln died in a just cause, then those who killed him must be evil. To many, the search for and prosecution of those believed to be responsible for the assassination became a crusade.

It is well known among historians that the Federal government felt it had good reason to believe that Booth had been sponsored by the Confederates and that the Confederate apparatus in Canada, in particular, had been involved in the assassination. The Federal authorities also learned shortly after the assassination that Booth and his associates had been working for some months on a plan to capture Lincoln.

In spite of the considerable volume of evidence available concerning this abduction plan, Secretary of War Edwin M. Stanton and Judge

FINALE of the "JEFF DAVIS DIE-NASTY."
"Last Scene of all, that ends this strange eventful History."

This 1865 cartoon drawn by "Burgoo Zac" illustrates the mood of many Northerners after Lincoln's assassination. Picking up on a Union soldiers' song, this shows Jefferson Davis hanging from a "sour apple tree." Courtesy of the Library of Congress.

Advocate General Joseph Holt decided not to prove that the abduction was a Confederate operation but instead to prove that the Confederates had planned to assassinate Lincoln. Naturally, some of the evidence concerning the abduction effort could be interpreted as supporting an assassination plot, but Stanton and Holt thought that they had even better evidence. Union detectives had found two witnesses who would testify concerning the involvement of Confederate representatives in Canada in plans leading to the assassination: Dr. James B. Merritt and Charles A. Dunham, alias Sandford Conover. Both men had spent some time in Canada and had been in contact with a number of the Confederates there, and both were prepared to swear that they had heard key Confederates in Canada discuss the possible assassination of Lincoln.

Booth was killed on April 26, 1865, but a fairly large number of people suspected of being involved in Booth's organization were arrested and interrogated. Finally, eight people were chosen to stand trial for complicity in the assassination. Their trial, beginning on May 13, 1865, became the forum in which the evidence of Confederate complicity in the assassination was presented.

There was only one problem with Merritt and Dunham as witnesses. They were liars. And the Confederates who remained in Canada after the end of the war saw to it that the perjury committed by Merritt and Dunham was exposed[1]—which did not destroy the case against the eight individuals on trial but did discredit the attempt to tie the Confederates directly to the assassination. Thus, the Federal focus on the assassination left the abduction plan and other Confederate clandestine activity incompletely explored—and even largely forgotten—and the question of why Booth shot Lincoln has remained unanswered.[2]

In the aftermath of the Civil War, it became convenient to explain the assassination as the work of a crazed actor who was solely responsible for recruiting the eight individuals who were brought to trial. There were many reasons for people to be dissatisfied with this simple theory; and as more and more was learned about the workings of the human mind, the explanation became even more unsatisfactory. Booth had not demonstrated the behavior patterns that could be reliably associated with a pathological murderer. So the question remained: "Why *did* Booth shoot Lincoln?"

Southern partisans developed a rationale to support their contention that the Confederate government had played no part in the assassination. According to their version of history, the surrender of Lee's army on April 9, 1865, marked the true end of the Civil War. With the war over, the Confederacy would have had no reason to attack Lincoln; on the contrary, as a defeated region, they had every reason to expect better treatment from Lincoln than from the radical abolitionists in Congress. It was said that at that point in history Lincoln was "the South's best friend."

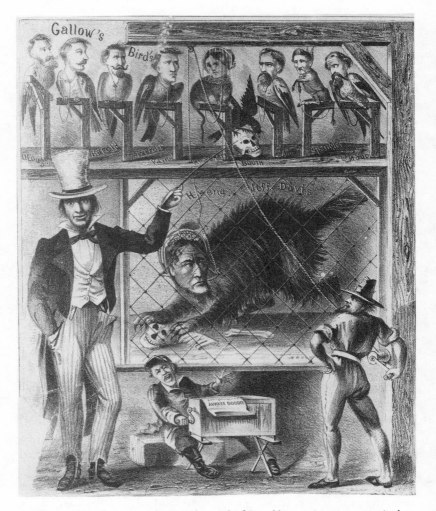

This unsigned cartoon depicts the trial of Booth's associates as a carnival act accompanied by an organ grinder. The hanging of the accused is a sideshow for the main attraction—the entrapment of Jefferson Davis. Courtesy of the Library of Congress.

This basic theme was reinforced by the interpretation of the Civil War as a romantic war of a chivalrous, rural South versus a materialistic, industrial North. The concept of a romantic war also generated a series of what Communists have called "personality cults." Jefferson

Davis, Robert E. Lee, "Jeb" Stuart, "Stonewall" Jackson, and John Singleton Mosby were all adopted by groups of admirers who believed ardently that their heroes could not have been involved in deception or covert operations.

The Southern rationale was widely repeated over many years. In 1915 it was even made into a landmark movie, D. W. Griffith's *The Birth of a Nation*, which showed the surrendered Confederate hero, who had returned to his home at the end of the war, plowing his farm before the assassination. Though Lee surrendered on April 9 and his men were not paroled until April 12, the movie would have its viewers believe that Confederate soldiers could have resumed their peacetime pursuits by the time of the assassination on April 14.

Griffith's movie was the respectable explanation of the Southern position. But there were other, less credible versions. One story had the incompetent Yankees shooting the wrong man and Booth escaping to live for many years in unreconstructed disdain. This version was even documented in the carnivals by the display of the mummified corpse of an obscure drifter, David E. George, touted as the remains of the "real" uncaptured John Wilkes Booth.[3]

The lack of a believable explanation of the assassination has attracted its share of unscrupulous hacks and forgers, but the greatest damage to the truth was done in 1937 by a successful Chicago businessman named Otto Eisenschiml. In that year his book, *Why Was Lincoln Murdered?*,[4] popularized the thesis that Lincoln was killed as the result of a secret plot involving Secretary of War Edwin M. Stanton and a group of Northern industrialists. Eisenschiml had done a substantial amount of research into the events surrounding the assassination—more than most of the professional historians who should have provided an informed evaluation of his work—and his expository technique was to pose leading questions that could be answered best by the conclusions he provided. Though his argument could not stand up to careful criticism, he attempted to answer a question that held a great deal of interest: his answer was sensational, and before the professional historians could challenge him, his thesis had captured the imagination of the public.

The net effect of his argument was to support the Confederate position that the South had nothing to do with the assassination and, at the same time, to blacken the reputation of Stanton, the man who had actually taken the lead in 1865 to search out the truth. Responsible historians saw through the "Stanton theory" readily enough, but it put a pall over the history of the assassination that lasted for nearly fifty years. As recently as 1971, Allan Nevins described the current view of the assassination:

> the consensus of serious historians is that the basic facts of the assassination are clear. Abraham Lincoln was shot in Ford's Theater in Washington shortly after 10 P.M., April 14, 1865, by the actor John Wilkes Booth. William H. Seward was viciously assaulted. It is known that Booth had collaborators, but that perhaps the role of one or two accused associates has been exaggerated, and that at least Mrs. Surratt and Dr. Mudd were falsely punished. It is generally agreed today that there was no plot made by President Jefferson Davis or anyone else in high position in the Confederacy to assassinate Lincoln, and that Booth and his array of miscreants acted on their own initiative. Most students agree that it was John Wilkes Booth who was killed in the Garrett barn in Virginia. Nothing in the flood of words written on the assassination seems really to contradict these general conclusions.[5]

Nevins recognized that the Stanton theory was false, but he accepted many of the other myths, and his summary of the conventional belief of the period contained both factual errors and a gross oversimplification of the events leading to the assassination.

Some good work was done in researching specific problems of Civil War history that might have had some bearing on the assassination and in organizing and publishing important source material, but it was not until the 1980s that the professional historians began to exert serious effort to understand the assassination. One such effort was Thomas Turner's book *Beware the People Weeping* and another was William Hanchett's *The Lincoln Murder Conspiracies*.[6]

Hanchett's book, in particular, served an essential purpose. It addressed systematically all of the previously advanced theories concerning the causes of the assassination and exposed the defects in fact and logic that made each of them untenable. With regard to the Stanton theory Hanchett said, "When scrutinized point by point, Eisenschiml's grand conspiracy thus falls apart, and one wonders how Eisenschiml, professing scientific objectivity all the while, could present it as a work of honest scholarship."[7] Hanchett's work did not drive the Stanton theory entirely from the field of popular imagination, but it did eliminate any scholarly underpinning that might have remained. It was an important stepping stone in the search for an explanation of the assassination.

The publication of *Come Retribution* in 1988 represented an effort to provide an explanation of the assassination supported by documentation and to avoid the errors in logic that Hanchett had found in previous theories.[8] It presented evidence, much of it circumstantial, that permitted a reconstruction of the probable course of a Confederate operation to take Abraham Lincoln hostage.

Come Retribution recounted how, after several tentative starts, the Confederates settled on the man to carry out the actual capture: John Wilkes Booth, an intelligent and ardently pro-Southern actor. With the help of other Confederate agents, Booth organized an action team and an escape route through southern Maryland. In the meantime, the Confederate army organized the Virginia side of the Potomac River as the reception area for the hostage and his captors.

While these clandestine operations were going on, Jefferson Davis and Robert E. Lee decided on a course of action for the spring campaign of 1865. They would evacuate Richmond and Petersburg, leaving Gen. Ulysses S. Grant's army to cope with the mines and other barriers of Confederate defenses. With a day or two head start, Lee was sure that he could outrun Grant, who would have to move away from his supply base and follow along roads torn up by the retreating Southerners. Lee would unite with Gen. Joseph E. Johnston in North Carolina, where large quantities of Confederate supplies were in place. Once there, with the combined resources of his army and troops in North Carolina, Lee could defeat Gen. William T. Sherman and then turn with reinforced strength to face Grant.

The timing of the Confederate evacuation of Richmond was critical. If Lee waited too long, the roads would dry out from the winter rains, and Grant would be able to get around Lee's southern flank and block his retreat. Judging from the patterns of rainfall and freezing and thawing in the area, the latest feasible date for the planned evacuation would have been the middle of April 1865.

Booth failed his attempt to capture Lincoln on March 17, 1865, and by that time it was too late to try again. But there was another way in which Booth's organization could be exploited. The Confederates decided that it would damage coordination between Grant and Sherman

S	M	T	W	T	F	S
						1 Benjamin draws $150 in gold
2 CSA leaves Richmond	3 Union enters Richmond	4 Lincoln visits Richmond	5	6	7	8
9 Lee surrenders	10 Skirmish at Burke, Virginia	11	12	13	14 Lincoln and Seward attacked	15 Skirmish in St. Mary's County, M
16 Booth goes in hiding at Cox plantation	17	18	19	20	21 Mosby releases troops—retains 50	22
23 Booth reaches Virginia	24	25	26 Booth killed—Mosby soldiers paroled at Ashland	27	28 Mosby near Richmond	29
30						

April 1865

and enhance Lee's chance of success if the Union war command in Washington could be disorganized. They sent an explosives expert, Thomas F. Harney, with fuses and detonators to Col. John Singleton Mosby, the Confederate partisan leader behind Union lines in northern Virginia, in order that Mosby might infiltrate Harney and a hand-picked team into Washington to blow up the White House.

Mosby sent a substantial force with Harney to the outskirts of Washington to create a diversion and leave Harney and his team behind to infiltrate Washington. Unaware that Lee had been forced to surrender at Appomattox on April 9, Mosby's force ran into Union cavalry near Burke, Virginia, on April 10 and fought a brief skirmish. Harney was captured and put into the Old Capitol Prison in Washington on April 12, 1865. Booth, without the skills to blow up the White House, and understanding that the Confederates wanted to attack the Union high command about the middle of April, did not realize that Lee's surrender made further action useless. He decided to substitute direct attack for the explosion that could not be created without Harney's help.

Booth decided that the damage caused by blowing up the White House during a meeting of senior officials could be approximated by attacking simultaneously a number of key persons. On his list were the president, vice president, and secretary of state. There may have been others such as Secretary of War Stanton, but the evidence concerning the selection of these three is firm.

As it developed, at about ten o'clock on the evening of April 14, 1865, Booth attacked Lincoln at Ford's Theater at the same time as a member of his action team attacked Secretary of State Seward at his home around the corner from Stanton's, wounding him so severely that he was sure that he had killed the secretary. Another member of the team was supposed to attack Vice President Johnson at the same time but lost his nerve and got drunk instead.

Frank Abial Flower, who published a biography of Stanton in 1905 and, consequently, had access to the Stanton papers and conducted many interviews with people who knew the secretary, reported that, according to a neighbor, a man had approached the Stanton home at ten o'clock on the night of April 14 and tried to ring the doorbell. The bell wire was broken, however, and the man could not attract the attention of anybody in the house. (Stanton said that the wire had not been repaired because the repair man had prior commitments.) Before the man could take any other action, several people came to tell Stanton that the secretary of state had been attacked, and the mysterious visitor disappeared.

According to Flower, Stanton was convinced that the visitor had intended to kill him. Several witnesses at the trial of Booth's associates testified that a person identified as Booth's associate, Michael O'Laughlin, had visited Stanton's house on the night of April 13 and acted in a suspicious manner, as if he were familiarizing himself with the layout of the house. Several defense witnesses, however, swore that O'Laughlin was with them and could not have been at the Stanton house. The story sounds reasonable, given the logic that Booth used in picking targets, and it is possible that some as-yet-unidentified member of Booth's group was the person actually involved.[9]

The human targets were well chosen, for successful attacks would have left the Union government in disarray. Under the law of executive succession in force at that time, in the absence of a president and a vice president, the secretary of state would have been required to call for

This drawing, which was prepared for *Frank Leslie's Chimney Corner* in anticipation of a reception that never took place, shows President and Mrs. Lincoln greeting General and Mrs. Ulysses S. Grant. Standing near Lincoln are Vice President Andrew Johnson, Secretary of War Edwin Stanton, and (*extreme right*) Secretary of State William Seward. Elimination of these powerful men would have left the Federal government in chaos. Courtesy of the Library of Congress.

electors to assemble the following December to elect a new president; but if the secretary of state were also missing, a new secretary would have to be appointed by the president pro tem of the Senate as acting president and approved by the Senate before issuing the call for electors. If Lee had succeeded in his attempt to reach North Carolina, confusion in Washington would have helped the Confederates in the field.

Unfortunately, Booth did not understand the entire situation. He did not know the connection between the planned attack in Washington and Lee's abandonment of Richmond, and he did not realize how weak the remaining Confederate forces actually were. He did not recognize that Lee's surrender made the attack useless. He felt that he was executing a bold stroke to help those Confederates still in the field.

After the assassination, Booth, with the help of a number of Confederate agents, followed the general course of the route originally planned for his escape with a hostage Lincoln. He was finally cornered—almost accidentally—and shot before he could be interrogated.

In general, reaction to the explanation of the assassination presented in *Come Retribution* has been favorable. There were some problems, however, cited by those who did not agree with the explanation: an unwillingness to believe that the Confederates had an active secret service, a constant probing for the existence of a "rogue" underling who might have ordered Harney's attack on the Union leaders in Washington, and a reluctance to be convinced by a mass of well-documented small facts assembled to create the explanation of the events surrounding the assassination.

Clandestine tradecraft is not unique to the twentieth century. British clandestine capability in the sixteenth century and American undercover operations in the American Revolution have been well documented. Even fiction of the nineteenth century, such as that of Edgar Allan Poe, an early writer of detective stories, or Rudyard Kipling, who called clandestine operations "the Great Game," shows the extent to which clandestine tradecraft was common knowledge in that era.[10]

In the course of the research underlying *Come Retribution*, we concerned ourselves greatly with the question of the existence of a "rogue" underling who could have been responsible for the critical decisions. What we found was that the Confederate government was a small bureaucracy. There were few men in the chain of command, and we found no evidence to suggest that any of them was so radically inclined as to act against Lincoln in a manner not approved by Jefferson Davis.

Some people suggested that Secretary of State Judah Benjamin was the rogue, but this idea presents several problems. Benjamin was not in the military chain of command. He had been secretary of war early on, and he obviously had much influence in Richmond, but he could not have intervened in command matters, such as the assignment of Harney from the Torpedo Bureau, without some formal authorization to do so. Earlier in 1865 a number of men from the signal corps were placed under State Department control by a special order drafted personally by the secretary of war. No such order concerning the men in the Torpedo Bureau has been found.

Nor is there any direct evidence that either Davis or Benjamin was involved in the decision to send Harney to Washington. There is, however, evidence that Benjamin obtained secret service gold on April 1, 1865, and this information supports the view that Davis made the decision to send Harney and that Benjamin may have played a role in getting the operation under way. From the procedure used by the Confederates, we know that Benjamin had to have Jefferson Davis's personal approval for the withdrawal of secret service gold. Benjamin already had a substantial amount of gold accessible, but this was gold authorized for normal State Department use and conventional secret service purposes ("Necessities & Exigencies"); it was not gold authorized to be used for covert action projects ("Secret Service"). The amount Davis authorized and Benjamin withdrew on April 1 was money labeled "Secret Service" and was to be expended for action projects such as that in which Harney was involved.

John Harrison Surratt, a principal associate of John Wilkes Booth, said that Benjamin gave Surratt two hundred dollars in gold. Testimony at Surratt's trial in 1867 established the date of this event as March 31, 1865.[11] If Surratt's memory of the date was correct, the money would have had to have come from the secret service account designated for conventional secret service purposes ("Necessities and Exigencies"). On the other hand, Surratt may not have remembered the date correctly, or Benjamin might have given him money from one account and replaced it on April 1 with money from the correct account ("Secret Service"). Harney left Richmond on either March 31 or April 1. If his departure date was April 1, it would be reasonable to suppose that he too was given some of the money from the "Secret Service" account, since that account was to be used for projects involving unconventional action. No other activity under way at that time would have required similar amounts from the secret action account.

Benjamin appears to have acted for Davis in many secret service operations, but always in accordance with Davis's wishes. There are stories of people seeing the secretary on secret service matters and Benjamin excusing himself (apparently to confer with Davis) before making a final decision. Benjamin seems to have tried to carry out exactly what Davis wanted him to do, and there is nothing in Benjamin's record to suggest that he was likely to act against his chief's wishes. Even if he were the one who actually launched Harney on his deadly mission, he would have done it in accordance with what he believed Davis would approve. The only person who had the necessary power and opportunity to make the decision about sending Harney to Washington was Jefferson Davis.

In addition to the reviews of *Come Retribution* and comments from Civil War buffs, other recent developments indicate that views on the nature of the war and the significance of the assassination may be changing. In March 1990 *Civil War History* published William Hanchett's scathing critique of the scholarship of Otto Eisenschiml—an article that should have ended any serious interest in the Stanton thesis.[12]

Hanchett had also concerned himself with some of the consequences of the thesis of *Come Retribution*. In a 1991 article in *Civil War Times Illustrated,* he called the idea of an assassination generated by John Wilkes Booth and his personal associates acting on their own a "simple" conspiracy as opposed to a "grand" conspiracy involving support by an outside power such as the Confederacy. He pointed out that Confederate involvement in the abduction of Lincoln could have been based on rational considerations and said, "No matter if Booth acted at Ford's Theater in accordance with what he thought would be in the interest of his country or under its order, there is much more to the history of the assassination than is encompassed by the simple conspiracy."[13]

Judging by the general flow of comment, it would appear that Hanchett's prediction concerning the impact of *Come Retribution* is proving to be true. Traditional views of the Lincoln assassination are fading, but there is still no full agreement on what did happen. During the years since *Come Retribution*'s publication, a good bit of information has been turned up that supports its thesis. Nothing has been found that contradicts it. The following chapters present the additional information and show how it supports and enlarges on the explanation of the assassination of Lincoln. It is hoped that this material will lead to a general agreement on the major aspects of that sad event.

Chapter 1

CONFEDERATE GOLD

To UNDERSTAND a clandestine organization, look for the money. The amount of money that an organization has available, its sources, and the way in which the money is handled are critical factors in understanding that organization's methods and objectives. Specifically, the procedure for the handling of Confederate secret service monies provides a valuable clue in the case of the Lincoln assassination.

Until 1990 the search for information about the Confederate secret service involved tracking down and assembling hundreds of tiny, scattered fragments of information. But quite suddenly the problem changed when records were found that showed the amounts of gold withdrawn from the Confederate treasury for secret service purposes as authorized by Jefferson Davis. Now we have some facts around which to build our understanding of Confederate clandestine operations and the Confederate background of the Lincoln assassination.

During the war, Jefferson Davis personally approved the withdrawal of over $1,500,000 in gold for secret service activities. About $300,000 was spent in the first two and a half years of the war and over $1,200,000 in 1864 and 1865. Additional sums of Confederate dollars were spent that are not included in these figures,[1] and no record has been found of additional amounts of gold believed to have been withdrawn late in the war. (Some secret service activity was financed by Confederate currency instead of gold.) The gold-equivalent value for all

Confederate secret service allocations—gold and paper currency—was on the order of two million gold dollars, or six million Confederate dollars.

The pattern of secret service expenditures approved by Davis corresponds to a broad shift in the objectives of the Confederate government. During the early years of the war, Confederate hopes were focused on getting Britain or France to recognize the Confederacy, an act that the Confederates believed would lead to a negotiated end to the war.

After the fall of Vicksburg and the Battle of Gettysburg and after the British seizure of a pair of ironclad warships being built for the Confederacy, the Confederate government recognized that there was little hope of getting Britain or France to act in accordance with Confederate wishes. The Confederacy had achieved considerable success in the military arena but had failed in their attempts to erode the political position of the Lincoln administration in order to gain recognition by the European powers. It was now more apparent than ever that, for the South, the war had to be won among the citizenry of the North and that the Confederates needed help to make this happen.

During late 1863 and early 1864 the Confederates developed a broad program of clandestine action to demonstrate to the Northern electorate that the Lincoln administration's war effort was ineffective. Part of the program involved an increase in sabotage operations in the enemy rear and a major effort to capture Lincoln as a hostage, but the main element was to encourage and assist in the organization of an effective antiwar political movement in the North. This shift in Confederate strategy is reflected in a drastic increase in the allocation of secret service funds in 1864 and 1865. Of the total of approximately two million dollars in gold devoted by the Confederates to secret service work, one million was devoted in 1864 to secret operations to be conducted from Canada. A large part of this sum was intended to foster the peace movement in the North, but some of it spilled over into the sabotage program and some into Booth's operation to capture Lincoln.

Finding something like the secret service gold records is a bit like being hit by lightning: you can't make the lightning happen, but if you stand in the rain long enough there's a greater chance that the lightning will strike. In this case, it was James O. Hall who was standing in the rain. During the summer of 1990, while working at the Library of Congress on a different matter, he came across copies of several forms referring to "Secret Service" and signed by Jefferson Davis. These were mixed among copies of a number of forms for Confederate State Department expenditures in the manuscript collection familiarly known as the Pickett Papers.[2] Hall suggested that because of my intelligence background it would be useful for me to study these in greater detail. My son, Alan C. Tidwell, carefully went over the material and found copies of sixty-three printed forms signed by Davis.

> [serial number]
> Department of State, Richmond,————186_
> To The Secretary of the Treasury.
> Sir:
> Please cause a WARRANT for the sum of _____
> payable out of the Appropriation for _____
> to be issued in favor of _____
>
> Secretary of State
>
> Appropriation for _____$_____.

The majority of the forms in the Library of Congress collection were copies of forms signed by the Confederate secretary of state requesting the issuance of warrants for money for normal departmental business. These forms were also numbered in a continuous series. The requests for warrants signed by Jefferson Davis, however, had the "Department of State" crossed out and the words "Executive Office" written in by hand. These forms carried their own continuous number series, distinct from the series carried on the Department of State forms.

The Jefferson Davis forms in the collection included those numbered from one through sixty-three.[3] Form number one was dated August 9, 1862, and form number sixty-three March 1, 1865. Thus the forms covered most of the last three years of the war. Some of the entries appear to be in the handwriting of William J. Bromwell, the disbursing clerk of the Confederate State Department, and others appear to have been written by C. W. Volkman, another clerk in the State Department. The forms appear to be the record copies kept by the State Department when the originals were sent to the Treasury Department.

The forms for Davis's signature cited "Necessities and Exigencies" or "Secret Service" as the appropriation to be used for the warrant. Most of the forms specified that the funds requested were to be issued in gold or in British sterling. Others did not specify the form of the payment, and some express the amount of money desired in Confederate dollars. Throughout the series, wherever the comparison could be made, the exchange rate of three Confederate dollars per dollar of gold was used. In January 1863 the rate of $13.33 Confederate dollars per sterling was used, but thereafter the rate was steady at CS$14.50 per pound sterling.

A few of the treasury warrants issued as a result of these requests have been located and help round out the picture of the process followed in disbursing secret service funds. Request No. 17 of December 22, 1863, called for the issuance of a warrant for CS$29,100 to be issued to J. P. Benjamin as secretary of state as a bill of exchange for £2,000. As a result, the treasury issued warrant number 2247 on December 29, 1863, which drew $9,700 from the appropriation for "Necessities and Exigencies." The money was to be issued in the form of a draft on Fraser Trenholm and Company for £2,000, which was issued to Benjamin, who signed a receipt for draft number 5571 in the amount of $9,700 (CS$29,100 equals $9,700 in gold, which equals £2,000). The treasury account for "Necessities and Exigencies" appears to have been a gold account.

On April 16, 1864, Henry Hotze, Confederate commercial and propaganda representative in England, wrote to Benjamin requesting £1,000 for secret service work in France. He also asked that in view of the "increasing magnitude of the sums I am expected to disburse" three different accounts for secret service money be established—one for work in Ireland, one for work in England, and a third for work in France. On May 25 Request No. 37 was prepared for Davis's signature requesting that $29,100 in Confederate money be issued as a bill of exchange on England for £2,000, citing "Necessities and Exigencies" as the fund to be used. On May 27 the treasury issued warrant 6265 for £2,000. This warrant was sent to Hotze, who acknowledged its receipt on July 4, 1864, as an amount to be used for secret service expenditures. The sum covered the £1,000 requested by Hotze and provided additional monies as well.[4]

On August 31, 1864, Request No. 45 requested the issuance of a warrant for $242,500 charged to "Secret Service" payable to Benjamin as a bill of exchange for £50,000. This was handled by the treasury on September 1, 1864, as warrant number 2980 from the appropriation for "Secret Service (Act of 15 Feb. 1864)." This was issued as five drafts of £10,000 each, and Bromwell receipted on behalf of Benjamin for five drafts of $48,500 each. In this case, £50,000 equals $242,500 in gold, and the secret service account again appears to have been a gold account.

On December 6, 1864, Request No. 52 asked for $1,500 in gold to be issued to Secretary of State Benjamin and charged to "Necessities and Exigencies." The treasury issued warrant number 3178 on the same date. In this case the warrant has not survived, but the original request form is extant and has the warrant number written at the top of the document. This was probably travel money for E. G. Lee, who saw Benjamin on December 6 in preparation for his transfer to Canada.

A fifth warrant was issued on April 1, 1865 (the request being made on March 31 or possibly even earlier), for $1,500 in gold to be issued to Benjamin. Unfortunately, the request for this warrant was not found in the series of documents in the Library of Congress. At a minimum the warrant indicates that at least one request for the issuance of a warrant was prepared after Request No. 63, the request dated March 1, 1865.

Some of the forms signed by Jefferson Davis specify the amount desired in gold dollars and some express the amount in Confederate dollars without indicating which they are using. In most cases it can be demonstrated that they meant dollars in gold or sterling, which had a fixed relationship that was recognized on the international market. For convenience the Confederates spent gold as if a gold dollar were worth three Confederate dollars. In fact, the Confederate dollar changed in value on the international market. Fortunately, most of the forms indicate that the proceeds are needed in gold or sterling, which makes it possible to calculate the kind of dollars intended by the requester. In spite of this casual manner of filling in the forms, it would appear that gold was the accounting medium used for the exchanges between the Confederate Executive Office and the treasury. Jefferson Davis personally approved all expenditures of gold for secret service purposes,[5] and the forms provided a medium for recording his approval.

Additional information is provided by an article printed in the *Raleigh* (North Carolina) *Standard* on May 9, 1865. According to the article, on April 21, 1865, the writer (a correspondent of the *Philadelphia Inquirer*) visited the Customs House in Richmond, which had been used as the main office for the president and secretary of state, and found among the waste papers on the floor of one of the rooms several official papers, which he referred to as "Warrants." His story carried the text of three of these documents, and judging from the texts quoted, the documents that he found were actually the original requests for a warrant signed by Davis. The only difference between the text quoted and the copy in the Library of Congress is that the former included a four-digit number at the top of the form. The original signed by Davis had gone to the treasury, where a warrant was issued and the number of the warrant was written on the top of the request form which was then returned to the State Department. The documents found by the reporter were the original requests rather than the warrants themselves. Unfortunately, the originals on which the *Standard* story were based have disappeared. However, the original request signed by Jefferson Davis on February 29, 1864, for $290 is in the Museum of the Confederacy in Richmond. It carries the warrant number 2418 at the top of the page and illustrates the procedure. The three mentioned in the *Standard* article were Request Nos. 31, 32, and 33. Request No. 32, dated April 25, 1864, was for one million dollars (in gold) for "Secret Service." It is hard to see how the prosecutors at the trial of Booth's associates could have missed this sensational piece of information, but for some reason nothing was made of it, and this clear proof of Confederate secret service activity dropped from sight until the twentieth century.

In 1968 the National Archives published *Guide to the Archives of the Government of the Confederate States of America*, by Henry Putney Beers. This impressive work detailed the locations of all known collections of original Confederate records and gave brief descriptions of the material contained in each collection. Beers's discussion of the financial records of the Confederate State Department contained this sentence: "A secret service account book, with the Chicago Historical Society collections, is a remnant; most of the pages have been removed." The description of the book as a "remnant" sounded discouraging, but several Confederate ledgers in the National Archives that had been severely damaged by having pages torn out still had page stubs carrying names or dates that provided useful information. In the hopes of finding such items, the Chicago Historical Society made copies of all the pages remaining in the book, including pages that had major pieces cut away. The book proved to be an amazing complement to the requests for warrants. It confirmed the interpretation of the requests and added substantially to the solid information available on Confederate secret service.

The Chicago "remnant" turned out to be the remains of a ledger that originally held about one hundred pages but had been reduced to twenty-eight pages that hold some legible handwriting and several fairly long entries. From the original Confederate writing and from later notations on the remaining pages, it was possible to piece together some of the history of the book. The volume appears to have been picked up by somebody in Richmond at the end of the war, possibly as a souvenir. It found its way into the hands of a person who bought a drugstore from a Dr. Ladd in about 1874. At that point its blank pages or portions of pages were used to record an inventory of the drugstore. An index page survived showing that the inventory was on pages 1–17 and that pages 17–60 were used for invoices. Later most of the drugstore material was cut out of the book, and this process largely destroyed the Confederate content as well. What remained, however, was of great interest.

The Confederate writing in the book was largely in the handwriting of William J. Bromwell, the State Department disbursing clerk who kept the copies of the requests for warrants signed by President Davis. Bromwell appears to have devoted much of the book to double-page entries headed by "Dr. [name] in a/c with the Secretary of State for Secret Service Money." The headings survive for the following:

Rev. Father John Bannon
James L. Capston
Capt. George Dewson
James P. Holcombe
Colin J. McRae
James M. Mason
John Slidell
Jacob Thompson
Major N. S. Walker

The pages under the headings are either blank or missing for most of these names, but the page for James P. Holcombe, one of the Confederate commissioners in Canada, shows that he was issued $500 in gold and $7,500 in gold as a sterling draft for £1546.7.10. This agrees with the text of a letter from Benjamin to Holcombe dated February 24, 1864, in which Benjamin says that he is giving Holcombe these sums, which total $8,000 in value, and that Holcombe is to consider $3,000 as salary for six months with $5,000 to be used for operational expenses.[6]

The page for Jacob Thompson shows that he was given two payments (in gold), one on April 27, 1864, for $100,000 and one on April 29 for $900,000. This is confirmed in part by a note from Benjamin dated April 28 and addressed to Thompson in Wilmington, North Carolina.[7] The note forwarded the payment for $900,000 and asked Thompson to acknowledge receipt by telegram and by letter. This delay in issuing the larger sum suggests that the treasury may not have had a million dollars in gold or sterling immediately available and that Thompson had already left for Wilmington on his way to Canada before the money could be made ready.

Two other pages in the secret service ledger are entitled "Amounts withdrawn by Warrants," and they list seventy-one sums, beginning with $40,000 on April 10, 1861, and ending with $2,500 on February 25, 1865. The total amount listed is $952,942.14.[8] All of the items covered by requests for warrants and citing "Necessities and Exigencies" up through Request No. 62 are contained in this list, and beginning with Request No. 12 dated September 29, 1863, the list shows the serial number of the request form as well as the date and the amount. There are nine entries totaling $99,380.85 on the list dated before the beginning of the request forms. The earliest of these is for $40,000 and is dated April 10, 1861. There may well have been a separate page listing requests that cited "Secret Service," but there is no evidence remaining of such a page. There were six such request forms in the Library of Congress file, plus the missing request form that supported the April 1, 1865, warrant for $1,500. The total for all seven requests is $1,282,000 in gold.

It is important to note that both the funds citing "Necessities and Exigencies" and those citing "Secret Service" were considered to be funds for secret service use. One surviving page of the record book is headed "Appropriations for Secret Service Act of 15 Feb 64" and lists one appropriation for $5,000,000. Another page is headed "Appropriations for Secret Service," and somebody inserted the words "i.e. 'Necessities and Exigencies' etc." This view of the two terms as both referring to the same function is supported by a note in the same collection in the Library of Congress.[9] This note may have been associated with a budget preparation or review and appears to refer to the funds actually drawn in 1864 or to be expended in 1865. The note lists several categories of figures including:

"Secret Service"
"Necessities & Exigencies" $\Big\}$ 3,783,494.53.

There is no indication of the kind of dollars intended; but if the figure were Confederate dollars, it would convert to over $1,250,000 in gold and would be consistent with the money actually drawn from the treasury in 1864.

From the various pieces of information available, it is possible to reconstruct most of the procedure followed in issuing gold for secret service purposes. This procedure involved the preparation of a request for secret service funds to be addressed to Jefferson Davis. If Davis approved the request, it would go to the State Department (the next floor below Davis's office) where the form requesting a treasury warrant would be prepared. The original of the request form would go to Davis for signature and a copy would be retained by the disbursing clerk in the State Department. After the request had been signed, the disbursing clerk would write Davis's name on the signature block on the copy and send the original to the treasury, which would then prepare the requested warrant and write the number of the implementing warrant on the original request form. The original request form then would be sent to the State Department with drafts that had been issued in response to the warrant, and the disbursing clerk would send the drafts to their destination or cash them as appropriate. Money issued by the State Department to individuals in draft or as cash would be recorded in a ledger and a hand receipt would be obtained if possible.

Both the Confederate War and Navy departments conducted operations that would fall under the classification of secret service, but neither normally had access to secret service gold. Their operations appear to have been financed by Confederate dollars or by some form of economic activity to acquire greenbacks or sterling. So if the navy needed gold for its secret service work, it had to apply to Jefferson Davis for the money in the same way that anybody else did.

The Navy Department's secret service expenditures were mostly in support of their program to build or buy ships abroad, but that department also sponsored the Volunteer Navy, which engaged in a number of irregular warfare activities similar to those sponsored under the Secret Service Act of February 15, 1864. Unfortunately, records of expenditures by the Volunteer Navy do not appear to be available.

Some records of secret service expenditures by the Confederate War Department, however, are in the National Archives. One ledger contains a listing of "Incidental and Contingent" expenditures by the War Department for the period between October 1863 and March 25, 1865, which amounted to a total of $276,021 Confederate dollars and appears to reflect an accelerating trend in such expenditures.[10] The Confederate Congress appropriated CS$175,000 for the "Incidental and Contingent" category for the first six months of 1865—indicating that the rate at which these funds were used was now much higher than in the preceding year.[11] No doubt part of this increase was caused by inflation in the Confederate economy, but some of the increase doubtless came from an increase in clandestine activity as well.

Although not exactly comparable to the State Department's category of "Necessities and Exigencies," the War Department's category of "Incidental and Contingent" funds appears to have played a similar role in providing funds for purposes that could be expressed in deliberately vague or misleading terms. A portion of the funds appears to have been spent for normal wartime contingencies, but another was clearly expended on matters normally associated with secret service activity. A conservative estimate would be that a total of CS$500,000 was spent for "Incidental and Contingent" purposes during the entire war, of which about half, or CS$250,000, might have been used for secret service work.

As mentioned above, the list of appropriations for "Secret Service" under the act of February 15, 1864, carries only the one entry for $5,000,000. It is not clear whether this was in gold dollars or in Confederate dollars. It is possible that the legislators were thinking

Confederate dollars and the executive board was spending it as gold dollars. The list of appropriations for "Necessities and Exigencies," however, is longer. Two partial pages list four items for a total of $840,000:

March 15, 1861	$200,000	Act 73
May 21, 1861	$40,000	Act 151
February 10, 1863	$100,000	No number
January 1, 1864	$500,000	No number

There was nothing in the language of these acts to indicate whether the appropriation was intended to be valued in Confederate dollars or gold, but it is clear from the actual withdrawals cited above that gold was the medium of exchange actually used.

Some additional information about the appropriations can be derived from the records of the Confederate Congress. Act 73 is described as "an Act making appropriations for the Legislative, Executive, & Judicial Expenses of the Government for the Year Ending 6th/February 1862."[12] This act was approved on March 15, 1861: "for necessities and exigencies . . . there is hereby appropriated the sum of two hundred thousand dollars, subject to the requisition and under the control of the President of the Confederate States of America."[13] Act 151 of May 21, 1861, is described in similar terms but with an interesting addition: "For necessities and exigencies . . . forty thousand dollars—to replace same amount in the State Department." This wording suggests that the State Department had already advanced $40,000 for secret service purposes from its own appropriation and that this act was needed to restore the money to the State Department for its conventional expenditures. In fact, the money involved may have been the $40,000 in the first secret service warrant dated April 10, 1861. Of course the Confederacy was already engaged in clandestine operations, even though hostilities did not begin until Fort Sumter was attacked a week later.

The wording of the act of February 10, 1863, reverts to the earlier formulation: "For necessities and exigencies . . . one hundred thousand dollars." This is presumably Act 4 approved on February 10, 1863, and described in the "Register of Acts" as "an act making appropriations for the support of the government for the period from February 1st to June 30th inclusive, and to supply deficiencies arising from thereto."[14]

Table 1
Funds Available for Confederate Clandestine Operations

Source	CS Dollars*	Gold Dollars
Unnumbered Requests	99,380.85	?
Numbered Requests*	4,682,724.00	1,589,504.00
Missing Requests	?	?
Warrant of April 1, 1865	——	1,500.00
St. Albans Raid**	——	100,000.00
Navy Department	?	?
War Department	250,000.00	——
Totals	5,032,104+	1,691,004+

* The figure in the first column gives the Confederate dollar value of all requests for warrants; the figure in the second column gives the gold value of all of the requests that specified gold or sterling. Therefore, the figure in the first column includes the value of all of the items in the second column, but the second column does not include all of the items in the first column.

** Oscar A. Kinchen, in his book *Confederate Operations in Canada,* estimated that the St. Albans raiders captured about US$220,000. Using an exchange of 2.2 to 1, the gold value would have been about $100,000. The Canadian government confiscated about US$90,000 from the raiders that were captured and tried but returned the money to the Confederates after the trial. Presumably, the remaining US$130,000 remained in Confederate hands and was available for use in clandestine operations.

Confirmation of the entry for $500,000 for January 1, 1864, is not as clear cut as it is in the case of the preceding items, but it does throw some light on those cases in which persons associated with Confederate clandestine activities were referred to by military rank that could not be confirmed in the conventional records of the Confederate War Department. The Register of Acts lists Act 7 as being approved on January 1, 1864, but cites January 6 as the date on which it was passed. The register describes it as a continuation of an act originally approved on May 1, 1863, which is listed as "an act to pay officers, non-commissioned officers and privates not legally mustered into the service of the Confederate States, for services actually performed." The language of the act stated:

. . . all officers, non-commissioned officers and privates of any legally constituted military organization, which may have been actually received into the service of the Confederate States by any general office thereof, but were never legally mustered into service, in consequence of the loss of the muster rolls of such military organization, shall be entitled to receive pay from the time they were so received into the service and the time they served, is duly proved to the satisfaction of the secretary of war, under rules to be prescribed by him.

Notice that the language of the act left the secretary of war in complete control of the process of deciding who should be paid. This act may well have provided the authority needed for the secretary of war to grant military rank to those engaged in irregular military activity of various kinds. The original act was passed to cover 1863 and would thus expire on December 31. The follow-on act, appropriating $500,000, was passed on January 6, 1864, but made effective as of January 1 in order to avoid a gap in the authority for such payments. Because the State Department clerk listed the 1864 act as a secret service appropriation, it must mean that it was intended that the personnel paid under this act would be paid from secret service funds. This act could explain the mysterious references to "Captain" Booth and other people involved in Confederate clandestine operations who did not appear to have a conventional claim to military rank.

It is interesting to note that this 1864 appropriation listed under "Necessities and Exigencies" was for a considerably larger sum than had been allocated earlier. This is in keeping with the Confederate plans for increased clandestine activities. Although there was little reference to secret service in the records of these appropriations, the *Journal of the Confederate Congress* refers to secret sessions of the Senate in connection with HR101, a House-sponsored measure for additional secret service money. This bill was signed by Jefferson Davis on February 15, 1864, and is doubtless the $5,000,000 appropriation referred to in the secret service record book.

Senate Bill S194, dealing with "organizing bodies for the capture and destruction of the enemy's property by land or by sea and to authorize compensation for the same," was sent to Davis for his signature on

February 17. The two bills had clearly been under consideration by Congress at the same time. Their simultaneous consideration, so soon after passing the January 1, 1864, increase in the customary funding for secret service activity, suggests that all three measures were part of a single program.

Conventional clandestine operations, such as espionage, were presumably supported by "Necessities and Exigencies" and were to be increased in support of a major effort to influence the Northern electorate. The main effort, however, was to be the new campaign aimed at covert political and paramilitary action in the North with the intent of supporting the creation of a Northern peace movement. The Northern electorate was to be made aware of the need for a peace movement by a greatly increased effort to carry out acts of sabotage and other forms of irregular warfare behind Union lines. Those carrying out successful acts of sabotage were to be amply rewarded for their efforts, and the funds for this major new campaign were to be provided by the new "Secret Service" appropriation. Thus there were to be two funds for secret service, with money taken from one or the other in accordance with the purposes for which the money was to be used. Money from the "Necessities and Exigencies" fund was for routine secret service, and money from the "Secret Service" fund was for sabotage and other forms of violent action.

Given our current knowledge of the history of the Civil War and the history of various clandestine political movements around the world, we can question the soundness of the logic involved in trying to organize a peace movement by blowing up those we are trying to convince. It is another example of a decision that would have benefited from a more thorough and objective analysis of the problem, but it is a possible error in logic that has been followed by many other clandestine political movements in the years since the Civil War. Determined but weak political movements do not have many policy alternatives open to them, and a policy of combining force and political action sometimes works.

The distinction between the uses of the "Necessities and Exigencies" citation for "normal" secret service work and the "Secret Service" citation for unconventional action projects is important in assessing the role of Davis and Benjamin in the decision to attack the Union high command in Washington.

State Department clerk Bromwell made a summary accounting of the funds under his care as of April 1, 1865.[15] In the summary Bromwell noted that there were $480.66 in gold on deposit in the treasury credited to the incidental and contingent expenses account. He also noted that Benjamin had in his possession $1,000 in gold from the State Department account for "Foreign Intercourse." No mention was made of the $1,500 in gold that Benjamin received on April 1 from the "Secret Service" fund.

On April 1, 1865, the leaders of the Confederacy thought that they would be evacuating Richmond about the middle of April; they did not realize that they would be leaving the next day. Thus actions were not taken amid the panic of preparing for departure and were in keeping with the plans for the campaign of 1865 as the Confederates foresaw it.

Bromwell's figures suggest that on April 1 Benjamin needed money for clandestine action, not for espionage or other conventional secret service work. Even though he had access to a total of $1,480.66 in gold, Benjamin went through the process of getting Davis to sign a request for the issuance of a treasury warrant for $1,500 in gold from the "Secret Service" account. Either Davis knew what the money was to be used for or Benjamin was lying to him, but there is no reason to think that Benjamin would have risked lying to Davis on that date. In normal circumstances, such a lie could have been exposed at any time by a number of different events beyond the control of the liar; and as far as Benjamin knew on April 1, the situation was normal.

Even more convincing than the risk is the fact that Benjamin was neither disloyal to his cause nor a fanatic about Lincoln. One can never rule out completely aberrant behavior; but in this case, logic and the vast majority of the evidence say that normal procedure was followed. Davis approved the uses for which the money was intended, and Benjamin saw that the money went where it was supposed to go.

Two hundred of the $1,500 for "Secret Service" may have been the money given to John Surratt, but most or all of the rest probably went to Colonel Mosby and Thomas F. Harney, who left Richmond at approximately this time, to cover the expenses of the operation in Washington. No other projects under way at this time would have required such an amount of secret service money.

It becomes increasingly evident through this mundane investigation of procedures for the handling of money that Confederates were involved in the planning of covert action in Washington, an operation that was the beginning of a series of events that resulted in the assassination of Lincoln.

Chapter 2

THE ORGANIZATION
OF SECRET SERVICE

THE CIVIL WAR was fought before the development of organization charts and modern concepts of organization. Thus, even if historians had all the records of the various components of the Confederate secret service, it would still be difficult to understand exactly how they functioned. Unfortunately, there are no direct records of such operating organizations, and related information, such as the financial records, are scarce. So what remains is a collection of fragments of information upon which to build a few logical conclusions. These conclusions, however, can be helpful in understanding what the Confederates were trying to do with their secret service.

These conclusions reconstruct a history of how the Confederate leaders tried to invent a way to organize themselves into effective components that would use secret operations to help win the war. In their minds, clandestine operations formed an important weapon, and how they organized those operations reveals their understanding of the war and how they intended to win it.

Like the intelligence organizations of the United States in World War II, the secret service of the Confederacy evolved from a number of different organizations created separately, at different times, by different people, to accomplish discrete purposes. By 1864, however, the Confederates had acquired experience in clandestine operations, had developed a body of doctrine concerning such operations, and had created a cluster of organizations that, together, contained a considerable capability for secret service work. The most important elements of the Confederate secret service were:

- State Department Secret Service: This loose collection of agents with special qualifications or special missions was managed by Judah Benjamin with frequent intervention by Jefferson Davis.
- War Department Secret Service: These agents worked on assignments from the War Department but were sometimes assigned to work for specific field commanders. Their activity appears to have been managed for the War Department by personnel in the War Department Signal Bureau.
- War Department Signal Bureau and Signal Corps: The bureau provided Signal Corps personnel to the field commanders to transmit information over the battlefield and operated the Secret Line, which passed information and personnel across enemy lines between Richmond and Washington (apparently operated independently of the War Department Secret Service). The Independent Signal Corps and Scouts operated in tidewater Virginia.
- Provost Marshal of Richmond: Established in 1861 under Gen. John Henry Winder, this organization had a checkered career, being responsible at one time or another for military discipline in the Richmond area, counterespionage, the defenses of Richmond, the administration of prisoners of war, and the collection of information in support of these various tasks. It may also have assisted the State Department's secret service.
- War Department Torpedo Bureau: Primarily concerned with the employment of explosive devices on land—"subterra" mines— agents also planted underwater mines and controlled the mine fields in the James River.
- Navy Submarine Battery Service: This unit focused on the employment of underwater mines to defend the major harbors and rivers of the Confederacy.
- War Department Strategy Bureau: Never established officially, this undercover bureau was created in early 1863 to sponsor

sabotage teams known as "strategic corps" or "destructionists," which were concerned primarily with the use of explosives and newly invented weapons against targets behind enemy lines approved by the military department commanders.

- The Greenhow Group: This well-organized espionage service in Washington was formed originally under sponsorship of the state of Virginia. Although several key members, like Rose Greenhow, were arrested, the group continued to function during most of the war with the primary focus of providing direct support to the Army of Northern Virginia.

- Cavalry Scouts: A group of talented young men were recruited and trained by Gen. J. E. B. Stuart to operate in front of and around the army and, on occasion, behind enemy lines. The group reported to Stuart and General Lee. After Stuart's death, the group became less efficient, possibly because several of its outstanding members were drawn off into other missions.

- Operations in Canada: Confederates developed a number of clandestine assets in Canada, initially to support the passage of couriers and other tasks. In 1864 the Confederacy established what amounted to a field office capable of developing and carrying out complex clandestine operations. Jacob Thompson, the chief, reported to Benjamin and Davis, but he also had the support of a War Department team under the control of Clement C. Clay.

In addition to these organizations, there were a number of guerrilla units whose raids on occasion might have been hard to distinguish from the work of the Strategic Corps. And there was Colonel Mosby's partisan unit as well, which supported the Army of Northern Virginia primarily but also from time to time undertook missions of interest to the central government. Evolving out of the debate over how to conduct warfare against Union commerce at sea, secret legislation was submitted in 1864 to create a Special and Secret Service Bureau. This organization was intended to foster the development of secret weapons, provide a legal basis for the Strategy Bureau, and coordinate the operations of the other existing clandestine organizations. The legislation for this Confederate version of a central intelligence organization was not approved by Congress until March 1865.

Although there does not appear to be any surviving definition of just what the Confederates meant by the term "secret service," the organizations listed above describe what they had in mind, and some additional bits and pieces of information help in understanding the history of Confederate secret service. A prime source is the secret service record book, which contains a number of clues concerning the clandestine operations of the State Department.

State Department Secret Service

There does not appear to have been much of a central organization involved in the State Department's secret service operations. Secretary of State Judah Benjamin and Lucius Quintius Washington, his principal assistant, acted personally as case officers from time to time, and some central staff support might have been provided for clandestine operations by Gen. John Henry Winder and his detectives. Winder had been hand picked for his position by Davis and would have provided discrete assistance as required, but with Davis and Benjamin remaining in command. After Winder was reassigned in May 1864, the provost marshal, Maj. Isaac H. Carrington, who inherited the residue of Winder's organization, continued to carry out the same functions. Other assistance was supplied by the army Signal Corps and the War Department's secret service.

The State Department's secret service operations were often conducted by principal agents who were assigned missions and funds to carry them out. Davis and Benjamin were in a position to secure cooperation from other elements of the government whenever some sort of special assistance was needed. Jacob Thompson's mission to Canada is characteristic of the way many of these operations were carried out. Thompson had been given a mission and had full control of the one million dollars devoted to the operations from Canada. His fellow commissioner, Clay, received only $1,500 in gold, enough to get him to Canada in proper style but not enough to support serious operations. If Clay were to initiate an operation, he would have to get the necessary funds from Thompson.

The secret service record book contains further clues. On the end papers of the ledger somebody had accumulated a list of agents and their cipher keys:

Born a British subject, Judah Philip Benjamin (1811–84) represented Louisiana in the United States Senate and then served successively as attorney general, secretary of war, and secretary of state in the Confederate government. At the end of the war he escaped to Cuba. He spent the rest of his life in England, where he had a successful career as a barrister. Courtesy of the Library of Congress.

At Cassius F. Lee's, Hamilton, Canada
Morton T. Bledsoe   Rivers

Fide sed cui vide   Reynolds
The Women of the South   Baxley
Louis Napoleon   J. Thompson
Cowards only flee   Hines signs T. H. Hines
John S. Williams signs N. N. Simpson
McCulloh [*sic*] will sign Richard } key word
Harris will sign Alexander   } is Constantinople

Clement Clay does not appear on the list. The list may have been compiled after Clay left Canada, but it suggests that Clay had no private way of communicating with Benjamin. He may well have had a cipher arrangement with the War Department, but he was not on the "inside" with Benjamin and Davis.

Cassius F. Lee, a distinguished citizen of Alexandria, Virginia, staunch Episcopalian, and uncle of Robert E. Lee, was forced to leave his home because of his pro-Southern opinions. He arrived in Canada in late 1863 and established himself in Hamilton, Ontario, at the western end of Lake Ontario between Toronto and Niagara. There is no evidence that Lee was directly involved as an agent or operator, but it is clear that he provided support and acted as a message center. Messages could be sent to him, and he would know where the agent was currently located and could forward the message to the correct address. He may have been sent to Canada in preparation for the increased activity of 1864, but it is also possible that he made the move on his own initiative and that the Confederates merely took advantage of the presence of somebody they could trust.

The people listed with their cipher keys were agents working directly for Davis and Benjamin or those working on assignments that might make it necessary for Richmond to communicate directly with them. Thompson, "Louis Napoleon," is an obvious case. Captain Thomas Hines, "cowards only flee," is also fairly obvious. Hines had been assigned to Thompson but did most of his work with antiwar elements in Illinois, Indiana, and Ohio, having begun that work as an officer of the Confederate army before Thompson was given his mission to Canada. Hines's work was potentially so critical that Richmond might well have felt a need to get in touch with him directly.

David Winfred Gaddy, coauthor of *Come Retribution,* has reported firm evidence that Brig. Gen. Edwin Grey Lee, who was sent to Canada as a Confederate commissioner in December 1864, used the key "Morton T. Bledsoe" in his cipher messages to Richmond. In that case, "Rivers" must have been an alias used to further protect Lee's identity. "McCulloh" was probably Richard G. McCulloch, who was captured off the Florida coast on May 17, 1865. His capture was brought to the attention of Secretary of War Stanton with the note that McCulloch's name "appears in the documents captured at Richmond as being in the poison & dagger service of the Confederacy."[1]

"Harris" was undoubtedly Thomas A. Harris, former brigadier general of Missouri state troops and former representative from Missouri to the Confederate Congress. After being defeated for reelection to Congress in 1864, Harris was associated with McCulloch (note that they shared a common cipher key) in an ambitious project to attack all ships—foreign as well as U.S.—enroute to Northern ports by planting fire bombs or other devices on board, a project that involved establishing squads of operatives at numerous ports overseas. The war ended, however, before the project was fully organized, and Harris was captured with McCulloch near Cape Sable, Florida, on May 17, 1865.[2]

"Baxley" was certainly Catherine Virginia Baxley of Baltimore. On December 26, 1861, Jefferson Davis received a telegram from James F. Milligan, the head of the signal company operating in the Norfolk area, which asked, "Is Mrs. Baxley of Baltimore known to you? If so is she all right and to be trusted?" Davis commented, "Recently bore to me letters from reliable friends in Baltimore, had no previous acquaintance but believe her to be with us." The inquiry suggests that somebody was planning to use her for some sensitive work.[3]

But whatever Catherine Baxley's next assignment might have been, it led to her arrest and imprisonment with Rose Greenhow in Washington. Greenhow wrote a book about her experiences as a Confederate spy and Union prisoner, which was published in London in 1863, and in it lambasted Baxley and hinted that she might be unbalanced. Subsequent writers have tended to take Greenhow at her word and have dismissed Baxley as relatively unimportant. Before following their lead, however, it is important to remember that Greenhow was an ardent and sophisticated supporter of the Confederacy writing during the war. She knew that what she wrote would be read by Union authorities, and the cause would have weighed much more heavily than any personal pique. It is much more likely that Greenhow was deliberately trying to play down Baxley's importance and thus make it possible for Baxley to continue operating for the Confederacy.

The Union authorities sent Baxley south with Greenhow in the summer of 1862, but Baxley was arrested again and imprisoned in Washington in early 1865. Her name on the list in the secret service record book suggests that she had resumed operations for the Confederacy before she was arrested for the second time.

One of the things that makes it difficult to assign a specific individual to a particular part of the Confederate secret service is that the boundaries between organizations were quite loose. A person might work for the State Department on one mission and for the War Department on another. Cavalry scouts and other persons of established reputation could be recruited for a particular task for the State Department and then return to their parent unit when the task had been completed. And in other missions, the State and War departments collaborated on the operation.

With this in mind, others who may have worked covertly for the State Department at one time or another would include: William Cornell Jewett, who was on a mission to England in 1863 and later involved in the negotiations with Horace Greeley in the summer of 1864; George N. Sanders, who made several trips to Europe before joining Thompson in Canada in 1864; the Reverend Kensey Johns Stewart, who was sent by Davis to join Thompson in late 1864; and "Captain" Emile Longuemare, who did some of the early reconnaissance of the antiwar potential in the North.

War Department Secret Service

The War Department operated its secret service with Confederate dollars and the limited amount of Union currency it could get from prisoners of war or by economic activity. From time to time, for special operations, the department succeeded in getting Jefferson Davis to release some of the secret service gold, but such occasions were rare. In general, though, it got by on its own resources or on resources volunteered by those working with the department. Many of those working

A lawyer and U.S. congressman, James Alexander Seddon (1815–80) had withdrawn from politics before the war because of ill health, but Jefferson Davis appointed him Confederate secretary of war in 1862, a position in which he loyally served until February 1, 1865. Courtesy of the Library of Congress.

on secret activities were physically incapacitated for field service or ineligible for the draft, and many volunteered their services for patriotic reasons or in the hope of winning reward money from the destruction of enemy property.

The War Department appears to have drawn its secret service funds from its incidental and contingent expenditures. A list in a ledger in the National Archives shows War Department "Incidental and Contingent" expenditures made between October 1863 and March 1865 totaling CS$276,021, with CS$233,540 being spent in 1864.[4] The Confederate Congress appropriated CS$175,000 for the same category for the period from January 1 to June 30, 1865, which would total CS$350,000 intended for expenditure in 1865.

The largest single items paid out during the year and a half covered by the list of incidental and contingent expenditures were two payments of CS$50,000 each to Capt. C. Morfit, the quartermaster of the prisoner-of-war prison system in Richmond, made on June 9 and September 2, 1864. One of Morfit's major duties was to look after the money and other property taken from the enemy prisoners as they were processed into the Richmond prisons. On October 20, 1864, Confederate secretary of war Seddon sent a letter to Robert Ould, the commissioner on the exchange of prisoners of war, and to all the heads of War Department bureaus in which he pointed out that they were competing against each other in their attempts to buy Federal currency from the prisoners and that "Captain Morfit . . . is required to buy a large amount of that currency, and to avoid the evils resulting from competition it is deemed judicious that all the bureaus shall employ him."[5] Because most quartermaster activity would have been covered by funds normally designated for quartermaster use, the activity most likely to have been covered by the CS$100,000 issued to Morfit from the "Incidental and Contingent" fund was his attempt to purchase greenbacks.

It is interesting to speculate on the effort to collect such a volume of Federal currency from the prisoners. The purchase of arms and supplies through the blockade was normally handled by barter or borrowed funds, but there was no activity of this nature in 1864 that would appear to depend on Federal currency. On the other hand, War Department secret service operatives would always have need for Federal currency to facilitate their activities behind Union lines. There had been a surge of clandestine activity in 1864, which had failed to discredit the Lincoln administration, but there may have been plans to renew the effort in 1865, which would further increase the demand for U.S. currency.

The second largest "Incidental and Contingent" item was CS$10,500 paid to "A. Morris" on May 3, 1864, with another CS$441 paid on November 1, 1864. In 1861 Augusta Hewett Morris, who sometimes used the alias of "Mrs. Mason," had been acting as an agent for Colonel Jordan, the organizer of the espionage ring supporting the Confederate Army of Northern Virginia. In 1863 one of Union provost marshal Lafayette C. Baker's informants reported that a "Mrs. Mason" was staying with Thomas Green in his mansion at Seventeenth and Constitution, near the White House, and that he suspected that she and Green were traveling to Baltimore several times a week in order to send military information to the Rebels.[6] (Green is known to have supplied a safe house for Confederate agent Thomas Nelson Conrad, and Green and his wife were arrested in April 1865 for suspected complicity in the assassination of Lincoln.) Morris was arrested by Union authorities on February 1, 1862, and finally sent South with Rose Greenhow and Catherine Virginia Baxley on June 2, 1862, after which she doubtless returned to her work for the Confederate army. The payment on May 3, 1864, may have been in appreciation for her efforts, but the size of the payment more likely suggests that she was provided with the funds to cover an operation involving several people, with the November 1 payment made to cover travel expenses upon her return to Richmond.

Other major expenditures include $5,000 paid to Capt. Thomas H. Hines on March 18, 1864. With this money, he purchased cotton near the Mississippi River and then sold it in Union-controlled territory in order to acquire Federal currency with which to finance his operations with the Northern antiwar faction.[7] On August 18, 1864, $3,500 was issued to Col. R. M. Martin, who, with Lt. John W. Headley, was sent to Canada to report for duty with Jacob Thompson. Martin later bragged of meeting John Wilkes Booth during this assignment.[8] Other interesting recipients of incidental and contingent funds from the Confederate War Department were Commissioner on Exchange (of prisoners of war) Robert Ould; Maj. William Norris, the chief of the Signal Corps; Capt. William N. Barker, the number-two man in the Signal Corps; Judge S. S. Baxter, who was responsible for reviewing cases of disloyalty and treason involving persons held at the provost marshal's Richmond prison, Castle Thunder; Maj. John Ambler, an assistant quartermaster who sometimes paid accounts that may have been connected to clandestine operations; Col. Alexander G. Taliaferro, the post commander at Charlottesville; and Lt. Beverly Kennon, who asked for and received CS$500 for expenses in connection with his delivery of submarine mines to the shore of the Potomac in December 1864.[9]

In considering the value of the total War Department secret service effort, it should be recalled that these figures did not include the effort of volunteers or the salaries of the uniformed personnel engaged in these activities who had been formally mustered into Confederate service. Assuming that the sample of expenditures represents a late segment in a rising curve of such expenditures, the CS$276,021 spent during the last seventeen months of the war could be extrapolated into a total wartime "Incidental and Contigent" use of about half a million dollars.

Indeed, some of these expenditures were bound to have covered conventional army activities; but it is apparent that a large number of the items in this category—perhaps half, or about CS$250,000—were related to clandestine activities in some way. Using the standard rate of three Confederate dollars to one dollar of gold, the gold value of the War Department clandestine operations would be about $80,000 to $85,000 over the duration of the war.

War Department Signal Bureau and Signal Corps

The Signal Corps of the Confederate army played a unique role in connection with the War Department's secret services. When it was formally organized in 1862, the Signal Corps took over some crossborder clandestine lines organized earlier by the state of Virginia and by Confederate tactical units assigned in the Northern Neck of Virginia. These were reorganized and expanded into the Secret Line with alternative routes that provided regular mail and escort service for authorized personnel between Richmond and Washington. It provided a common service for other elements of the Confederate government, but its use was carefully controlled. It was necessary for a person traveling the line to have written authorization from the secretary of war or another senior authority and from the chief of the Signal Corps before gaining escort.[10] This line functioned throughout the war and remained in place for at least two weeks after Lee's surrender on April 9, 1865.

After the Signal Corps was organized, it became associated with the War Department's secret service operations as well. At the beginning of the war, the state of Virginia had organized an excellent espionage organization in Washington. Originally this espionage unit reported to an office in Richmond that provided it with guidance and distributed its information to those who needed it. When a Confederate army was organized in Virginia in June 1861, arrangements were made for pertinent information to be sent directly to its headquarters in the Manassas area. This direct contact was handled at first by Col. Thomas Jordan and then by Lt. Col. George W. Lay but eventually developed into an arrangement by which contact was maintained by Maj. Cornelius Boyle, who became the provost marshal and post commander at Gordonsville, Virginia. The key location of Gordonsville on the rail line made it possible for Boyle to forward messages rapidly to the headquarters of the Army of Northern Virginia, wherever it might be located.

The office in Richmond, however, evolved into the headquarters for the War Department's secret service operations. One of Union detective Allan Pinkerton's agents visited this office in early April 1862 before the Signal Corps was formally organized. According to the agent, the office, called the Subterranean Room, was a large room on the third floor of one of the main hotels in Richmond and was occupied by "a number of gentlemen—some reading, while others were engaged in writing at little tables that were ranged about the room." The agent was told it was a bureau of intelligence that was managed partly by the government and partly by wealthy merchants in Washington and Baltimore. He was also told that the bureau employed "nearly fifty persons, some of whom are constantly in the field carrying dispatches, gaining and bringing in information from the Yankee lines."[11] It is more likely that the "wealthy merchants" of Washington and Baltimore were sources and agents for the system, not its managers. (The description is remarkably reminiscent of some Allied intelligence offices in the early days of World War II.)

Perhaps because of the similarities of these activities to those of the Secret Line, the Signal Corps appears to have taken over the responsibility for managing the clandestine operations of the War Department. The Subterranean Room may have become what was later known to the Signal Corps as the Back Room, in which secret service matters were handled.

In June 1863, Major Norris, the commander of the Confederate Signal Corps, traveled to Charleston to meet visiting British dignitary Col. James Fremantle and escort him on his visit to Richmond. Fremantle, in his diary entry for June 14, 1863, referred to Norris as "the chief of the secret intelligence bureau at Richmond." Later he said that "Major Norris told me many amusing anecdotes connected with the secret intelligence department, and of the numerous ingenious methods for communicating with the Southern partisans on the other side of the Potomac."[12]

During this period, the War Department bureau responsible for the Signal Corps was sometimes referred to as the Signal and Secret Service Bureau. In 1864, however, Major Norris was assigned to special duty in South Carolina, apparently in connection with the defense of Charleston, and Capt. William N. Barker became acting chief of the bureau. Barker confined himself largely to the Signal Corps and Secret Line side of the business and was not much involved in the broader aspects of the War Department's clandestine activities. An inspector general's report on the Signal Corps, dated December 21, 1864, specifically quoted a Signal Corps spokesman as saying that the corps' duties included the operation of secret lines of communication on the Potomac and that this required it to "transport across the Potomac all agents or Scouts, who shall present orders for the same, from the War Department, Heads of Bureaux, [and] Generals of Armies, approved by the Chief of [the] Signal Corps." The Secret Line also required the Signal Corps to "forward letters for War & State Depts. to agents in foreign countries." Sources of information for the Signal Corps were described as "accredited agents in N. York, Washington, and Baltimore."[13]

The inspector general was also told that there was no secret service fund. Presumably, the Signal Corps did not have its own secret service fund and had to use the army's "Incidental and Contingent" fund or make a case for the secretary of war to ask the president for secret service gold. On January 23, 1865, as the effort to capture Lincoln drew toward its climax, Secretary of War Seddon personally wrote out paragraph 30 of Special Order No. 18 assigning a number of Signal Corps personnel to special service with the secretary of state.[14]

One of those men was Alexander W. Weddell, who withdrew $40 in gold on January 28, in order "to defray expenses of Foreign Intercourse" (not a secret service fund), and signed the receipt "Sergt. in ch. S.S.,"[15] which could be interpreted as "Sergeant in charge, Secret Service" or "Sergeant in charge, Special Service." This is the basis for some interesting speculation. Weddell, having served as an officer before being wounded and finding a new post in the Signal Corps, was a man of some competence. It is possible that by January 28 many of the assets of the War Department secret service had been dedicated to specific missions in the field and there was not much need for coordination and direction from Richmond. By then the department's secret service operations may have dwindled to a care-taker cadre with Sergeant Weddell in charge, in much the same way that the army Torpedo Service had diminished at about the same time. On the other hand, it is also possible that the abbreviation referred to Weddell's status as the senior person in charge of the army signal and secret service personnel who had been transferred to the State Department a few days earlier. Weddell might have been completely unaware of the many other individuals engaged in clandestine missions for Davis and Benjamin and thought of himself as being in charge of all the secret service people working for the State Department.

Throughout the war, most of the War Department's clandestine activity was in direct support of field operations. It was almost as if the secretary of war kept a pool of agents from which he could assign to a mission in accordance with the tactical needs of the moment. An example is the famous "Harrison" assigned to Longstreet at the time of Gettysburg—Henry Thomas Harrison of Tennessee and Mississippi. At different periods in the war, he was assigned to work for General Longstreet, Gen. D. H. Hill, and, late in the war, some special assignment in the New York area.[16] Another agent was John Williamson Palmer, who wrote dispatches for the *New York Tribune* under the name "Altamont" while at the same time keeping the Confederacy posted on Union movements. Later Palmer worked in Richmond, where he was employed in generating "black" propaganda (propaganda generated by the enemy but pretending to be from a friendly source) to use against the North.[17]

Other hints of War Department secret service activity are contained in telegrams received by the Confederate army's adjutant and inspector general (A&IG), who, in military procedure, acts as an authenticating message center, passing correspondence on to the person who had the authority to make a decision about it.[18] On May 26, 1864, Gen. D. H. Maury at Mobile, Alabama, asked Gen. Samuel Cooper, the adjutant and inspector general, for permission to send two men into Memphis on a secret mission. Also on May 26, Cooper received a telegram from "Columbia 26" that said, "Yours of 25th in cypher rec. I have no key, telegraphed for one some time ago to be sent by hand or mail" (distribution of cipher keys was a normal Signal Corps function). The identity of "Columbia 26" might make the matter clear, but since the sender is not otherwise identified, it remains a tantalizing mystery as does Gen. E. Kirby Smith's March 26, 1865, message to General Cooper: "The following dispatch rec'd from Genl. Walker at Houston. 'A very reliable agent of the Secret Service has just arrived from New Orleans.'"

Provost Marshal of Richmond

The Department of Richmond's Brig. Gen. John H. Winder was the "PooBah"[19] of the Confederacy's secret service. Since Winder held so many different jobs and was responsible for so many different duties, it is difficult to establish exactly what his role was in the clandestine operations—but his importance is indisputable.[20] Winder taught at West Point during the cadetship of Jefferson Davis, and Davis appears to have developed great confidence in him, appointing him brigadier general in the Provisional Army of the Confederate States (PACs) effective June 21, 1861.[21] Winder was assigned to command Camp Lee, the training camp near Richmond; made commander of the guards at the hospitals in Richmond; given the job of organizing the original defenses of Richmond; made responsible for maintaining discipline among the military personnel in Richmond; given charge of detecting Union spies; and charged with the care of Union prisoners of war. Originally he was the provost marshal of Richmond, but the job grew in size and complexity, and eventually he became the commander of the Department of Henrico, which in due course became the Department of Richmond.

For some time Winder engaged in a jurisdictional squabble with Judge John A. Campbell, assistant secretary of war, over who had the right to issue "passports" entitling civilians to leave the Richmond area. Winder argued from the standpoint of his police and counterintelligence responsibilities, and Campbell invoked the superior position of the War Department. In connection with his counterintelligence duties, Winder prompted another sort of controversy over his staff of detectives. Because he was from Maryland, and because at the beginning of the war there were several Marylanders floating around Richmond looking for jobs, a number of the detectives he recruited were from Baltimore. This prompted considerable criticism from the Richmond newspapers, who called Winder's detectives "Plug-Uglies," a reference to the notorious 1850s Baltimore thugs.

Two surviving rosters of the employees of the Department of Richmond show that in 1863 Winder's staff included six men in his immediate office, a chief of police, four deputies, twenty-six detectives, three wardens, twenty clerks, and six messengers. Captain Alexander, in charge of Castle Thunder under Winder, had a staff that included an adjutant, clerk, messenger, warden, two deputy wardens, a clerk of the guardhouse, a warden of the guardhouse, a deputy warden, a stockkeeper, and nine detectives. Total personnel reporting to Winder in 1863 numbered eighty-five. In 1864 there was a determined effort by the Confederate War Department to identify and reassign redundant personnel. After the hunt for military manpower—aided by his political enemies—had worked the organization over, Winder's staff dropped to forty-six, with nine in his office, six at Castle Thunder (including three detectives), and thirty-one in the provost marshal's office, including fourteen detectives. Though Winder was the head of the Department of Richmond, and the provost marshal was a subordinate office within that department, clearly he no longer had the political influence he had wielded in the early days of the war.[22]

Quartermaster payrolls give additional clues concerning Winder's actual activities. In 1863, Major Parkhill, the assistant quartermaster who paid Winder's personnel, recorded paying ninety-seven people whose salaries were charged against a fund known as "Arresting Deserters." In 1864, Parkhill paid only forty-two people from this fund but paid fifty-three people from a fund labeled "Special Service." (Some employees were paid from both funds.) From these records it would appear that in 1864 Winder's subordinates were less concerned with military police work than with clandestine operations. Unfortunately we cannot tell to what extent the clandestine operations were concerned with counterintelligence and to what extent they were involved in supporting more positive secret service.[23]

Of the numerous important responsibilities heaped on General Winder, the most challenging was the handling of Union prisoners of war. Because of his initial position as provost marshal of Richmond, it was only natural that Winder would have responsibility for the approximately one thousand Union prisoners taken to Richmond after the First Battle of Manassas. Winder housed his unhappy guests in a warehouse rented from the ship chandler firm of Libby & Co. Libby Prison, as it came to be called, was eventually used for officer prisoners; an island in the James River, Belle Isle, was used for enlisted prisoners; and Castle Thunder, a building near Libby Prison, was used as a prison for Confederate deserters and persons suspected of disloyalty. The hordes of prisoners eventually overwhelmed these facilities as well as additional prisons in Danville, Virginia, and Salisbury, North Carolina.

On November 21, 1863, Winder ordered his son, Capt. W. Sidney Winder, to travel to Georgia to select a site for another military prison that could absorb the overflow of prisoners from both the Virginia and Tennessee theaters of operation.[24] The site selected by Captain Winder became the notorious Andersonville prison, which was used for only a few months in 1864 but was the scene of more than its share of misery and death.

General Winder eventually became too unpopular politically, and in May 1864 he was reassigned and put in command of all prisoner-of-war camps. He died on February 7, 1865. What was left of his organization, however, remained part of the Department of Richmond and as late as March 1865 was still performing errands for the Confederate secret service.[25]

War Department Torpedo Bureau

An extension of War Department's secret activity into the world of combat was the Torpedo Bureau. In describing the activities of the bureau, however, it is important to lay to rest another of the many myths about Jefferson Davis and his attitude toward explosive devices: that he was opposed to the use of explosive weapons because they were secret and underhanded and that no gentleman would approve of such unfair practices.

Compare that notion with the following letter written on May 15, 1864, on the stationery of the Confederate Engineer Bureau and addressed to Col. W. H. Stevens, chief of construction for the Department of Northern Virginia.

> Col,
>
> This note will be handed you by Mr. G. W. Thompson associated with Capt. McDaniel on Torpedo Service. By special request of the President he is sent with orders to report to you & will have a supply of sub terra shell with sensitive fuses. His excellency the Presdt thinks they should be planted in front of the work called by your name Fort Stevens, say within musket range on the slope of the hill. The Presdt. counts on this producing by explosion great demoralizing effect on the enemy. If any other point occurs to you where it would be specially well to use them, the Presdt. desires you to take action—some two or three thousand can be had. Lt. Tucker formerly serving with Genl. Rains, now paymaster in the Navy may be ordered to report to you, to direct such enterprises as the above under your direction.
>
> Very resply. your obt. ser.
> A L Rives
> Col. & Actg Chf. Bu.[26]

It is obvious from this letter that Davis thought that hidden explosives made effective weapons, that he was willing to concern himself with the appropriate application of such weapons, and that he knew some of the players in the clandestine explosives game. Captain Zere McDaniel was an old-timer in the explosives business, having blown up the USS *Cairo* and other targets long before the Strategy Bureau was established. A joint resolution of the Confederate Congress authorized the treasury to pay CS$76,726.30 in Confederate 8-percent bonds to McDaniel and Francis M. Ewing as their reward for sinking the *Cairo*. Unfortunately for McDaniel, the executive branch was not as forthcoming, and he never received the reward.[27]

Although Gen. Gabriel J. Rains had been experimenting with explosives, fuses, and detonators for some time, the War Department Torpedo Bureau was not formally authorized until October 1862. In addition to developing and procuring "torpedoes," the bureau was authorized to employ them against the enemy. The items developed, therefore, tended to involve timing devices to control the moment of explosion or characteristics to make them suitable for clandestine emplacement behind enemy lines. Thus, they had to be simple and capable of concealment.

Navy Submarine Battery Service

The Navy Submarine Battery Service was organized parallel with the Torpedo Bureau in the autumn of 1862. It was begun under the command of Matthew Fontaine Maury, but when he left for England shortly thereafter, the operation was placed under the command of Lt. Hunter Davidson. The service's main function was the defense of the major ports of the Confederacy—Richmond, Wilmington, Charleston, Savannah, and Mobile. It laid mine fields to defend the harbors against intrusion by the Union fleet and built torpedo boats with which to attack the blockaders.

One of the first devices used was a torpedo placed on the end of a long spar attached to the prow of a torpedo boat. The explosion was set off by ramming the charge against the hull of the enemy ship, while the crew depended on the length of the spar to escape the resulting blast. One variant of the torpedo boat was the CSS *David,* a small vessel with only the pilot and crew's cockpit and the ship's smokestack above water. The *David* attacked the USS *New Ironsides* near Charleston and exploded her torpedo against four and a half inches of armor and twenty-seven inches of wood backing. The armor held firm, but the Union ship was badly shaken and a number of the crew injured. As a result, the Union fleet adopted drastic new measures to guard against torpedo boats.[28] The most radical experiment was with a crude, hand-powered submarine. Over thirty men were drowned in accidents during its development, and another volunteer crew lost their lives when they successfully used the vessel to sink the USS *Housatonic* off Charleston.

The Submarine Battery Service was a very professional organization with great esprit de corps. The unit was also very conscious of a need for secrecy and required its personnel to sign a security agreement. As a result of their professionalism, their torpedoes sank or damaged forty U.S. naval vessels, and the threat of their mine fields helped keep several Confederate ports out of Union hands.

War Department Strategy Bureau

This shadow organization came into being in the first half of 1863, but it was never formally established as a bureau. The name was given to it later by B. J. Sage, one of the intellectual godfathers of the activity, at the suggestion of General Rains of the Torpedo Bureau. What the men actually working in the endeavor called it is not clear. To them it may have been nothing more than "Secret Service."

The function of this bureau was to recruit men with ideas for new weapons or with an interest in operating behind enemy lines. These covert agents were assisted in developing their ideas or trained in the use of existing weaponry by experts from the Torpedo Bureau. They were also trained in the tradecraft needed for clandestine operations in enemy territory. Once trained, they were allowed to choose the part of the country in which they wanted to work; furnished the necessary munitions (explosives, fuses, detonators, timing devices, etc.); and assigned to the engineer company in the military department responsible for that area. The company provided them an administrative home, but otherwise the agents were organized into teams, called "destructionists" or "strategic corps," and sent out to destroy targets of interest to the department commander.

The central functions appear to have been carried out by Maj. William S. Barton, operating as a member of the staff of the adjutant and inspector general of the Confederate army. Orders to military departments and the individuals involved were signed by the chief of the Engineer Bureau in Richmond, but they were probably drafted by Barton.

Legislation passed in February 1864 broadened the authorization for the recruitment of agents to operate against the enemy behind his lines. This sanctioned the creation of sabotage teams that were not part of the engineer companies, but it is probable that the same people in Richmond looked after the organization, training, and support of both the engineer teams and the teams created under the new legislation. Some of these nonengineer teams, however, came into existence before the February 1864 legislation was approved, and their exact history is a bit murky.

One of the units not attached to the engineers was "Company A, Secret Service," under the command of Capt. Zere McDaniel. In function, this unit was similar to the bands of destructionists or strategic corps operating in the military departments. McDaniel, a veteran of the clandestine sabotage business, having served before the strategic corps was established and involved in the sinking of the USS *Cairo* in December 1862, received authority to organize this company on February 29, 1864. Around September 1864 the twenty-eight men in the company were assigned as follows:

Richmond	12
Kentucky	4
Mobile, Alabama	3
Augusta, Georgia	2
Mississippi	2
Lynchburg, Virginia	2
Missouri	1
Tennessee	1
Pittsylvania County, Virginia	1

Of the twelve men in Richmond, four were listed as operating behind enemy lines, six were listed as awaiting orders, one was sick, and one was in charge of the company's office.[29]

From the list of assignments, it would appear that the men in this company were also engaged in attacking targets in the enemy rear but that some were not operating under the control of a department commander. Possibly this company was a blue-ribbon unit kept at the national level to take care of work on targets of interest to Davis and others in Richmond. Part of Davis's interest might well have been to support specific department commanders from time to time, thus accounting for the men assigned to Mobile.

Later in the war, Capt. Thomas E. Courtney developed a torpedo of cast iron in the shape of a lump of coal. The idea was to mix these devices among the lumps of real coal in a pile of fuel to be used by a steam engine in a locomotive, on a ship, or in a factory. At some point the device would be shoveled into the firebox of the engine along with the coal. Within a few seconds or minutes the bomb would explode and tear open the boiler, causing a secondary explosion of steam. The steam explosion would mask the cause of the disaster, making it appear to be an industrial accident instead of enemy sabotage.

In August 1863, Courtney was authorized to raise a secret service corps of up to twenty men presumably to employ this device. On March 8, 1864, Major Norris of the Confederate Signal Corps recommended to the secretary of war that the use of the disguised torpedoes be extended to additional places behind enemy lines.[30] The "Courtney torpedo" was apparently used with great success, and Jefferson Davis kept a souvenir example of the bomb in his office in the Confederate White House.[31] It is rarely possible to tell from the reports available which method, Courtney or a match, was used to set fire to a boat, but there is ample evidence that a large number of river steamboats were destroyed by the Confederates.[32]

On April 27, 1865, after the surrender of Generals Lee and Johnston but before all Confederate forces had been rounded up, the steamer *Sultana* sank in the Mississippi River just after leaving Memphis. An explosion set her on fire, and strong winds fanned the flames so that the vessel burned extensively before sinking. The *Sultana* was grossly overcrowded with former Union prisoners of war returning to the North, and the estimates ran from over 1,200 to about 1,800 lives lost. There were many theories concerning the cause of the explosion. An investigation of the wreckage showed that several of the boilers had been torn apart, but nothing was said about the firebox, which could have contained a Courtney torpedo. It was concluded that one of the boilers had burst, causing the others to explode and starting the fire. On May 8, 1888, however, the *Memphis Daily Appeal* published an article claiming that a Confederate agent named Robert Lowden, alias Charles Dale, had planted a lump of coal that contained a bomb on the coal pile in front of the boilers.[33] The whole truth about the *Sultana* may never be known, but the circumstances surrounding its sinking are almost exactly what they would have been if it had been "hit" by a Courtney torpedo.

Other leaders of sabotage operations included Minor Major, who had a successful campaign of boat burning on the Mississippi River and turned up on January 26, 1865, at St. Lawrence Hall in Montreal, a hotel frequented by people involved in Confederate clandestine activity; Edward Frazier, who was interrogated about Confederate explosives activity at the trial of the Lincoln assassination conspirators; Maj. E. Pliny Bryan, who served in the Signal Corps and planted torpedoes in the James River; and John Maxwell, who blew up General Grant's supply base at City Point on August 9, 1864.

The Greenhow Group

John Letcher was not a rabid secessionist, but as governor of Virginia he was conscious that civil war was a possible outcome of the political trends of 1860 and that he was responsible for preparing his state for that eventuality. Letcher had previously served in Washington as a congressman and had many friends in the city, and during the winter months of 1861 he spent several weeks in Washington arranging for sympathetic army officers to join Virginia in the event of the outbreak of war. There were a number of these officers in Washington at that time—such as John B. Magruder and Thomas Jordan—who later resigned and joined a group of former regular officers, mostly West Point graduates, nominated by Letcher for commissions in the Provisional Army of the State of Virginia on May 7, 1861.[34]

Whether Letcher was involved personally is not known, but he probably participated with Magruder and Jordan in the creation of an espionage organization to keep the state of Virginia posted on events in Washington. The organization that they evidently created included a number of citizens well placed in Washington society, as well as a number of people of more humble background who had good access to key points in the Washington bureaucracy.

One of the members of Washington society involved in the organization was Rose O'Neal Greenhow, the widow of a U.S. State Department official. She was instrumental in getting word of Gen. Irvin McDowell's sally from Washington to Colonel Jordan in anticipation of the First Battle of Manassas and continued to report useful information until she was arrested on August 24, 1861. Thereafter Greenhow was able to play up her role as the beautiful society matron imprisoned by the dastardly Yankees to attract publicity for herself and the Southern cause. In fact, she attracted so much attention that subsequent historical investigation has concentrated on her rather than on the elaborate organization that made her successes possible. It is clear, however, that the Confederates continued to receive good information from Washington long after Greenhow's arrest.

Cavalry Scouts

Many Confederate generals used cavalry scouts to provide tactical intelligence, but Gen. J. E. B. Stuart, as the senior cavalry commander in the Army of Northern Virginia, established an exceptionally able group of bright, active, young men to serve as scouts for the army. General Lee depended so heavily on these men and was so involved with Stuart in their assignments and reports that it is difficult to tell exactly how Lee and Stuart divided the responsibility of using the scouts. In essence, they appear to have followed the aggressive policy of knowing where the enemy was at all times. Some commanders, and some intelligence officers, would have been content to use their scouts merely to avoid surprise, but such a policy surrenders the initiative to the enemy. Lee and Stuart, on the other hand, appear to have wanted to hold the initiative and to have thought that up-to-date knowledge of the whole battlefield was necessary.

Most of the work of these cavalry scouts was connected with conventional tactical problems, but it is necessary to consider them in connection with the secret service, because the scouts themselves constituted a pool of trained and disciplined talent close to Richmond that could be borrowed for specific secret service tasks. Benjamin Franklin Stringfellow, Thomas Nelson Conrad, and Channing Smith are examples of men who served as cavalry scouts for part of their military career and later turned up in secret service projects.

Following Stuart's death, none of the other cavalry commanders appears to have had his success in handling the scouts. Consequently, while at the war's end several of the scouts were still on secret service assignments of interest to the highest levels of the Confederate government, in general the group was not as successful as it had once been. The Battle of Five Forks is a good case in point. Completely unaware of the troop movement, Gen. Fitzhugh Lee allowed General Sheridan to get several large units of Federal infantry onto the battlefield. As a result, General Pickett thought that he had won the day when in fact the real battle had not even begun. Five Forks became the Union victory that precipitated the Confederate retreat from Richmond.

Operations in Canada

The activities of the Confederates in Canada in 1864 have been re-counted a number of times, but the genesis of the Confederate organization there goes back to a much earlier date. How the organization was created, some of its operating practices, the role that it was expected to play, and the role it played as a postwar quasi-Confederate-government-in-exile are discussed at greater length in chapter 5.

From the array of organizations described above, one can draw some obvious conclusions about the Confederate secret service. Part of the effort was clearly devoted to the collection of political intelligence at the national level. The information was evaluated by the senior members of the Confederate government without the intervention of "objective" analysis by "independent" intelligence officers. These senior officials also used the secret service for political action and propaganda operations. Other parts of the secret service were primarily interested in military intelligence—some of it strategic and some of it tactical. Other parts of the secret service were involved in complementing the actions of the Confederate armies by employing clandestine tradecraft and secret weapons to attack the enemy's military establishment and logistic facilities.

Some of the functions performed by the Confederate secret service were better executed than others, but on the whole the Confederacy showed ingenuity in adapting existing concepts and developing new ideas to meet the circumstances of the Civil War. Their own view of the matter was well stated by the Reverend Stephen Cameron, who worked in the secret service in England and in Canada:

Every government has its own secret service, even in time of peace, and sometimes the most important results are effected through their agency. The universality of its adoption by nations supposes its efficiency, and the importance of such an arm of the service and the character of the agents appointed only consist of those in whom the greatest confidence can be placed and who have already won reputation and distinction in the political scene. . . . Perhaps no contest in the world ever afforded similar opportunities for acts of individual daring than did the late embittered feud between the North and the South, and in no department was there more scope for the exercise of adroit courage than was afforded by the Secret Service.[35]

Chapter 3

THE GREENHOW
ORGANIZATION

THE STORY of Confederate espionage in Washington has been dominated by the personality and adventures of Rose O'Neal Greenhow (1817–64). This colorful friend of presidents, politicians, and generals, sent to the Confederate government a mass of information on the early preparations of the Union for war, her chief success being when she sent warning of the Union movement which resulted in the First Battle at Manassas on July 21, 1861.

Rose Greenhow was arrested on August 23, 1861, and subsequently a number of her associates were also arrested or forced to flee Washington. The Confederate espionage organization continued to function, but as a result of these various arrests and the writings of Allan Pinkerton and his detectives, as well as copies of a number of reports prepared by Greenhow's group, a great deal of information is available about her and her espionage associates. Greenhow herself published a book in London in 1863 describing her arrest and imprisonment.[1]

In addition to her reputation as a hostess at the center of Washington society, Pinkerton's detectives and others suspected that some of Greenhow's success with highly placed informants was due to her exploitation of sexual attraction. One such beneficiary of her boudoir charm appears to have been Henry Wilson, a Republican senator from Massachusetts, who succeeded Jefferson Davis as chairman of the Senate Military Affairs Committee.[2] This view of Greenhow's sexual prowess was shared by some of her contemporaries. After her tragic

1864 death by drowning while running the blockade on her return to North Carolina from London, Stephen R. Mallory, Confederate Secretary of the Navy, wrote to Mrs. Clement Clay, wife of one of the Confederate Commissioners in Canada, commenting on Greenhow's character.

> She was a clever woman, much more clever than was ever admitted by her associates. She started early in life, into the great world, and found in it many wild beasts; but only one to which she devoted special pursuit, and thereafter she hunted man with that resistless zeal and unfailing instinct which made Gordon Cumming so successful with elephants. She was equally at home with Ministers of State or their doorkeepers, with leaders and the led, and she had a shaft in her quiver for every defense which game might attempt, and to which he was sure to succumb. If, like Gordon Cumming, she had displayed the fruits of her bow and spear, her collection would have been far more rare and interesting than was his museum of tiger, leopard and lion skins. What scalps she might have shown, only think of it! And if she had at the same time shown the weapons with which death was inflicted, the special arrow and particular spear, her skill and success would have appeared wonderful. She was very slender—beautiful.[3]

The romance of the espionage game and the attraction of Greenhow's personality have focused attention on her immediate activities, with the more general context of her role as an agent being slighted. There is, however, useful information about Confederate secret service activity scattered throughout the Greenhow story.

In the first place, Rose Greenhow was not a neophyte in the world of political intrigue. Although she did not have much formal education, she had been thoroughly indoctrinated in politics by John C. Calhoun, the great spokesman of states' rights, and by other politicians in Washington. In 1835 she married Robert Greenhow (1800–1854), a Virginian who was trained as a physician and lawyer but, because of his familiarity with foreign languages and world affairs, was employed by the State Department. In 1850 Robert Greenhow, with Rose and their daughters, was sent to Mexico as a special agent to investigate fraudulent claims rising from the Mexican War. Later he moved to San

Francisco, where he opened a law office. In 1854 he died from an accidental injury while his wife was in the East with their daughters, and Rose traveled to California via Panama to settle his affairs. On July 14, 1854, she wrote to Jefferson Davis, then secretary of war, asking him if a house had been found for her in Washington. This could have been the result of close friendship, but the manner of expression suggests a more formal one and may indicate that Robert Greenhow had been working on a confidential assignment for the United States War Department.[4]

The net effect of all of her exposure to world affairs was to provide Rose Greenhow with an unusually valuable background for the role of espionage agent. It is even possible that through her husband's associations she had learned some of the more technical aspects of espionage tradecraft. Given this experience, coupled with her obvious intelligence and personal contacts, her familiarity with leaders of the Southern party in Washington, and her personal commitment to the Southern cause, she was an obvious candidate for any group planning a serious pro-Southern espionage effort in Washington. And in view of her prominent connections, the Confederate organizers of the espionage net would also have been inclined to treat her with the utmost respect.

On January 12, 1861, a congressional caucus of representatives of the seceded states voted to leave the U.S. Congress immediately instead of following Jefferson Davis's recommendation to wait for the inauguration of the new Congress on March 4. This precipitate departure of the leading Southerners left the task of organizing their friends in Washington in others' hands. Fortunately for the South, there remained in the capital a number of people of considerable talent and technical expertise, including: Robert E. Lee; Lee's oldest son, 1st Lt. George Washington Custis Lee of the West Point class of 1854; Capt. John Bankhead Magruder of the West Point class of 1830; Capt. Thomas Jordan of the West Point class of 1840; and 2d Lt. Lunsford L. Lomax of the West Point class of 1856. All of these men were Virginians who later became general officers in the Confederate army. There were also a number of capable civilians who strongly supported the Southern point of view. These included William T. Smithson, president of the Farmers and Merchants Bank; Thomas Green, who represented persons with claims resulting from the War of 1812; Col. Michael Thompson, a prominent attorney from South Carolina; and Benjamin Ogle Tayloe, reputed to be the richest man in America with property holdings in Virginia, Maryland, and the District of Columbia.

The governor of Virginia, John Letcher, visited Washington for several days between January 21 and February 11, 1861. Letcher had been a member of Congress from Virginia 1851–59 and knew Greenhow and most of the pro-Southern members of Washington society. There is no direct information concerning the governor's activities during this visit to Washington; as soon as Virginia voted to secede on April 17, 1861, and began to organize its own army, however, it became obvious that there was an understanding between Virginia and several of these army officers. On May 7 Letcher nominated Magruder, Jordan, and Lomax to receive commissions in the Virginia army, and on May 9 he nominated Custis Lee. Jordan, however, did not apply for a commission until May 8, apparently formalizing an already existing agreement.[5]

On April 21, 1861, Lomax's mother noted in her diary that "Colonel John Bankhead Magruder, Ogle Tayloe and Custis Lee spent the morning in a serious discussion. This evening Lindsay told me that he had sent in his resignation; Colonel Magruder has also sent in his resignation from the army and will go to Virginia tomorrow where Lindsay will join him."[6] Ogle Tayloe, as the stay-behind member of this group, was doubtless concerned with the organization of pro-Confederate activities in Washington.

A more important demonstration of the existence of an agreement with Letcher, however, is that before he left Washington Jordan organized an espionage ring that included Rose Greenhow and Augusta Morris. Jordan also arranged for the chief agents in the ring to report in cipher, later apologizing for leaving them with a relatively rudimentary system for encrypting their findings.[7] In addition to evidence that the organization had other "leaders,"[8] in Greenhow's writings it is clear that there was money available to buy supplies for Confederate prisoners in the Old Capitol Prison. While there is no direct clue as to the source of this money—and at this early stage of the war it is possible that it came entirely from donations from local pro-Confederate citizens such as Tayloe, Green, and Smithson—the first allocation of Confederate government secret service funds on April 10, 1861, of $40,000 would have provided ample funds for the Washington operation as well as for operations elsewhere. Could it be that prior to its secession the state of Virginia was already cooperating with the Confederacy in clandestine matters?

Also clear is that, while Greenhow collected some secret information from her own contacts, such as Massachusetts senator Henry Wilson, and also received data amassed by others, possibly subagents, there were other principal agents organizationally parallel with Greenhow, because the apparatus continued to provide useful information after she was arrested and sent South in 1861.

An espionage organization as ambitious as the one to which Greenhow belonged needs other capabilities as well as agents. For example, Greenhow may have been able to encipher her own messages on occasion, but encipherment takes time and attention to detail and usually works best when there is a specialist in charge. It is likely that an unnamed somebody was keeping track of who had cipher systems, what the systems were, and what problems were encountered in using them. In addition to cipher expertise, there was obviously at least one team of operatives who could "work" the streets of Washington. These individuals moved around the city to observe activity, checked on reports of new fortifications, trailed persons of interest, and provided security screens to help threatened individuals avoid arrest. Greenhow mentioned several incidents that would have required this sort of expert assistance and claimed that the organization had warned former vice president John C. Breckenridge and former minister to Spain William Preston of plans to arrest them (both men later became general officers in the Confederate army).[9] Greenhow also cut clippings from newspapers and magazines with sketches of Washington fortifications and annotated them with information that must have been obtained by on-site observation of those installations.[10]

From Virginia, Jordan managed the network in Washington by correspondence. For a while in the spring of 1861 he was in Richmond, but when P. G. T. Beauregard established a Confederate command in northern Virginia, which eventually became the Army of Northern Virginia, Jordan joined the general's staff and continued to direct the activities of the espionage apparatus in Washington.

Jordan began as the responsible manager, sending requirements to the field and distributing the information received to those who needed

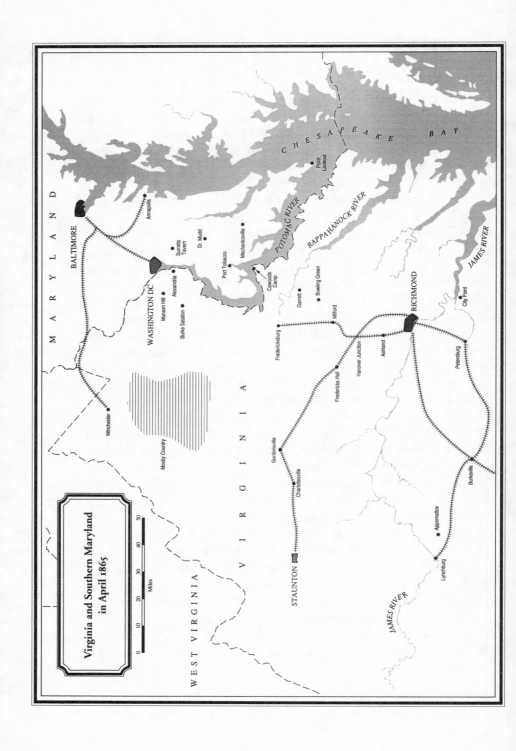

Virginia and Southern Maryland
in April 1865

Miles
0   10   20   30   40   50

MARYLAND

BALTIMORE

Annapolis

WASHINGTON DC

Munson Hill
Alexandria
Burke Station

Surratts
Tavern

Dr. Mudd

Port Tobacco

Mechanicsville

Cawoods
Camp

CHESAPEAKE BAY

Point
Lookout

POTOMAC RIVER

RAPPAHANOCK RIVER

JAMES RIVER

Winchester

Mosby Country

WEST VIRGINIA

VIRGINIA

Garrett

Bowling Green

Milford

Fredericksburg

Fredericks Hall

Hanover Junction

Ashland

RICHMOND

City Point

Petersburg

Gordonsville

Charlottesville

Burkeville

Appomattox

STAUNTON

Lynchburg

JAMES RIVER

it. In this he had the assistance of Maj. Cornelius Boyle, the provost marshal at Manassas. Boyle, who had been a successful physician in Washington, had headed a pro-Southern militia unit in Washington known as the National Rifles in spite of a walking impairment. When war broke out, the National Rifles moved to Alexandria and most of the men joined the Alexandria battalion of the Virginia Volunteers. Boyle was appointed to command the unit on April 29, 1861, but on May 11 was transferred to the provost marshal post.

Jordan soon became Beauregard's chief of staff, and his duties grew so numerous that he had to delegate responsibility for the Washington espionage group to someone else. The man chosen was Lt. Col. George W. Lay, West Point class of 1842, who served for the first half of 1862 as the inspector general for northern Virginia. In due course Lay followed Beauregard when he was assigned to Charleston and was replaced in part by Maj. Charles S. Venable of General Lee's staff. In the meantime, Boyle, having become more experienced in his job, took on more responsibility and was transferred to the key post of provost marshal at Gordonsville, where he remained for the remainder of the war.

In addition to its managers in Virginia, the Greenhow group needed an efficient communications system. While there are abundant romantic tales of agents carrying secret messages through enemy territory—such as beautiful Bettie Duval wrapping Greenhow's key message about General McDowell's offensive in her hair and riding her mount through Union lines—the network had to arrange for a complicated chain of couriers, boats, horses, and whatever else was needed to get messages from Washington to their proper points of contact. Greenhow says that on one occasion she sent a message to Beauregard's headquarters at Manassas and that it was received at Manassas by eight o'clock that same evening and that she had a reply to her message by noon the next day. Considering that Manassas was a good twenty-six miles from Washington, the ride alone would have taken about five or six hours each way, plus the time it would take to get past Union sentries and evade patrols. Fortunately, from Beauregard's description of how he received a message from Greenhow, it is possible to trace what was probably the main communications route employed to get messages from Washington to General Beauregard's headquarters.

The extension of McDowell's pickets had now interrupted our "underground mail" between Washington and Manassas; but it had fortunately happened a few days before, that a gentleman, Mr. D[onnellan], formerly a clerk in one of the departments at Washington, was introduced at headquarters by Colonel Chestnut [*sic*][11] as perfectly trustworthy, and capable of performing the delicate office of communicating with the friendly agencies we had managed to establish in Washington. He was provided with a paper, having neither signature nor address, but upon which was written the ciphered message, "Trust the bearer," and with it immediately despatched to the residence of Mrs. G[reenhow], our secret emissary in the Federal Capital. The result was that, at about 8 o'clock P.M. on the 16th [July 1861] a sealed communication was received at headquarters, despatched by relays from General Holmes's picket line near Eastport [Evansport, located where the Marine base at Quantico now stands]. It had been brought that morning from Washington, to a point on the opposite shore, by Mr. D[onnellan], from Mrs. G[reenhow], and announced in cipher, this simple but important piece of news: "McDowell has been ordered to advance tonight"; confirming General Beauregard's belief as to the intended Federal movement, which was otherwise apparent to him.[12]

Further detail on the communications route is provided by a slip of paper that appears to have been the cover letter for this sealed package. On one side it says,

To Col Danl. Ruggles
near Matthias Point.
Commanding Confederate forces

and on the other side,

Let this go thro by 11 or 12 A.M. [*sic*] of the 16th inst. This must go thro' by a *lightning express* to Beauregard. Incur any expense upon authority of my instructions and I'll certify to the bills when I return.—G. Donnellan

To Col. Danl Ruggles.[13]

The address to Colonel Ruggles[14]—who lived a few miles from Mathias Point and was headquartered at Brooke's Station on the Richmond, Fredericksburg, and Potomac Railroad where the tracks cross Accokeek Creek, three miles from the end of the line at the mouth of Aquia Creek—indicates that the message was to be taken through southern Maryland for transfer across the lower Potomac, but the note was not intended to be delivered to Ruggles before action was taken. The note was more a formal bit of military correspondence telling the officer who received it that it was a serious matter and should be acted on immediately. It also indicated for the record that expenses incurred in carrying out the instructions would be approved. (Similar messages are exchanged today among headquarters without the addressees ever actually seeing the message. These messages are the grease that keeps the wheels of military bureaucracy turning with a minimum of friction.)

Obviously, the only way that this message could have been delivered to Beauregard by "lightning express" was for such a system to already exist. One could not create such a system upon the arrival of an unexpected communication from Washington. The troops assigned to Ruggles and stationed along the Potomac north of Brooke's Station included fifty-eight cavalrymen from the Stafford Rangers; thus, there were in the vicinity of Evansport mounted troops who could support a courier relay system between Ruggles's headquarters and General Beauregard's headquarters at Manassas.[15]

The shortest and most practical route for a courier system between Brooke's Station and Manassas would run through the village of Aquia at the head of deep water on Aquia Creek, then past Evansport to Dumfries, and then almost due north to Manassas. The total route from Brooke's Station to Manassas covered twenty-eight miles; the distance from Evansport to Manassas was approximately twenty miles.

Standard speeds for horses were four miles per hour at a walk, eight miles per hour at a trot, and twelve miles per hour at a gallop.[16] These speeds could not be continued over long periods, so the normal practice on a long march was to alternate periods of walk and trot with short rests interspersed, resulting in an average speed of about six miles per hour. Therefore, for a speed courier system using a galloping horse to achieve a speed approaching twelve miles per hour, it was advisable to have stages of ten or twelve miles with fresh horses available at each stage.

If the distance between Brooke's Station and Manassas had been organized in this manner, it would have made sense to have one relay point below Dumfries, about where the road from Evansport intersected the main north-south road, and another about half-way between Dumfries and Manassas. Allowing for time to change horses and minor mishaps of the road, such a system would have enabled the two headquarters to receive messages regularly within two and a half hours of origination. If a message unexpectedly entered the system at Evansport, the travel time to Manassas would probably be less than two hours. Additional time would be required to bring the message to the attention of the proper officer, but with proper alertness on the part of the troops at Evansport, the message from Donnellan should have arrived at Manassas within two or two and a half hours of its receipt at Evansport. So, subtracting two and a half hours from its 8:00 P.M. arrival time in Manassas, the message should have reached Evansport near 5:30 P.M. on July 16, 1861.

While the Union's Potomac flotilla was not yet in full operation, it would still have been necessary to observe caution in crossing the river, which at that point is over a mile wide. And since the exact launching point is unknown, the actual distance traveled by boat may have been somewhat longer. It would be safe to assume, however, that the total trip across the Potomac would have taken at least an hour, and thus the message arriving at the launch area at about 4:30 P.M. The approximate launch point in Charles County, Maryland, is about thirty miles from the Anacostia River, which marked the southern edge of Washington. At an average of six miles per hour, a courier could have left Washington at 11:30 A.M. and delivered the sealed package to the launch site in time for the message to reach General Beauregard by 8:00 P.M. It would have been perfectly feasible for a single horse and rider to have made the Maryland segment of the trip.

So in addition to good fortune, the courier who would maximize the success rate of such a system had to be a person of skill and experience with the physical stamina to cope with the demands of travel and the courage to take risks in hazardous circumstances. George Donnellan, the first to fill this role, had been a former employee of the U.S. Land Office and had considerable experience in surveying and field engineering. Donnellan continued to operate successfully until he was relieved in the spring of 1862 and given a commission as an engineer in the Confederate army.[17] He faced two problems in his courier duty: getting information to the army headquarters in northern Virginia and relaying information to Richmond. Fortunately, through papers captured by the Union army,[18] it is known that the line to Richmond involved Dr. Edward H. Wyvill who lived in southern Prince George's County, Maryland, and George Dent, a wealthy planter who lived in Charles County, Maryland. This line was partially broken up by arrests in the fall of 1861, but most of the individuals involved later became part of the Confederate Signal Corps' "Secret Line" between Richmond and Washington.[19]

When George Donnellan withdrew from the secret service network in the spring of 1862 and took a commission as an engineer in the Confederate army, he was replaced by a Marylander named Walter "Wat" Bowie. Tracing his career in the Confederate service is difficult because there were three men of the same name who served in the Army of Northern Virginia, and two of them served with Mosby's Rangers. One Walter Bowie was born in Westmoreland County, Virginia, and trained as a lawyer. Early in the war he enlisted in the 40th Virginia Infantry and rose to the rank of captain. He was wounded at Gettysburg and disqualified for field service. In April 1864, Gen. A. P. Hill gave him a strong recommendation as an inspector to Brig. Gen. R. H. Chilton, the chief inspector under General Cooper, the adjutant and inspector general of the Confederate army. One of Bowie's first tasks as an inspector was to write a report on conditions at Andersonville Prison. At the end of the war he was on active duty in South Carolina.

Another Walter Bowie was also born in Westmoreland County, Virginia. The youngest of the three, this Bowie graduated with a distinguished academic record from the Virginia Military Institute in 1861 (class of 1862). He participated in the First Battle of Manassas as a member of an infantry unit, and when classes at VMI resumed on January 1, 1862, he was appointed an instructor. Instead of serving at VMI, however, he enlisted in the 9th Virginia Cavalry and was wounded in mid-1862. Upon recovery, he obtained an appointment as an acting master in the Volunteer Navy; but finding that he did not have the nautical skills that he felt he needed, he resigned the position after three months. In September 1863, Bowie led a party of naval partisans from a base in Westmoreland County on a raid into southern

Maryland. The camp was located between two signal corps camps and attracted some unwelcome Union attention to the area. In December, the head of one of the Signal Corps units complained of the circumstance, and Bowie's group was apparently moved. Shortly thereafter, in the fall of 1863, Bowie joined Mosby's Rangers and was assigned as a private in Company A (a postwar roster of the company lists him as "John W. Bowie"; but in his VMI record, his letters to VMI superintendent Gen. Francis H. Smith, and letters from his daughter, he is always "Walter Bowie"). Possibly, Bowie and his whole party of Naval Partisans were shipped off to Mosby.[20]

In the autumn of 1864, Mosby asked for three volunteers for a "risky" job. Two of those who responded were Lewis Thornton Powell, who later joined John Wilkes Booth in Washington, and "Bowie of the Northern Neck," the Walter Bowie from VMI, men one comrade described as "first class men, always ready for any duty, and game." The operation involved the three Confederates galloping into Salem, Virginia, and firing on the Union pickets and then leading the pursuing Bluecoats into an ambush. The operation appears to have been quite a success.[21]

The Walter Bowie of primary interest to the understanding of the Greenhow organization was Walter Weems Bowie, born in Prince George's County, Maryland, in 1837 to a locally prominent family. Practicing law in Upper Marlboro, Maryland, when the war broke out, he joined the Confederate army in Richmond, where he served in a staff position as a captain for a short time. In early 1862, however, he began to travel back and forth across the Potomac, ostensibly recruiting soldiers for the Confederate army. He was actually providing a regular connection between the espionage organization in Washington and the Army of Northern Virginia. In this role he delivered information requirements to key agents in the Washington organization, picked up reports from them to carry to Virginia, and on occasion used several reports from various sources to summarize and interpret a situation covered by the reports.

In October 1862, Bowie was captured on a visit to southern Maryland and imprisoned in the Old Capitol Prison. With clandestine assistance, he escaped on November 17 and returned to his work for the Army of Northern Virginia. Some of his activities are described in the diary that he kept for a few months in early 1863. At the beginning of January, he scouted the crossings over the Potomac in Montgomery County, Maryland, just north and west of Washington. (Was General Lee already thinking of his next sweep north?) On January 11 he left Luray, Virginia—possibly after delivering reports to Maj. Cornelius Boyle at Gordonsville—and moved on to visit Capt. George Emack's Company B of the 1st Maryland Cavalry, then in camp at the foot of the mountains near Luray.

In February Bowie was in Bowling Green, Virginia, visiting friends in the 1st Maryland Artillery. Presumably he had been back in Maryland at least once since the stop at Luray. It is possible that Bowie was delivering his material directly to the Army of Northern Virginia's headquarters on this occasion, since the army was wintering in the area along the Rappahannock near Bowling Green.[22] In July 1863, Bowie was surprised by Federal troops at the home of his cousin, John H. Waring, in Prince George's County. Bowie escaped, dressed as a black woman, but his relatives were arrested and their property confiscated.[23]

On April 27, 1864, Bowie wrote for General Lee an excellent summary of information about Grant's preparations for the Wilderness campaign, including a description of the tactics that Grant later followed. The report appears to have been based on several more detailed reports from agents writing on various aspects of the situation.[24] Shortly after this, Bowie joined Mosby's Rangers.[25] Based on subsequent events, it appears that Bowie had taken his primary mission as liaison with espionage groups in Washington with him when he joined Mosby. After that time, Mosby's troopers began to make fairly frequent clandestine contacts in the Washington area, contacts they were still making in March 1865. Mosby may have originally provided a secure base from which Bowie could operate, but as time went by Mosby and his organization assumed more and more of the routine responsibility of maintaining communications between the espionage organization in Washington and the Army of Northern Virginia. With Mosby playing this role, there was no longer any need for a single person to play the part originally played by Donnellan and then by Bowie.

Bowie was obviously a man of considerable competence. Mosby recognized his ability on September 13, 1864, by organizing a new company, Company F, which elected Walter Bowie as one of its lieutenants. It is an interesting coincidence that on this same date Thomas Nelson Conrad was making preparations to leave Richmond with his team to establish a surveillance of Lincoln's movements and investigate the prospects for capturing the president and taking him into Confederate territory. On September 15, 1864, Secretary of War Seddon gave Conrad a piece of paper that read, "Lt. Col. Mosby and Lieutenant Cawood are hereby directed to aid and facilitate the movements of Captain Conrad."[26] Conrad asked that a similar order be issued to his associate Mountjoy Cloud, who was going on a mission similar to Conrad's via the "upper Potomac," which would have caused him to pass through Mosby's area of operations.[27]

If Mosby's partisans were involved in the same operation as Conrad, their involvement would indicate that the mission to capture Lincoln had backing at the highest levels in the Confederate government. One might interpret Conrad's surveillance of Lincoln as Conrad's own distortion of a clandestine mission originally intended for other purposes, but if Mosby were also involved in the Lincoln project, it could only mean that the Confederate government was behind the project and that Conrad's surveillance was an essential part of his mission.

Conrad received his orders from James A. Seddon, the Confederate secretary of war. Colonel Mosby normally received his orders from General Lee. The letter Seddon gave to Conrad was a means of identifying him to Mosby; it was not an operational order. There is no record of such an order from General Lee to Colonel Mosby, but it is possible to deduce what it might have been by analyzing the timing of Conrad's activities and those of some of Mosby's men during the last part of September 1864.

After the war, Mosby claimed that Walter Bowie had conceived the idea for a raid into Maryland to capture pro-Union Maryland governor Augustus W. Bradford at Annapolis.[28] Such a raid would have been very much out of keeping with Mosby's normal operations, which were concentrated on helping the Army of Northern Virginia.[29] Approval from the commanding general of the Army of Northern Virginia, however, would have put a very different light on the matter. Bowie's operation would have made sense as a dress rehearsal for an operation that carried a captured Lincoln through southern Maryland on the way to Richmond.

Most of what is known about Bowie's trip into Maryland comes from an account given by Lt. James Wiltshire and printed in a Baltimore paper in 1900.[30] According to Wiltshire's account, on about

September 25, 1864, Mosby got the idea of sending a detachment to capture the governor of Maryland and use him as a hostage to exchange for Confederates from southern Maryland in Union hands. Mosby assigned the command of the operation to Bowie and gave him twenty-five hand-picked men. Bowie's detachment then traveled to Mathias Point in King George County, the location of the Confederate Signal Corps station that moved agents, reports, and newspapers across the Potomac. Bowie and two men (one was James Wiltshire) crossed the river to reconnoiter and camped near "the Walnut Tree."[31] On the third day after crossing, they were approached by two men from nearby Port Tobacco, Maryland. After the men left, Bowie sent Wiltshire back across the river to bring a few selected men across the river and send the rest of the detachment back to Mosby.

Bowie and his select group walked to Port Tobacco, where they captured the horses of a small Union cavalry unit, and then continued on to the vicinity of Bowie's family home, north of Upper Marlboro, Maryland. Bowie left the group in hiding near his home for a day or two. On his return he announced that Governor Bradford was too well guarded to attempt to capture.

According to Wiltshire's story, Bowie's group would have been in King George County at about the same time that Conrad would have been passing through on his way to Washington. A detailed analysis of the itineraries of the two parties is necessary in determining whether or not Bowie and Conrad could have met and coordinated their activities. If such an opportunity existed, it would support the idea that the two groups were part of a single Confederate secret service operation.

Bowie's itinerary can be traced beginning with the report of the detachment's capture of the horses at Port Tobacco, among other information. The October 3 *Washington Star* reported the incident by quoting a story taken from September 29 issue of the *Port Tobacco Times*, which refers to the raid as occurring "last night," meaning that it occurred on September 28 (or on September 27, if the type for the paper was set the day before its release).[32]

On September 14 Mosby was wounded in a skirmish with a small detachment of Union cavalry in Fairfax County, Virginia, near Washington.[33] The wound left him on crutches, but he was able to get around; according to an ambiguous statement in his memoirs, Mosby may have had a meeting with General Lee a few days after he was wounded.[34] The wounded Mosby was taken immediately to The Plains, Virginia, and then to Lynchburg.[35] During the trip to Lynchburg, he would have had to cross the Virginia Central Railroad and would thus have been in a position to take the train to Richmond or Petersburg.

Working backwards from September 27 or 28 and taking into account known activities, one can deduce that Bowie and his detachment must have left Fauquier County around September 21 or 22, meaning that if Mosby did see General Lee in time to discuss the Bowie raid it would have had to have been no later than about September 19. As it turns out, Lee was in Richmond September 12–15, while Conrad was preparing to leave for Washington, but after September 15 was back at his headquarters near Petersburg. Beginning their trip, Bowie and his twenty-five rangers traveled through Fairfax County, south to Falmouth, and east to Mathias Point in King George County. According to Wiltshire, this trip, totaling over ninety miles, took the party two days to accomplish.

Reaching the vicinity of Lieutenant Cawood's Signal Corps camp on Mathias Point in the evening of September 22 or 23, Bowie quartered his men in nearby farms and arranged for a local blockade runner named Long to row him across the Potomac with Wiltshire and another man. Wiltshire commented that Long appeared as if by prearrangement and also indicated that Long had worked with Bowie in the past. Long was most likely necessary because the expected burden of a large group of men was probably too great for the signal corps boat stationed at the same location on Mathias Point.

Bowie's familiarity with the Mathias Point area and the Potomac crossing is confirmed by a letter written by Mary Dent Washington, of King George County, widow of Col. John Taylor Washington, to her mother on September 27, 1864: "Walter Bowie is on a secret expedition to Maryland, and some eight or nine of his men have been eating here for several days. They did not come this morning. . . . Tell Sallie that now Walter has come back, I won't be able to give her the buttons I promised her, as I have sent him word to come and get his bundle, if he ever returns from Maryland." The Washingtons lived at Albion, a plantation on Mathias Point, not far from Lieutenant Cawood's signal corps camp.[36]

Thomas Nelson Conrad and his party left Richmond on September 17 and probably did not arrive at Lieutenant Cawood's camp until

September 20 or 21. Later Conrad claimed to have reached Washington within ten days after leaving Richmond (September 27). If Conrad left King George County as late as September 25 or 26 (a perfectly reasonable date to get him to the District of Columbia by September 27), both Conrad and Bowie would have been on Mathias Point at least on September 23. Thus, there was an opportunity for Bowie and Conrad to coordinate their operations.

Certainly the missions of Bowie and Conrad fit together: Conrad was to investigate the possibility of capturing President Lincoln, and Bowie was to investigate the possibility of capturing the governor of Maryland. Thus, Bowie's mission could well have been a cover, with his true mission being to see whether it was feasible for a small armed unit with a captive VIP to travel unimpeded through Maryland.

Bowie crossed the Potomac into Maryland on September 23 or 24. Once across the river, he spent three days acquiring "the information he desired." "In the afternoon of the third day [September 26 or 27], [Bowie and his associates] encountered two of Bowie's friends, who had come out from Port Tobacco to see him, having been secretly informed that he was in the neighborhood."[37] The visit paid Bowie becomes more meaningful when one realizes that on the Maryland side Bowie was in the immediate presence of Thomas A. Jones, the Signal Corps agent on the Maryland side; the Watson family, who collaborated with Jones; and another member of the Lincoln operation, Thomas Harbin, who lived near Bryantown in Charles County, Maryland, and operated in the area.

One of the visitors was James Brawner, the owner of the Brawner Hotel in Port Tobacco, a favorite stopping place for Confederate agents. It is possible that one of the Watson sons was at home and that either he or Harbin was the other. It is also possible, of course, that the second visitor was somebody not familiar with the area and that Brawner was acting as a guide to put the visitor in touch with Bowie. There is also the possibility that the unknown visitor had nothing at all to do with the Lincoln operation. But the possibility of his association with Jones, Harbin, or Watson is another fact to keep in mind when evaluating Bowie's raid.

After talking to his visitors, Bowie decided that twenty-five men were too many to take into Maryland; seven would be enough. He sent James Wiltshire back across to the Virginia side to return with those chosen for the mission and to send the remainder back to Mosby. All this activity was accomplished on the same day, probably on September 26.[38] With his seven troopers on foot, Bowie reached Port Tobacco on the second night (September 27 or 28), captured a detachment of Union cavalry, took the horses that they needed, paroled the cavalrymen, and headed north through Charles County, Maryland, where they spent the next day in the woods, arriving near Bowie's home at about four o'clock the following morning (September 29 or 30).[39]

At the trial of Booth's associates in Washington in 1865, former slaves of Dr. Samuel A. Mudd testified that the previous year Bowie and some Confederate soldiers had been fed by Dr. Mudd. On the roads that existed in 1864, the doctor's home was about twelve miles from Port Tobacco (about a four-hour journey for horses traveling at night at the rate of about three miles per hour), and Bowie's home territory near Upper Marlboro was about twenty miles beyond. Was this the occasion on which Bowie stopped at Dr. Mudd's house?

Bowie left part of his team holed up in a forest near his father's home and went off for an overnight trip with three of his men, presumably to Annapolis to investigate the governor's accessibility. Upon their return on about October 2 or 3, Bowie told the rest of the detachment that the governor was too well defended and that capture was not possible. This may have been an accurate statement, but it is also possible that it was part of the cover story. Bowie could just as well have met Conrad or others from Washington to describe his experiences as a clandestine traveler in southern Maryland. Conrad later said that after investigation his team had decided to recommend southern Maryland as the route to use for moving a captive Lincoln to Richmond.

Bowie chose to return to Virginia by passing north of Washington through Montgomery County in order to cross the Potomac directly into Loudoun County. Along the way, his party raided a store for new boots and other items. Angry citizens pursued the raiders, and Bowie was killed in a brief skirmish on October 7.[40]

Bowie's story has been told many times, but usually as an adventure story with no context other than being an example of a prank carried out by Mosby's troops in the enemy's rear. In fact it was not a typical Mosby operation. Rather, its timing, which coincided with other clandestine operations in progress, and Bowie's past connection with the espionage organization supporting the Army of Northern Virginia indicate that he might very well have been selected to play a critical role in preparing for the capture of President Lincoln.

If Bowie was working on the same project as Conrad, it has some interesting implications for the organization and operating procedures being employed. Conrad said that he was furnished with gold in preparation for his trip to Washington. That means that the issuance of the gold was approved by Jefferson Davis and executed by Judah Benjamin. Jefferson Davis signed Request No. 47 on September 14, 1864, for $500 in gold to be drawn from the "Secret Service" fund. In other words, Conrad, an army scout, was working on a matter of direct interest to the highest level of the Confederate government. If Bowie was working on the same project, it would mean that Mosby had to have received word through his normal command channel (General Lee) to cooperate in an operation not within Mosby's normal mission.

There is also the possibility that Mosby may have been given only general instructions—like "Go along with whatever Bowie asks of you"—while Bowie was given the details of the operation through his previous secret service channels. That could account for Mosby's comment that Bowie originated the idea and requested the assignment of men to help him. The Bowie operation was a departure from his normal contact with the Confederate espionage organization in Washington, but regular contact with the organization continued.

In spite of occasional reverses, such as Greenhow's arrest, the extensive and well-organized Confederate espionage organization in Washington did continue to produce useful information. It continued to operate after Lee's surrender, and many of its agents passed into their postwar lives without any public recognition of their wartime roles. Naturally much of the information collected in Washington was of value to Jefferson Davis and other senior members of the Confederate government. Washington's geographic location, however, at a major junction of transportation lines, together with its military headquarters and its normally large population of troops meant that information gathered in Washington frequently was important for the Army of Northern Virginia. The Confederates recognized this duality of focus and devoted considerable effort to maintaining the flow of information to both Richmond, the national command center, and to Lee's headquarters, the major operational headquarters in the field.

The Confederate espionage organization in Washington was prepared to continue to support the Army of Northern Virginia in its campaign of 1865. Because Lee planned to leave Richmond and revert to a war of maneuver, the secret communication lines from Washington to the organization's two main customers would be much longer and harder to keep in operation. But Mosby, Major Cornelius Boyle, and the Confederate Signal Corps' Secret Line all remained outside the area of Union control and prepared to carry out their responsibilities. Thus, they were in place and prepared to assist the Confederate cause when Booth fled Washington after the assassination of Lincoln.

Chapter 4

SAGE AND THE
DESTRUCTIONISTS

IN THINKING of the Civil War, we think of battles, death, slavery, bravery, and a portion of the country so ravaged that it took nearly a hundred years to recover. And, if we push the search, we may even consider the ironclad ships, Walt Whitman, and Lincoln's articulation of the political rationale of the winners. We do not, however, readily recall intellectual achievement in connection with the Civil War.

This failure to look for or recognize new, creative thinking during the war is the result of several mutually reinforcing factors. In the first place, the war overwhelmed everything else to such an extent that most creative thought was devoted to some aspect of the war. In some cases the issue was as broad as "How should wars be fought," in others as narrow as a single weapon or a single tactic. Furthermore, in a war in which both sides shot at each other in close-order formation, there seemed to be such an absence of intellectual achievement on both sides that there was little incentive to look for any.

When the war ended, both winners and losers turned their attention to the need to find a common basis or common understanding on which to establish a new, different United States. It became a time for myth building, not for logical, probing analysis. Forums that might have concerned themselves with serious lessons learned from combat, like the Southern Historical Society Papers and the MOLLUS[1] papers, were instead devoted to stories of gallantry, descriptions of battles, and explanations of wartime events calculated to support the political rationales of the former foes. In addition, each side, former Unionists and former Confederates, set out to describe three things about the war: how each side wanted to think about itself in terms that would be acceptable to the other, mutually acceptable explanations of why the events of the war happened the way they did, and how each side thought about the other in terms that would be acceptable to both. As time went by, the positions of both sides drew nearer each other, and in the course of doing so became more myth and less reality.

This process of myth building was a serious matter. Agreed-upon myths affected the course of elections, national economic policies, those who held appointive office at the national level, and the personal fortunes of millions of Americans. It is small wonder that few people cared whether or not there had been any original development of the art of irregular warfare or clandestine operations.

The myth building of the South in particular, had the effect of drawing attention away from the secret service. The mainspring for this development was the Lincoln assassination. In the immediate postwar period it would have been devastating to the Southern self-image that was being created to have admitted any responsibility for the assassination. It might also have been fatal to a number of the individuals involved in Confederate secret service work. The best Southern tactic, therefore, was to block all logical paths that could have led from the assassination to the Confederate government. Some of those roadblocks were:

- Booth was mad.
- The war was over and the South had nothing to gain from Lincoln's death.
- The plan to capture Lincoln was Booth's idea and was financed by him.
- The Torpedo Bureau was concerned only with underwater mines, a legitimate and overt wartime activity.
- The Confederate government would never trust an important task to erratic amateurs like Booth and his associates.
- Scouting and guerrilla warfare were dashing and heroic but had no connection to secret activities like espionage, sabotage, propaganda, or political action.

• The South had no secret service and therefore had no mechanism for dealing with people such as Booth.

Scouting and guerrilla warfare may, on occasion, be dashing and heroic; the Torpedo Bureau did have a legitimate overt mission in addition to its covert ones; the assassination accomplished nothing good for the Confederacy. Nothing else is true in this array of assertions. True or false, however, the arguments were successful in preventing students of military affairs from investigating how the South handled its intelligence problems or the role that irregular warfare was intended to play in the total Confederate effort.

This lack of attention is unfortunate. If that original thinking about how clandestine activity and irregular warfare as a unique contribution to the Southern cause had been widely known, it might not have had the same impact on warfare as the writings of Alfred Thayer Mahan, but, in the realm of clandestine operations, Confederate thinking would have been of distinct benefit when the United States found it necessary to revive an interest in these matters during World War II. It is possible that we might still learn something from the Confederacy's efforts if we integrate their thoughts into the body of clandestine lore that is now accepted.

Several Confederates contributed substantially to the idea of using clandestine operations in support of the Confederate war effort. The contributions made by two of them, Jefferson Davis and his principal assistant, Judah Benjamin, first as secretary of war and then as secretary of state, must be deduced from the record of their actions, because neither man wrote about this aspect of the war. The intellectual contributions made by Matthew Fontaine Maury, "the Pathfinder of the Seas," are more obvious, if not more influential.

Maury came to the Confederacy with a well-established reputation for intellectual achievement based on his oceanographic work for the United States Navy. His first wartime association was in 1861 with the state of Virginia, after it seceded from the Union but before it joined the Confederacy. During a period of about two months, before the Confederate army was ready to assume responsibility for the defense of Virginia, the state organized its own provisional army and navy. To this end, Governor John Letcher created an advisory council composed of Judge John J. Allen, chief justice of the Virginia Court of Appeals;

From a Virginia family known for intellectual achievement, Matthew
Fontaine Maury (1806–73) served in the U.S. Navy before the war and
established a worldwide reputation for his oceanographic scholarship.
After joining the Confederate navy, he became one of the originators of
naval mine warfare.

Col. Francis H. Smith, the superintendent of the Virginia Military Institute; and Capt. Matthew Fontaine Maury. Shortly afterward, Col.
Robert E. Lee was appointed major-general to command all Virginia

forces and became an ex officio member of the group. The council worked hard, meeting nearly every day.[2] During that time Maury must have thought a great deal about the problem of defending the navy-less South against an efficient Federal navy of forty-two ships. As soon as the council ended its duties in June 1861, Maury turned his attention to two courses of action. One of his ideas has had a profound effect on warfare since that time; the other never had a true test.

Maury first acted on the development of underwater explosives as defensive weapons to be used in Southern rivers and harbors, devices referred to, in the language of the day, as "torpedoes." (Only later, after the invention of motors to drive underwater vehicles loaded with explosives, did the term "torpedo" take on its modern meaning.) In June 1861 Maury demonstrated that explosives could be detonated mechanically underwater, proving the feasibility of creating weapons operating on that principle.[3] His demonstration convinced the Confederate government that the idea had merit, and there were several talented officers available in both the army and navy to pursue the development of the weapons and the techniques for employing them. It should be noted, however, that the Confederates considered the torpedoes to be secret weapons; hence their employment came to be considered a secret service activity.

Maury's other idea brought him into direct conflict with Stephen R. Mallory, the Confederate secretary of the navy, with whom he already had a checkered relationship dating back to the time in which Mallory was chairman of the U.S. Senate's Naval Affairs Committee. For a number of years before the war, Mallory had sought unsuccessfully to have the U.S. navy build an ironclad warship.[4] Now, as head of the Confederate Navy Department, he had an opportunity to put his ideas into practice. He began the construction of five large ironclad warships: the *Virginia, Arkansas, Tennessee, Louisiana,* and *Mississippi.* Completely absorbed in building the ironclads were the capacities of Norfolk, New Orleans, and Memphis, the only three shipyards in the South capable of building such large vessels.[5]

Maury's idea was almost the exact opposite of Mallory's. According to Maury, the best defense for the Confederacy to adopt against the North's wooden navy was to build a large number of small, fast gunboats, each armed with a large swivel-mounted cannon. These were to swarm like mosquitoes around their larger and slower opponents and use their speed and numbers to reduce the effectiveness of the enemy's broadsides. Not only were these gunboats much cheaper to build than the ironclads, but they could be assembled in many different places. Aside from the minor issue of cannons and crews, there was little competition between the two types of vessels for the scarce resources of the South.

The gunboats, however, did compete for the attention of the harassed and overworked men who were trying to create a navy. Mallory had little faith in the gunboat idea and pushed hard to get the large ironclads built. Maury, with political support from the Virginia state government, persuaded the Confederate Congress to authorize the construction of one hundred gunboats to be built mainly in Albemarle Sound in North Carolina. Only six were in operation, however, when fate and the Union navy intervened.

In February 1862, a Union amphibious operation defeated the small Confederate fleet defending Albemarle Sound and seized Roanoke Island. The six gunboats took part in the defense. But instead of outnumbering their opponents, they were outnumbered. Thus, they were unable to operate in accordance with Maury's concept. Out-gunned and unarmored, the tiny ships were easily defeated. This defeat was followed within weeks by the startling victories of the ironclad *Virginia* over the largest wooden ships in the blockading Union fleet. The armored protection offered to the crew of the *Virginia* was compared favorably to the vulnerability of the unarmored gunboats. A crewman on one of the gunboats who had his head blown off during the battle near Roanoke Island became a symbol of the futility of a gunboat navy. The defeat in battle overwhelmed Maury's logical argument that his idea was still sound and had not been truly tested.

One result of Maury's rebuff was that the Confederacy never did build the numbers of small warships that it could have used to advantage in defending its coasts and rivers.[6] Another was that Maury was sent to England to help with the procurement of ships to be used as raiders against Northern commerce and to take advantage of the scientific and technical facilities there to continue his research into underwater explosive devices. In effect, he was sent into exile for intellectual incompatibility.

Thinking about naval warfare, the Confederacy reached an understanding of the role of clandestine operations that is unique in the history of the ninteenth and early twentieth centuries. The man mainly responsible for this accomplishment was Bernard Janin Sage, a Louisiana planter and lawyer.[7] Sage was born in 1821 in Connecticut and during his teens spent three years as a cadet officer on a merchant ship. This experience introduced him to a number of ports around the world and gave him some invaluable practical experience in the operation of ships at sea. Later he studied law in New Orleans, developed a lucrative practice, and eventually acquired a sugar plantation in southern Louisiana. From this remote position and modest background, Sage sought to advise the Confederacy concerning the conduct of the war at sea.

It is difficult to evaluate the reaction of Confederate authorities to Sage and his ideas. He had not been active politically, and therefore did not operate from any base of political influence. He had no established reputation among those concerned with naval matters; he had few friends, if any, in Richmond; and at first he may have been thought of as a busybody or a crank because of the radical new ideas he presented to people of conventional wisdom. Yet by the soundness of his ideas and the clarity and persistence of his arguments, he eventually had an impact on the Richmond establishment, and by the end of the war he had become a major influence in the creation of the Confederate Volunteer Navy and in the establishment of the Confederates' Special and Secret Service Bureau. Writing in his diary after meeting Sage, Maury captured his essence when he characterized him as a "Great talker but in spite of ego a useful man."[8]

Sage began his campaign of ideas by talking about Confederate privateering, a form of naval warfare little known or understood in the modern age. For centuries before the Civil War, however, the nations of Europe had developed a series of practices recognized in treaties and international law that allowed a nation to issue a license to an individual or group authorizing the recipient to arm a privately owned vessel for the purpose of making war on the commerce of an enemy. The license was known as a Letter of Marque and Reprisal and was subject to a series of customs and international regulations concerning the treatment of captured ships, cargoes, and crews. In the days before governments became so efficient at collecting revenues, it was a way of attracting private capital to support a war effort. In return for purchasing, arming, equipping, and crewing a ship, the owners were allowed to benefit monetarily from the capture of enemy merchant ships. Officers and crews were attracted to privateers because they, too, were allowed to share in the profits of the voyage (as were the officers and crew of regular naval vessels).

Privateers had been very effective in a number of earlier wars, such as those between England and France in the seventeenth and eighteenth centuries, but there were some obvious problems with this rather unorganized approach to warfare. Once a Letter of Marque had been issued, the government had no control over the quality of the ship used, its armament, the training of the crew, or the movements of the vessel. A privateer might do damage to the enemy's commerce, but he could not be counted on to do anything specific—he could not be given an assignment to be at a specific place at a specific time. Furthermore, on occasion, Letters of Marque might be abused through attacks on unauthorized targets or the mistreatment of captives.

In 1856 a number of European powers agreed in the Declaration of Paris to abolish privateering. The United States and various other countries did not subscribe to the declaration. At the time of the Civil War, privateers were still generally regarded as useful in many parts of the world, and the United States in particular had favorable memories of the performance of privateers during the War of 1812. It was also recognized, however, that privateers were guaranteed to create problems for the sponsor as well as the victim.

On April 17, 1861, Jefferson Davis issued a proclamation inviting citizens of the Confederacy to apply for Letters of Marque and Reprisal, and on May 6 the Confederate Congress passed an act authorizing their issuance. This followed closely the Union announcement of a blockade of the Southern coast. On May 14 the British issued a proclamation of neutrality that recognized the Confederate states as belligerents, which would have had the effect of giving privateers and their prizes in British ports the same rights as the regular naval vessels of the sponsoring nation. The British proclamation was followed by similar actions on the part of France, Netherlands, Spain, and Brazil. Other nations refused to accept the entry of Confederate privateers or prizes, and shortly thereafter Britain announced that because of its policy of neutrality it would not allow privateers to receive aid.[9] In effect, these declarations meant that Confederate privateers would be limited to the ports of the Confederacy.

On May 18, 1861, the first Confederate privateer authorized under the new legislation, the *Savannah,* was commissioned at Charleston, South Carolina. A fast schooner with an eighteen-pound swivel cannon mounted amidship, the *Savannah* sailed on June 3, made one capture, and was promptly captured itself. Another privateer, the *Jefferson Davis,* sailed from Charleston on June 28 and had a much more successful career, capturing or destroying a number of Union ships before running aground while trying to enter the harbor of St. Augustine, Florida, on August 16. Several other privateers operated successfully in the summer of 1861, some under Confederate Letters of Marque and some under authorization of individual states. By August 1861, the privateers had destroyed nearly sixty Union ships at the cost of two privateers captured or destroyed. On August 10, 1861, the *New York Herald* estimated that twenty million dollars' worth of property had been destroyed by the Confederate operations. This campaign had the effect of driving much of the Northern cargo into foreign-flag vessels.[10]

In a note written long after the war, Bernard Janin Sage said that in late May or early June 1861 he wrote to "the Government" expressing a wish to fit out and command a privateer. There is no official record of his letter or of a reply to it, and Sage gives no further clue concerning whom in "the Government" he might have addressed. He does say, however, that the letter discussed "other matters," including the desirability of creating a navy of two classes. Based on his subsequent writings, Sage must have advocated the creation of a more regulated form of privateering as one of the two classes. In 1863, he stated that he had proposed in 1861 the establishment of a bureau or board for the examination and testing of new inventions or contrivances for destruction and for the organization of action teams to carry out the destruction behind enemy lines. These may have been among the "other matters" discussed.

On July 22, 1861, Sage wrote to "the Government" again. In a note written long after the war, he said that this July 22 letter, written from his "Australia" plantation in Louisiana, unfolded a plan to get arms through the Union blockade. In addition, the letter promised another letter within "a few days" to expound a plan to "inflict great damage on the enemy." This third letter, dated August 5, 1861, began to develop more complex ideas about how the war might be conducted:

In the first place, Northern commerce is all over the world, and it is everywhere defenceless, except on the coast of the old United States. Hence privateers should go far abroad. Lincoln's cruisers must be mainly employed at home.

2nd. Abroad, fast sailing-vessels will answer. They cost much less, are far more easily procured, avoid the inconvenience of coaling—and having to depend on that—when it is often impossible to get coal. It is for these, and other reasons that with sailing vessels, in the most of seas, the same capital will do the enemy the most harm.

3d. Our privateers or cruisers hanging about home, can be of little or no service under present circumstances, while they are in danger of being taken—whereby our naval capacity of offense is impaired. Abroad, out of danger, their capacity for harm is greatly increased. All of Lincoln's vessels, attracted in pursuit, would be so much aid at home.

4th. . . . Lincoln's government threatens to treat privateers as pirates, though it will probably reconsider that absurdity.[11] But to remove, or obviate these and other difficulties, I propose that our government . . . avail itself of unquestionable character and capacity from the Mercantile Marine—men with which the country abounds, and give regular Naval Commissions to proper men. By this means, in one or two years, a Confederate Navy should be improvised of both ships and men partly at home and partly abroad, able to cope with the United States Navy. . . . I take it for granted that ships thus made public armed, and commanded by regular commissioned officers of the Confederate Govt., would not come under [the definition] of privateers. . . .

5th. I would start from Europe with a good vessel (taken from here or there as might be best) laden with sufficient arms & munitions of war (to furnish other vessels) and with a perfectly reliable crew, which I could obtain—all or nearly all of whom would be competent to be officers of prizes, turned to privateers or men of war; and go to far distant seas to cruise. Every fit vessel taken would in turn become a privateer—the rest being disposed of as might be proper or required by law. This might be the best mode to eviate [sic] all privateering expeditions hereafter.

6th. After cruising a while & becoming notorious, so as to attract Lincoln's cruisers, I would change my cruising ground,
taking all vessels in my way. . . . It is obvious that all the U.S.
cruisers I could provoke to leave our coast, would be so much aid
to our cause. In conclusion, two objects should be held in view,
1st to harm the enemy and destroy his ships & commerce. 2nd,
To lay the foundation of our future mercantile marine I
then propose, if my modification of privateering be adopted, to
submit a project of law, and further state that these propositions
are for the good of the cause, and the Government is welcome to
carry them out without me, if it find merit in them. . . .[12]

Sage went on to state his desire to serve as a privateer but with a regular commission in the Navy. This was the first full articulation of his
idea: to gain the benefits of private initiative found in privateering but
to avoid the abuses and improve the performance by careful selection
and commissioning of officers who would be required to operate in accordance with established naval regulations.

While conventional privateering was getting under way, and Sage
was developing his ideas for reforming the process, other activities that
played an important part in defining how Sage's ideas would be applied were taking place.

The U.S. Navy sloop *Pawnee* had tried to relieve Fort Sumter in
Charleston harbor in April, before the Confederates forced the surrender of the fort. Thereafter, for several months, the *Pawnee* served in the
Chesapeake Bay–Potomac area.[13] Because of its activity at Charleston
and its power relative to the generally unarmed shipping in the Bay,
the sloop attracted quite a bit of notoriety.

Soon after the secession of Virginia on April 17, 1861, two young
men called on Governor Letcher with a proposal to organize a regiment of Maryland troops on Virginia soil. These were Richard Henry
Thomas (he later operated under the name of Zarvona) of St. Mary's
County in southern Maryland, who had served with Garibaldi in Italy
and therefore had some military experience, and his friend, G. W.
Alexander. Shortly thereafter, George N. Hollins, a lieutenant in the
U.S. Navy, resigned his commission and traveled from Baltimore by
steamer to southern Maryland, where he disembarked and made his
way secretly to Virginia. In Richmond, Hollins pointed out that the

notorious *Pawnee* was visited regularly by the mail steamer *St. Nicholas,* which performed its duties by steaming alongside the *Pawnee* while transferring mail and other items. He believed that it would be feasible to capture the *St. Nicholas* by positioning among its passengers an action team, who at a signal would take over the vessel. The *St. Nicholas* then could take on a number of Confederate troops who would remain hidden until the steamer was alongside the *Pawnee,* at which point they would board and capture the Union ship.

Governor Letcher proposed Thomas as the ideal man to head the action team and had Matthew Fontaine Maury review the proposal. Maury approved the plan, and Letcher arranged for several hundred Virginia troops to be sent to the mouth of the Coan River, a tributary of the Potomac in Northumberland County, Virginia. Thomas and about a dozen men boarded the *St. Nicholas* in Baltimore on June 28, 1861, and were successful in capturing it after it had left port. They proceeded to the Coan River to take on the extra troops but learned that the *Pawnee* was in Washington and not on its usual voyage. Therefore, they decided to make the most of their opportunity and took the *St. Nicholas* out into Chesapeake Bay, where they captured several small merchant ships. These were taken up the Rappahannock to Fredericksburg, where they were stripped of all useful items.[14]

Thomas, or Zarvona, as he was more popularly known, became a popular hero with the Confederate public. More importantly, he demonstrated that it was possible to carry out successful irregular naval warfare by using clandestine techniques. When Thomas tried to repeat the exploit by capturing another ship in July 1861, he was recognized, captured, and imprisoned, and finally exchanged in June 1863. His successful operation was remembered, however, and people recognized the possibility of carrying the war to the enemy's maritime power by means other than privateering or conventional naval operations.

By late 1861 the Union blockade had become tighter, and it had become more difficult for privateers based at Confederate ports to operate. That factor, plus the drain of manpower out of the economy into the Confederate army, made it more and more difficult to find entrepreneurs and crews to organize and man privateers. The decline in privateering and the lack of positive response from his suggestions prompted Sage to go to Richmond to see what he could do to bring about needed action. While there during December 1861, he published articles promoting his ideas in the city newspapers.[15]

Sage's ideas were competing for the attention of Secretary of Navy Mallory and others in the Confederate government at a moment when every effort was being devoted to the completion of the ironclad warships and at the same time that Matthew Fontaine Maury was pushing for the construction of his gunboats. The idea of privateering or of striking back at the enemy at sea, however, had a large constituency (particularly in seacoast towns like Charleston) that could not be ignored by responsible officials.

On January 6, 1862, Mallory submitted a short memorandum to President Davis proposing to "divest privateering of its exclusively private, and invest it with a public, character, and connect it with the Government by judicious checks." He pointed out that this measure would remove the objections being raised against privateering. As Sage proposed in his August 5, 1861, letter, Mallory would accomplish this objective by creating a provisional navy led by regularly commissioned officers operating under government regulations. Officers and crew would receive nominal salaries and would share the money gained from the sale of ships captured; the Confederate government would get 10 percent of the prize money. Mallory concluded that through these means the provisional navy would be recognized in foreign ports as a national service and would therefore have the privileges usually accorded to the naval vessels of all nations.[16] It was a good way to get around the provisions of the Declaration of Paris.

Mallory's proposal was referred to the Committee on Naval Affairs in the Confederate Congress, and a bill to establish a volunteer navy was submitted by Colin J. McRae. The provisional Congress expired on February 17, 1862, before action could be taken, but the permanent Congress met the next day, and on March 10 a similar bill was submitted. On April 16, however, Henry S. Foote, a future defector to the Union, managed to have the bill tabled.[17]

In the meantime, Sage had written another long presentation of his arguments in favor of a volunteer navy to replace the conventional privateer. He quoted the arguments he made in August 1861 and went on to argue that "We must reform and elevate privateering." He apparently had seen a copy of the legislation based on Mallory's memorandum, which required the owner of a ship to present the government with full particulars concerning the vessel and its crew before being commissioned, for he commented:

Objections—
This necessitates the obtainment of vessels in the Confederacy, and there are few or no fit vessels in the Confederacy—or the bringing of them in through the blockade, and taking them out again—a double risk, from which few would escape. . . .
2nd. If we have to buy, (and we cannot build without great cost and delay) in the Confederacy vessels will cost triple or quadruple their price in foreign posts, and hence such ventures could hardly be profitable inducements to capital & enterprise.
3d. We can buy vessels abroad at fair prices, so that if peace soon supervene [sic], causing frustration of our arms against the enemy, we could turn over all war materials to the Government at cost, and use the vessels profitably in the carrying trade, thus helping to found a home commercial marine. Whereas heavy losses would result if we paid the triple or quadruple prices of Confederate vessels.
4th. To say nothing of men, we have not arms, powder, munitions, and supplies to spare to be carried away [on ships fitted out in the Confederacy] while we are barely manufacturing and importing enough for home use.[18]

Sage went on to argue that the most efficient way of organizing the ships and crews would be to appoint trusted agents who could inspect them and issue a commission in foreign ports. Such a course would take advantage of foreign economies and minimize the impact of the effort on the Southern economy. (When, long after the war, Sage submitted a copy of this lengthy memorandum to the U.S. government for historical use, he added a note at the bottom that said, "This was read by the President [Davis] who characterized it as 'well considered views and deserved that it should be submitted to the Naval Committees.'")
The tabling of the legislation based on Mallory's proposal brought a temporary end to active work on the idea of a volunteer navy. Congress took action, however, on another aspect of Sage's ideas. On April 21, 1862, Act No. 90 was passed, amending an earlier act concerning Let-

ters of Marque. It stated that "in case any person or persons shall invent or construct any new machine or engine, or contrive any new method for destroying the armed vessels of the enemy, he or they shall receive fifty per centum of the value of each and every such vessel that may be sunk or destroyed, by means of such invention or contrivance, including the value of the armament thereof, in lieu of the twenty per centum, as provided by said Act."[19] This new language showed clearly the importance attributed to the development of new weapons. While the language referred to naval matters, it required only a small leap in logic to apply the same concept to other forms of warfare.

Meanwhile, as Gen. George B. McClellan began to move up the peninsula toward Richmond, Brig. Gen. Gabriel J. Rains, in command of a brigade at Yorktown, tried to delay McClellan's advance by planting artillery shells in his path. Rains graduated from West Point a year ahead of Jefferson Davis and two years ahead of Robert E. Lee, but his influential friends did not prevent him from being roundly criticized by officers on both sides of the battle for using unethical tactics. In due course the conflict of views concerning the use of land torpedoes was referred to George Wythe Randolph, the Confederate secretary of war, who decided in favor of using explosives in situations of genuine military value. Randolph's words are interesting because they reflect the attitude of some in the Confederate government toward potential targets of clandestine action:

> Whether shells planted in roads or parapets are contrary to the usages of war depends upon the purpose with which they are used. It is not admissible in civilized warfare to take life with no other object than the destruction of life. Hence it is inadmissible to shoot sentinels and pickets, because nothing is attained but the destruction of life. It would be admissible, however, to shoot a general, because you not only take life but deprive an army of its head.[20]

Randolph recognized the realities of hierarchical relationships, however, when he said that since Rains was junior to General Longstreet, who disagreed with Rains, that the latter should defer to Longstreet's view.

The upshot of the dispute involving Rains's torpedoes was that when Lee took command of the Army of Northern Virginia he asked to have Rains put in charge of the defenses of the James River. On June 18, 1862, Rains took command of the "submarine defenses of the James and Appomattox Rivers." The next day, the navy relieved Matthew Fontaine Maury of his assignment on the James. Maury had completed a field of fifteen large electrically detonated mines, and Rains was to plant mechanically detonated mines in other parts of the river.[21]

If this transfer of a command from one service to another had occurred in many armed forces, one would have expected a certain amount of parochial, interservice rivalry. But it would appear that in this case those who understood the technology of torpedoes shared an interest more important than pride of service: the masters of technology were a fraternity united against the conventional world. Given Sage's interest in new weapons and new ways of fighting, it is a logical assumption that Sage arranged to meet Rains during this period. Rains appears to have shared many of Sage's views on warfare and corresponded with him later in the war.

Whatever the cause, Sage began to think seriously about the problem of attacking the enemy on land as well as on sea. Philosophically, the problems were similar: how to develop weapons that might provide an advantage, how to find men with the skill to employ the weapons, how to find men with the initiative and character to operate the weapons in a hostile environment, and how to motivate those men to take serious risks to accomplish their objectives. These problems existed whether one was on the high seas dodging a superior enemy navy or behind enemy lines trying to blow up a well-guarded arsenal. In addition, both land and sea activities could benefit from many of the same inventions, and both naval and ground operations might be influenced by many of the same regulations. In particular, since money was considered to be a major motivating force, the same structure of rewards for missions accomplished could be used for both types of operations.

Although Sage appears to have recognized that his ideas had broader application, he could not tear himself away from his first love—irregular warfare at sea. During the winter of 1863 he wrote a number of articles for newspapers urging the passage of a volunteer navy act. A bill to create a volunteer navy was introduced into the Senate, and Sage submitted a number of proposed amendments of the draft to Mallory, who then added his comments. Presumably, this document was then turned over to the Senate for consideration. The bill was finally passed and approved by President Davis on April 18, 1863. On April 25, Sage applied for a commission to enhance his status in his work for a volunteer navy.

In his application, Sage said that he had lost a great deal of property in the war, including 250 bales of cotton burned. That loss would have been worth $12,000 to $15,000 in the postwar period; during the war, that amount of cotton, successfully gotten past the blockade, would probably have been worth a great deal more. In any case, the value of the loss would probably have covered the cost of a good sailing vessel purchased abroad.

The passage of the volunteer navy legislation brought a flurry of correspondence from Sage, in addition to his request for a commission. He wrote to the secretary of the navy suggesting how the ships commissioned abroad might rendezvous with a navy agent at isolated points off the coast to receive their orders, thus establishing that they were sailing from Confederate territory. On June 1, 1863, he wrote again to stress the importance of commissioning officers before they obtained their ships, and he requested his own commission to outfit a ship for the volunteer navy. And on June 20 he wrote to object to the president's view that a vessel had to be inspected before commissioning, arguing again that there should be agents abroad with the power to inspect and commission.

On June 6, 1863, Sage wrote to say that he had organized a group of investors in Richmond to meet on June 9 to discuss the formation of a company to finance a ship in the Volunteer Navy. He used this event as an argument to plead for haste in the issuance of his commission. The organization of a group of investors was the beginning of a bizarre episode in the history of the Volunteer Navy, but it was not the first group of investors to be attracted by the new legislation. Even before the law was passed, a different group was organizing itself to take advantage of the idea behind the law. In February 1863 John Yates Beall, a member of a wealthy family from Jefferson County, Virginia, sent a memorandum to Gen. Samuel Cooper, the adjutant and inspector general of the Confederate army proposing what amounted to an authorized privateering raid on Union shipping in the Chesapeake Bay.[22] Beall, a wounded veteran of the 2d Virginia Infantry regiment, had many influential friends and relatives, and his position in Virginia society would have guaranteed him a hearing. Cooper referred the matter to the secretary of the navy, who approved the idea and appointed Beall as an acting master in the navy.[23]

Beall had a close friend and neighbor from Jefferson County in the convalescent ward in Richmond's Chimborazo Hospital, Edwin Gray Lee, colonel of the 33d Virginia Infantry, who was recovering from an attack of tuberculosis. Lee and a number of other convalescent soldiers decided that, while not fit for normal field duty, they would still be able to make a useful contribution to the war effort and earn some money on the side. Lee and Beall recruited Edward McGuire, William Webb, and a number of others and organized themselves into a raiding party.

On April 2, 1863, Lee was given a pass by the War Department to leave Confederate lines on "special service." The next day Gen. John H. Winder, the head of the Department of Henrico (the Richmond area), gave him a pass for his command and baggage to pass all pickets and guards.[24] The raiders proceeded to Mathews County, Virginia, on the Chesapeake Bay and began to fit out a boat to use in their operations.

In June the Union navy learned of the arming of the boat and sent the USS *Crusader,* an armed, three-masted, 545-ton bark to destroy the raider. The *Crusader* landed a party of twenty-seven men who went directly to the house where Beall and four others were living. The Confederates took shelter in the woods and engaged the shore party in a fire fight that cost the Union several men, killed and wounded, and drove the remainder back to their ship. The *Crusader* left, apparently afraid of being ambushed in a narrow creek, but at a nearby location burned eight houses in retaliation.

Soon after this episode, Colonel Lee was called back to duty with the army and left Beall in command of the raiding party. In August Beall began active operations, capturing a schooner and four fishing boats, cutting the submarine cable between Fort Monroe and Washington, and destroying the Cape Charles lighthouse at the southern tip of the eastern shore of Virginia.[25] The interest raised in Richmond by these events involving prominent Virginians caused a favorable public climate for the idea of a volunteer navy. This was reinforced when

President Davis's aide, John Taylor Wood, led a party of regular Confederate troops transported in boats—carried overland on specially built wagons—to capture the USS *Satellite* and the USS *Reliance,* gunboats of the Potomac River Flotilla, at anchor in Chesapeake Bay near the mouth of the Rappahannock River on August 23. Naval raiders were very popular in the Confederacy! The activity in the Chesapeake Bay in 1863 may have helped attract interest in Sage's effort to form a group to invest in the volunteer navy.

On August 5, 1863, the Virginia Volunteer Navy Company met and elected its officers. Sage made speeches urging investors to subscribe to the company.[26] He apparently felt that he was slated to go to Europe to purchase and command the first vessel for the company, but he was due for a disappointment. A British adventurer, one "Captain" Decie, turned up in Richmond and quickly established himself as the true expert on operations at sea in the current environment.

Decie had arrived in Savannah in 1861 aboard his yacht, the *America*. He lived aboard it for some months masquerading as "Lord" Decie. The yacht was found sunken and abandoned in the St. Johns River in Florida in 1862 and was raised and refitted by the Union navy.[27] There is no record of Decie thereafter until he arrived in Richmond in July 1863 claiming to be a post captain in the British navy. Challenged over his apparent youth for such a high rank, he admitted that he was only an "acting" post captain.

Introduced to the board of the Virginia Volunteer Navy Company, Decie was scornful of Sage's preference for a sailing vessel. He assured the board that he knew what needed to be done and so convinced them that they should listen to him rather than to Sage or representatives of the Confederate navy. Only a steamship should be used, he asserted. This would be keeping up with the progress of technology, whereas the era of sailing ships was passing. The board was so mesmerized by Decie that it no longer listened to Sage's rationale concerning the cost-effectiveness of sailing raiders. By early September Sage was being ignored by the company.[28] There is no evidence that Captain Decie found a ship for the Virginia Volunteer Navy Company and seems to have dropped out of their activities. The volunteers finally bought the steamer *Hawk,* which got as far as Bermuda in 1864 but ran into financial difficulties and never saw active service.

Sage continued with his preparations for traveling to Europe in search of a ship to purchase on his own behalf. On August 29, 1863, Secretary of State Benjamin issued Sage a passport to leave the Confederacy and travel abroad.[29]

Presumably he continued his quest, encouraged by the Confederate navy, which appointed him to the rank of "master." The navy would doubtless have agreed with Sage's rationale. (On September 22 a friend reported to Sage that Mallory had promised that he would give Sage the first commission issued under the new legislation.) On September 30, 1863, Sage was still urging a committee of the Virginia legislature to act favorably on authorization for a stock subscription for his Volunteer Navy Company. During this same time he was writing articles for the Richmond papers urging support for the volunteer navy.

In the meantime, the Confederate War and Navy departments appear to have acted together to expand unconventional warfare against the enemy. For a time Sage appears to have been involved in a double life. On the one hand, he was continuing to pursue the creation of a volunteer navy company in Virginia to finance a ship to be purchased abroad and commanded by him. On the other hand, he was also involved in broadening the application of his volunteer navy concept to cover land warfare as well. In early 1863, the secretary of war asked Sage for suggestions on the organization of such increased activity. Sage provided several alternatives, of which one was adopted. The War Department decided to attach personnel trained in sabotage and unconventional weaponry to engineer companies being formed in each of the military Departments of the Confederacy. These specially selected persons would be recruited and trained centrally by the War Department and then assigned to the engineer company in the department of their choice. The engineer company would provide them with an administrative home in the army, but they would devote their time and energy to attacking targets approved by the department commander.

The Navy Department appears to have used the same central apparatus to develop teams for naval unconventional warfare. In other words, a bright young fellow with a strong back and a taste for explosions could join the central enterprise, get his training, and then choose duty in any military department or in the volunteer navy.

The task of organizing the central apparatus for the unconventional warfare teams was given to Maj. William S. Barton, formerly an attorney in Fredericksburg and a member of the Virginia militia.[30] Barton had served in the Fredericksburg area during April and May 1861 and had organized a clandestine courier system into Maryland that probably formed one of the activities on which the Signal Corps Secret Line was based. He was personally acquainted with Governor Letcher and Matthew Fontaine Maury, who had been a neighbor in Fredericksburg. In June 1861 Barton was commissioned as a major in the Provisional Army of the Confederate States (PACS). Such an appointment indicated that Barton was believed to have unusual capabilities. Later he was assigned to General Winder's Department of Henrico.

Barton's compiled service record shows a number of minor assignments to courts and boards but nothing concerning his main duties. Given General Winder's involvement in clandestine activity, it is probable that Barton was also assigned to secret tasks. On February 26, 1864, a detailed description of the Adjutant and Inspector General's Office shows Barton as head of the "Office of Organization."[31] His personal office was in a building adjacent to the main War Department building on 9th Street in Richmond; a larger building on an alley in the rear of the War Department was also assigned to the Office of Organization. The Office of Organization was in charge of what the modern American army would term "Tables of Organization and Equipment"—that is, keeping track of the various units of the Confederate army as units.

This is the sort of assignment that would have provided Barton with every opportunity to look after the recruitment, training, and assignment of individuals as part of the unconventional warfare effort. In fact, a review of Barton's file suggests that he could have spent the entire war looking out for likely recruits for Confederate clandestine operations. In such a case, his association with the sabotage teams would not be surprising. At the end of the war, Barton did not leave Richmond with the Army of Northern Virginia, and there is no record that he went with the War Department staff to Danville, Virginia. There is also no record that he ever signed a parole or sought a pardon after the war. In other words, he could have stayed on in Richmond, keeping out of Union sight, continuing to do what he could for Confederate clandestine operations, and eventually fading into his postwar life without ever formally recognizing the defeat of the Confederacy.

As part of the preparation for expansion of irregular warfare operations, a school was established at Buffalo Springs, a spa in southern

Virginia, to train personnel in the tradecraft necessary for working behind enemy lines. Personnel recruited for such operations were sent to a four-week course at this school and then sent to their permanent post.[32]

In early September 1863, two parties of navy irregulars containing people trained at Buffalo Springs crossed over into southern Maryland to operate against Union targets. One team was headed by Capt. John W. Hebb and the other by Walter Bowie, the former VMI cadet.[33] The operations of these groups were conducted too close to the Signal Corps Secret Line and attracted too much Union attention to the area. As a result, their operations appear to have been shut down. Barton, however, continued in his post.

Sage does not appear to have allowed his disappointment with the Virginia Volunteer Navy Company to keep him from constructive thought. Sometime after John Taylor Wood captured the USS *Satellite* and USS *Reliance* on August 23, 1863, Sage wrote a proposal that appears to have marked a turning point in the Confederate use of irregular warfare. Sage called his proposal "Organization of Private Warfare," with the subtitles "Bureau of Destructive Means and Measures" and "Bands of Destructionists and Captors." This proposal has survived in the form of a printed copy that Sage used as a final proof copy.[34] (Whether Sage paid for the printing himself or it was printed for use by congressional committees is not clear.)

Much of the first part of Sage's memorandum was dated at Richmond on April 25, 1863. This portion of the document arrayed all of the arguments for the establishment of a central bureau to encourage the invention of new weapons and the creation of bands of "destructionists" to employ against the enemy. Sometime after August 23, 1863, when Wood captured the *Satellite* and *Reliance,* Sage rewrote the document to provide references to examples of successful action, like Wood's, to add his objections to the way the bands of destructionists were operating currently and to urge special legislation to correct the defects that he found.

Since writing the foregoing, the want of proper legislation has been demonstrated in the repeated and earnest endeavors of the Secretary of War to form satisfactory organizations of such ingenious and daring men as sought authority, protection and aid in carrying out plans of destruction against the enemy. Acting for some of these parties, the undersigned had the honor to submit to him [the Secretary of War] several propositions to choose from. . . . It was finally proposed . . . to organize them under the Engineer Bureau, according to act approved March 19th 1863. This was adopted, and the men were individually authorized to proceed to the department or district where they wished to operate, and be enlisted and organized with an engineer company; and then be detailed for their special purpose-the commanding General being requested or recommended to furnish them with transportation, workshop aid, ordnance stores, and military protection and assistance, at his discretion.

Under this plan, some of the most ingenious, enterprising, daring and patriotic men in the Confederacy have gone to the South and South-west, who will form the nuclei of many organizations, of the progress of which, in the work of destruction, I hope we shall soon hear favorable and loud reports.

To get them into the field at once on the Mississippi and elsewhere, during the low water, and give them the necessary protection, facilities and aid it was proper to contrive a temporary arrangement, as Congressional action could not be had.

Sage then listed the defects that he discerned in the current arrangements. These included the need to organize them and focus their activities entirely on the task of destruction. Furthermore, he felt that they should be increased in number and stationed according to the numbers of targets available, not assigned to military units that might be moved for tactical reasons not related to the availability of sabotage targets.

The band of destructionists needed commissioned officers in charge, but engineer officers who commanded the units to which the bands were attached were not trained for sabotage or other clandestine duty and had duties prescribed by law that did not include sabotage. Even more important, however, was the matter of the personnel. The men in the bands had peculiar characteristics that were not compatible with conventional engineering duties. As an example, Sage pointed out that one team included a fifty-year-old former attorney general of Texas and a sixty-year-old former secretary of state of Texas. The personnel situation was further complicated by the mixture of volunteers and regular members of the military establishment. The volunteers were eligible to receive monetary rewards for the destruction of their targets, but there was some doubt as to the eligibility of the regulars to receive such payments. Another evidence of the irregularity of the status of the destructionists was the practice used by the secretary of the navy of appointing an "Acting Master without pay." The Confederate Court at Mobile had "virtually" decided that this was no commission at all and that it left the holders without legal protection.[35]

Sage went on to urge legislative action to establish a bureau on a legal basis and to correct the other defects of the situation. The increased range of Sage's thinking is clear from the titles that he gave to the memorandum. Sage's thinking was no longer confined to private warfare at sea but now covered all theaters of private warfare. In a manner of speaking, Sage was now part of a spreading wave of opinion that recognized an opportunity to employ explosive devices aggressively against the enemy. The army had begun to refer to its bands of destructionists as "strategic corps," and Sage may have had that in mind when he corrected the subtitle of his paper to read "Bureau of Strategy."[36]

Sage's memorandum may have represented views that were no longer unique to him, but the document is particularly noteworthy because it is a very clear expression of the arguments for clandestine action and contains a number of the points that were later incorporated into the legislation that eventually approved the creation of a "Special and Secret Service Bureau" to consolidate and regularize the development of new weapons and the means to employ them. The following are examples of the way in which the legislators creating a Special and Secret Service Bureau echoed the ideas expressed by Sage in his writing.

> *Sage:* "If our destructive means and measures of a novel or unusual character be made known they may become possessed by the enemy, who, thereupon, is, in the first place, put on his guard, and secondly, enabled to use them equally with us. Hence every man who thinks he has made discovery, should be encouraged to carry it to an examining and testing place of the government, established and operating with a due degree of secrecy. With such a

bureau as proposed, it could be speedily and conveniently examined, tested, and either adopted or rejected, thus satisfying the
proposer, stimulating—instead of discouraging inventive genius,
enterprise and patriotic aid."

Legislation: ". . . that a bureau in connection with the War
Department, for the examination, experiment and application of
warlike inventions, and direction of secret agencies is hereby established . . ."

Sage: "How far such Bureau should control this service in
the field, I will not undertake to say. Perhaps some aid can be
found in the analogy between this and the Engineer Bureau and
service."

Legislation: ". . . forms and regulations of the engineer bureau
not inapplicable shall be those to be observed and conformed to
by this bureau."

Sage: ". . . corps or bands of destructionists and captors,
should be organized .·. . for destructive purposes."

Legislation: "The companies and parties now irregularly organized for the application of submerged or other defenses, and
known as torpedo corps, and for the construction and use of new
warlike inventions or for secret service, shall if approved by the
President be incorporated into and form a part of the organization contemplated by this act."

An example of the implementation of the bands of destructionists
as members of the Engineer Corps is contained in the *Official Records,
Navies.* On September 15, 1863, Lt. Col. A. L. Rives, the chief of the
Engineer Bureau in the War Department, wrote to Gen. E. Kirby
Smith commanding the Trans-Mississippi Department.

. . . list of men who . . . are to be employed in your department
on special service of destroying the enemy's property by torpedoes and similar inventions. These men should each be enlisted
in and form part of an engineer company, but will, nevertheless
be employed, so far as possible, on the service specified above
when the public interest, in your judgment requires it. Details of
additional men may be made either from the engineer troops, or
from the line to aid them in their particular duties, and they may

be furnished by the military authorities with the necessary am-
munition, their compensation to be 50 per cent of the property
destroyed by their new inventions and all the arms and munitions captured by them by the use of torpedoes or of similar
devices. Beyond this they will be entitled to such other rewards
as Congress may hereafter provide.

This was accompanied by another from Rives:

R. W. Dunn, having been selected for special service, is authorized by the Secretary of War to proceed to the headquarters of
Lt. Gen. E. Kirby Smith, commanding Trans-Mississippi Department, to be attached to one of the companies of engineer
troops now being organized in that department under the act of
Congress, "to provide and organize engineer troops to serve
during the war," approved 20th March 1863.[37]

The letters from Colonel Rives to the Trans-Mississippi Department
are clear statements of the procedure and organizational relationships
being followed in the development of sabotage teams.

Sage sent a copy of his pamphlet "Organization of Private Warfare"
to General Rains, for the latter wrote to Sage on October 5, 1863, expressing interest in its ideas and strongly seconding the idea of a
bureau to handle inventions systematically.[38] However, Rains objected
to the term "destructionists" and urged that the bureau be called the
Bureau of Strategy. Rains, therefore, may have been the originator of
the idea that caused Sage to cross out "destructive means and measures" and insert "strategy" on the copy that found its way into the
National Archives.

Shortly after writing his pamphlet, Sage wrote on October 9 to navy
lieutenant R. D. Minor saying that he had heard that Minor was going
abroad and proposing to him a scheme for the temporary opening of
the harbor at Mobile. The idea was a wild one, and Minor had already
left for Canada, where he took part in an abortive attempt to free the
Confederate prisoners on Johnson's Island in the harbor at Sandusky,
Ohio.[39]

In October 1863, Sage at long last had an opportunity to participate
personally in some of the activity that he had been advocating. On

October 15 he was given a pass by the secretary of war authorizing him to go to Texas and then proceed to Europe, and on October 16 he was directed by Mallory to report to a board of examiners for consideration for appointment as a commander in the volunteer navy. Presumably he received the appointment, for he is listed in the navy records as "Master not in the line of promotion." Thus, he was equipped with the passport to leave the country, the pass to get him through the lines, and the commission that would entitle him to act for his investors with the permission of the Confederate government.

In December, Sage was in the field promoting the use of bands of destructionists. On 12 December 1863, the chief of staff of the Trans-Mississippi Department wrote to Gen. Richard Taylor at Shreveport, Louisiana:

> The lieutenant-general commanding desires me to commend to your favorable consideration the various measures that may be undertaken to annoy the enemy by organizing small parties, which acting under your supervision, shall destroy their gun-boats, transports, and depots. The lieutenant general takes a warm interest in this matter, and would be pleased if, upon investigation, you find it possible to do anything.
>
> He directs me to say Mr. B. J. Sage, a gentleman who will wait upon you, is just from Richmond, and is in possession of the views of the Government on the subject. Mr. Sage has for some time devoted himself to these matters, and can give you information, both as to men and means, which may be valuable in carrying into effect the desires of the commanding general.[40]

Sage must have spent a considerable amount of time in Louisiana helping the Confederate army organize its sabotage effort and suggesting ideas for impeding the operations of the Union army in the Louisiana rivers. One of the papers that Sage saved from this period is a lengthy memorandum to General Boggs, the author of the above letter. In this memorandum Sage listed a number of people in the vicinity of the lower Mississippi River who might be useful in secret service operations. He also included some ideas for blocking river traffic.

During his time in Louisiana, Sage was also trying to send some of his cotton out through the blockade in order to accumulate enough foreign exchange to finance a sailing vessel. He apparently got some out, but not enough to buy a ship. Finally he decided to go on to Europe to see if he could arrange additional financing. On March 26, 1864, General Boggs issued him a pass to leave Confederate lines. On April 20, however, he had gotten no farther than Texas, where from Houston he wrote to Gen. E. Kirby Smith asking for permission to ship two hundred bales of cotton through the blockade to raise money for his ship.

Before leaving Louisiana, however, Sage committed one of the greatest sins of a clandestine operator—he violated security. With apparent naive goodwill, Sage tried to help a team of destructionists including R. W. Dunn, E. C. Cooper, and J. D. Breaman, by giving them a letter of introduction to about fifty people, scattered over Louisiana, that Sage thought might be useful in their operation—meaning that a large number of pro-Confederacy individuals capable of assisting in clandestine operations were listed in a single document. A copy of the document was captured by the Union navy in March 1864 and circulated with arrest orders for all named in the document.[41]

Presumably, Sage traveled to Europe via the long route, from Texas to Mexico to Europe. He must have waited for a reply to his letter to General Smith but probably left the Confederacy in May or June 1864. By August he was in England. On August 15, 1864, Matthew Fontaine Maury, researching new technology in the English Midlands, noted in his diary that Sage had been by to see him and added the comment that Sage was a "great talker but in spite of ego a useful man."

Maury and Sage appear to have been reasonably congenial. On September 6 Maury noted that "Sage came yesterday, went back today." This visit must have been the occasion for one of those lovely "bull sessions" in which men of imagination stimulate each other to pour out their ideas. On September 11 Sage wrote to Maury to continue some of the discussion. After the war Sage filed an extract of this letter with U.S. naval archives.[42] The extract dealt with the purchase of the *Hawk* by the Virginia Volunteer Navy Company and mentioned that Sage had quoted some of Maury's views to Capt. Rafael Semmes, late of the CSS *Alabama*. (The *Alabama* had been sunk on June 19, and Semmes had been rescued by a British yacht. He was still in England at this time before returning to the Confederacy.) Maury doubtless knew personally several of the men on the company's board and would have appreciated Sage's problem with them being ignored in favor of Decie.

On September 26 Sage wrote to Maury asking that he write down his views on the steam-versus-sail-raider controversy, views that Sage had no doubt explored thoroughly in their face-to-face meetings, but he wanted something that he could quote. Maury obliged on September 28 with a concise statement of the arguments favoring the use of sailing ships in the Confederates' situation.

During this period Sage was continuing to try to arrange financing for a ship and writing to Secretary of the Navy Mallory asking him to intervene to get Gen. Kirby Smith to release his cotton for export. All the while he continued to fight his personal intellectual battle with the Virginia Volunteer Navy Company. On August 15, 1864, immediately after seeing Maury for the first time, Sage wrote to Samuel J. Harrison, the president of the company, citing the views of Maury and Semmes that agreed with his position on sailing raiders. Sage did not mail the letter until after September 22, when he added a postscript commiserating with Harrison on the financial problems of the *Hawk* and pointing out that if he had known about the problems he might have been able to raise money to resolve them.

While Sage was pursuing his ideas in person in England, back in the Confederacy his ideas were being taken a step further. In late 1864 the Confederates began to organize a large-scale operation to attack ships leaving foreign ports for the North. The Confederate raiders had successfully driven a large portion of the U.S. merchant trade into foreign-flag ships. There was little opportunity for the Confederacy to continue a major overt campaign using raiders, but it still was possible to use the Courtney torpedo and other devices to set fire to the ships carrying goods to the North. This was a campaign that would have to be carried out by clandestine means, but it could be counted on to have a major political impact, even if only partly successful.

The U.S. consul in Halifax, Nova Scotia, got wind of the project and reported it to Washington, but apparently not much credence was placed in this report until the end of the war when additional details came to light. The consul's information attributed the concept for the operation to Secretary of the Navy Mallory. It further claimed that the operation would involve a force of three hundred to four hundred men stationed in squads at locations like Nassau and Vera Cruz with head-quarters in Havana. Actually running the operation were Missouri general Thomas A. Harris and "Professor" Richard G. McCulloch, who provided much of the technical knowledge involved in manu-facturing the sabotage devices.[43]

Apparently unaware of the extent to which his ideas were being em-ployed, Sage searched for money in both London and Paris but was still without adequate funds when the war ended. He spent the next few months researching the Treaty of Paris that ended the American Revolution and preparing a defense brief in anticipation of represent-ing Jefferson Davis at his trial for treason. His brief was published in London in 1865 and later in the United States as "The Republic of Re-publics." He died in Louisiana in 1902 in reduced circumstances.

Bernard Janin Sage devoted much critical thought to the Confeder-acy's strategic situation. By spending his own money to promote his ideas and volunteering to test his ideas personally, he established his sincere interest in and concern for the Southern cause. With raid-ers like the CSS *Alabama,* owned by the government, the Confederate navy exploited some of his ideas, but it never fully implemented his volunteer navy concept of many privately owned ships hunting down Union commerce abroad.

The extension of Sage's ideas into the realm of war on land, however, met with much more success. The developments of 1863, including the formation of bands of destructionists under the cover of the Engineer Corps, appear to have contributed to the ideas incorporated by the Confederacy in Senate Bill S194, signed on February 17, 1864, dealing with "organizing bodies for the capture and destruction of the enemy's property by land or sea and to authorize compensation for the same." This bill and its companion appropriation (signed on February 15, 1864) of five million dollars for secret service became the foundation of the major Confederate secret service efforts in 1864 and 1865 on both land and sea. But even in this matter, Sage has not received the credit that he deserves.

Chapter 5

THE CONFEDERATE
SECRET SERVICE
IN CANADA

In 1864 the Confederacy launched a clandestine operation of unprecedented size and importance. Based in Canada, it involved the expenditure of a million dollars in gold, approximately half of all the money spent by the Confederacy on secret service activity. The story of this operation and all of its various projects is much too long and complex to detail here, but this chapter will describe some of the clues to the genesis of the operation, its successes and failures, and activities that illustrate the Confederate solution to various problems of clandestine tradecraft. In particular, it will discuss the role played by Confederate agent George N. Sanders in connection with the Lincoln assassination and the subsequent trial of the associates of John Wilkes Booth.

Originally intended to support the growth of a peace movement in the North, with a strong focus on the defeat of Lincoln in the election of 1864, the operation also involved a wide range of actions intended to interfere with the Northern war effort. These actions included paramilitary raids, the encouragement of sedition, pro-Confederate propaganda, attempts to release Confederate prisoners held in Northern camps, manipulation of monetary exchange rates, and the creation of "disinformation." One of the most ambitious operations was the attempt to take President Lincoln hostage, and, in the end, the most successful effort was to divest the Confederacy of any apparent responsibility for his assassination.

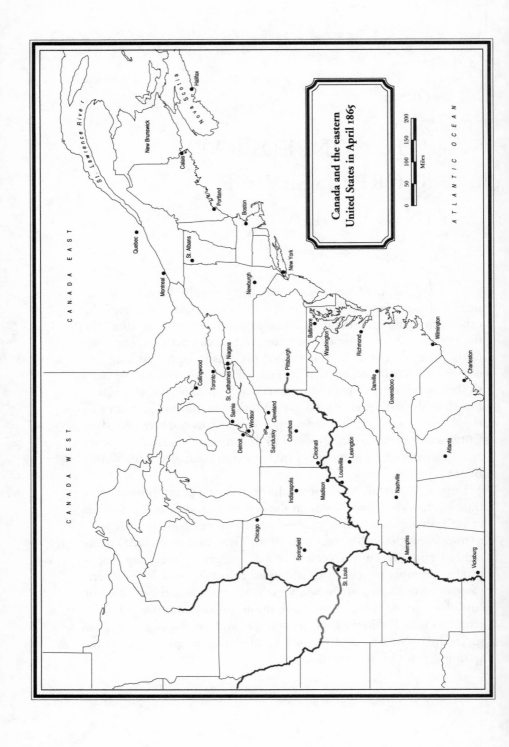

Canada and the eastern
United States in April 1865

CANADA EAST

CANADA WEST

St. Lawrence River

NOVA SCOTIA

New Brunswick

Halifax

Calais

Portland

Boston

Quebec

St. Albans

Montreal

Newburgh

New York

Toronto

Niagara

Collingwood

St. Catharines

Sarnia

Windsor

Cleveland

Detroit

Sandusky

Columbus

Cincinnati

Pittsburgh

Baltimore

Washington

Richmond

Wilmington

Danville

Greensboro

Charleston

Atlanta

Indianapolis

Madison

Louisville

Lexington

Nashville

Chicago

Springfield

Memphis

Vicksburg

St. Louis

ATLANTIC OCEAN

Miles

0   50   100   150   200

The genesis of the operation in Canada goes back at least to 1863. As the leadership of the Confederacy became convinced that there was little chance of recognition by either England or France, it began to focus on the critical importance of civilian support in the North. In February 1863, Gen. Robert E. Lee wrote to his son, George Washington Custis Lee, who was at that time a colonel on the staff of President Jefferson Davis. In a letter that mixed fatherly matter with semi-official business he said,

> You see the Federal Congress has put the whole power of their country into the hands of their President. Nine hundred millions of dollars & three millions of men. Nothing now can arrest during the present administration the most desolating war that was ever practiced, except a revolution among their people. Nothing can produce a revolution except systematic success on our part. What has our Congress done to meet the exigency? I may say extremity, in which we are placed![1]

Although his expression was more optimistic than it had been in February, the matter was still on Lee's mind on April 19 when he wrote to his wife: "If successful this year, next fall there will be a great change in public opinion at the North. The Republicans will be destroyed & I think the friends of peace will become so strong as that the next administration will go in on that basis."[2]

The subject of how to erode Northern public support for the war must have been discussed by Lee, Davis, Secretary of War Seddon, and any number of political leaders in Richmond often during mid-1863. With the passage of time and more thought given the subject, Lee seems to have recognized that victories by the Confederate army alone could not change the attitude of the Northern electorate toward the war. On such matters Lee occasionally wrote letters in which he summarized his views on a particular subject (what today we might call "position papers"). The letters appear to have been written in such a way that Davis or Seddon could show them or read them to others as support for a particular policy. They were not frank letters giving intimate reactions; they were carefully worded letters written with the ultimate audience in mind.[3]

Lee's letter to Jefferson Davis on June 10, 1863, would appear to have been aimed particularly at members of the Confederate Congress. He pointed out that the hostile reaction of "journalists and others at the South" to advocates of a pacific policy on the part of the Federal government had not encouraged the development of a peace party in the North. Confederate politicians had spoken for their Southern audience and forgotten that their remarks would also be read in the North where they might have caused an undesired reaction. Instead of encouraging the peace party in the North, the remarks of the Southern politicians had discouraged their potential friends in the North.

Lee also pointed out the inevitable erosion of Southern manpower in the face of a united North. Against this discouraging trend, he offered a specific course of action:

> Under these circumstances, we should neglect no honorable means of dividing and weakening our enemies, that they may feel some of the difficulties experienced by ourselves. It seems to me that the most effectual mode of accomplishing this object, now within our reach, is to give all the encouragement we can, consistently with truth, to the rising peace party of the North.
>
> Nor do I think we should, in this connection make nice distinction between those who declare for peace unconditionally and those who advocate it as a means of restoring the Union, however much we may prefer the former.
>
> We should bear in mind that the friends of peace at the North must make concessions to the earnest desire that exists in the minds of their countrymen for a restoration of the Union, and that to hold out such a result as an inducement is essential to the success of their party.
>
> Should the belief that peace will bring back the Union become general, the war would no longer be supported, and that, after all, is what we are interested in bringing about. When peace is proposed to us, it will be time enough to discuss its terms.[4]

This letter with its calm, objective tone, must have made an impression on the politicians to whom it was read. Here was the most successful general of the Confederacy saying that defeat was almost inevitable unless an unprecedented political campaign was waged to assist the development and ultimate victory of a peace party in the North. Any good politician would get the message: it was essential that the Confederate government take aggressive action outside of the conventional military area.

Given the time that it normally took for legislation to be prepared, introduced, debated, amended, and finally approved, this June 1863 letter of Lee's may mark the beginning of the effort to enact the laws finally passed by the Confederate Congress in February 1864 that established a program of awards for successful secret action against the enemy and appropriated five million dollars in secret service funds to support the program.

In considering the North as a target for political action, it was necessary to think of two distinct areas: the northern group of original states, New England, New York, New Jersey, and Pennsylvania, which had been settled for generations; and the states of the old Northwest Territory, which were still being settled. In the "West" as most people thought of it, Ohio, Indiana, and Illinois were settled first, and most of their population was originally in the southern parts near the Ohio River. For example, as late as 1850, Madison, Indiana, on the Ohio River, was the largest city in the state.

The settlement pattern also reflected the nature of many of the settlers in the West. Kentucky, admitted to the Union in 1792, lay just across the river from Ohio, Indiana, and Illinois. Many people from this slaveholding state moved into the newly open territory north of the river. Many other newcomers came from Maryland, Delaware, and Virginia—all slaveholding states. Only after the opening of the Erie Canal in 1825 made the Great Lake route accessible did people from the New England states and New York begin to move west in large numbers. Many Kentucky families had come to the state from Virginia, and many members of the same families (like the Lincolns) had moved on to Indiana and Illinois. Thus, there were many kinship ties between Kentucky and the new states, as well as similarities of background. Many Kentucky Confederates believed that they were uniquely qualified to understand the Yankee—particularly those across the river who were not abolitionists and who had previously given their votes to Democratic candidates. Many opposed the policies of the Lincoln administration, especially emancipation. If a crack was to be created in the popular support for the war policies of the Yankee government, the southern part of Ohio, Indiana, and Illinois was the place for it to begin.

There is no way of knowing who all the men were who participated in the formulation of a decision to do something to help the peace party in the North, but Jefferson Davis had been investigating the grass-roots political situation in the North since at least early 1862 when he sent young Emile Longuemare to contact Democratic leaders in the northwestern states.[5] It seems clear from subsequent events, however, that a group of Kentuckians were particularly influential in shaping the clandestine operation that was created to implement the Confederate political campaign in the North.

Though Jefferson Davis himself was born in Kentucky in 1807 or 1808,[6] his family moving to Mississippi while he was still small, his main association with Kentucky came later when he attended in 1816–18 the College of St. Thomas Aquinas near Springfield and Bardstown and in 1822–24 Transylvania University in Lexington. The associations that he developed during these years are not well known, but they did include various members of the Hawes, Coleman, and Sanders families, who later played critical roles in the clandestine operation in Canada.[7]

One member of this group was Richard Hawes, Jr. (1797–1877), of Bourbon County, Kentucky, who was made the Confederate governor of Kentucky. Hawes's wife was Henrietta Morrison Nicholas, whose sister, Anne Nicholas, was the mother of George Nicholas Sanders, the most notorious political action agent of the Confederacy.[8] These family connections reveal the close relationships of the families that took an active part in the political affairs of Kentucky, as well as Jefferson Davis's many points of association with this group. This is not to say that he knew the members of the group intimately, but the common associations provided many avenues of approach if members of the group wished to make their views known to the president of the Confederacy.

Family associations were important in another way. In the days before the invention of fingerprinting, the polygraph, and other modern police techniques that help in determining trustworthiness, the safest course in any secret endeavor was to deal with people that one knew well from personal contact. In that way, the confidence man

This photograph of the president of the Confederacy, Jefferson Finis Davis (1808–89), shows a man determined to do his duty. Courtesy of the Library of Congress.

and the informant planted by the enemy could be more easily avoided. Family members, neighbors, classmates—particularly classmates from West Point or VMI—and members of the same lodge, club, or church congregation were people that one knew best. They provided a pool from which one might, with minimum risk, recruit helpers in a clandestine enterprise.

An example of the role played by family in recruitment for sensitive positions is William Walter Cleary (1831–97), who was chosen to act as secretary to Jacob Thompson, the Confederate commissioner who ultimately headed the secret service operation in Canada. Cleary was born in Lexington and attended Transylvania University, graduating from the law school in 1851. The next year he moved to Cynthiana, Kentucky, and shortly thereafter married Ann Wherritt, whose mother was a member of the Morrison family. Governor Richard Hawes also had Morrison connections (viz. his son, James Morrison Hawes). Thus, Cleary may have come to the attention of Hawes through some Morrison association.[9]

At the outbreak of the war, Cleary saw fit to engage in serious anti-Union activity. There is no information available concerning its nature, but in June 1862 he felt compelled to flee to Canada to avoid arrest. Cleary went first to Clifton, Ontario (now Niagara), where he stayed at the Clifton House for two weeks and then proceeded to Toronto where he stayed at the Queen's Hotel until General Bragg invaded Kentucky in early September. Upon hearing the news of the invasion, Cleary returned to Kentucky, reaching Lexington on September 20, 1862. The Confederate tide in Kentucky, however, had already turned by the time Cleary arrived. He spent subsequent months following Confederate forces into Tennessee and Georgia, working in various staff positions as a volunteer and keeping a diary of his activities.[10]

Richard Hawes had also gone south with the retreating Confederate army. In keeping with the effort to establish at least the appearance of a Confederate government in Kentucky, Hawes had created a provisional government with Robert McKee as secretary of state, H. F. Gimball as president of an eight-member council, and William Cleary as clerk of the council.[11]

Cleary eventually reached Richmond on January 7, 1863, and began work as a clerk in the claims division of the Second Auditor's Office on January 20. (In a purely practical sense, there was very little for a provisional government of Kentucky to do.) On March 8, 1863, he noted that he had called on Jefferson Davis. He also wrote letters to his family in Kentucky using both the Signal Corps channel and the Flag of Truce boat.[12] On June 15, 1863, he recorded that somebody had asked him if he would be interested in undertaking an important job in Canada. He was careful not to say who had made the proposition or what the job involved; but in view of General Lee's letter of June 10 and Cleary's later assignment in Canada, it is reasonable to assume that the idea of a mission to Canada was already being discussed.

An enterprise as ambitious as that of imposing organization on a nascent antiwar movement in the North must have involved extensive planning—necessarily clandestine planning. Such planning must have been going on even before the beginning of the legislative process and would have continued in parallel with the enabling legislation as that worked its way through the Confederate Congress. And it had to include the selection of key people to run the organization that would be required to carry out the enterprise.

On the basis of figures from past elections, from their contacts with selected political figures in the North, and from their knowledge of the area involved, the Confederates decided that there was sufficient likelihood of success to justify their attempt to encourage a peace movement. In the area of personal knowledge, however, they were led astray by their Kentucky experts. In the early 1860s the Kentuckians knew the Ohio, Indiana, and Illinois of the past, even if just a few years earlier; they did not recognize the rapidity of change in the area. The northern parts of these states were being populated by immigrants from abroad and from the "old North," and most of these newcomers supported the war. The traditional Democrats were still strong in the area, but they were no longer the majority.

Not recognizing the extent of the shift in the strength of their target population, the Confederates continued their planning. Now the question was what mechanism should be used to organize the antiwar movement. What was the best way of mobilizing the people who were against the war and persuading others to join them?

The answer must have seemed obvious to the Confederates involved in the planning. In the unsophisticated West, secret societies were popular. The oldest and most socially acceptable were the various orders of Freemasonry, with chapters established in Ohio in 1808, in

Indiana in 1807, and in Illinois in 1822.[13] Secret societies, although they were not religious organizations, frequently had religious overtones. In addition to providing some education, entertainment, and a focus for community activity, they also inevitably had political influence.

In the years immediately before the war, there existed a secret society known as the Knights of the Golden Circle, made up of men opposed to the new Republican party. The election of Lincoln and the outbreak of the war, however, distracted the population at large, and the society fell into decay. In 1862 Jefferson Davis sent Capt. Emil Longuemare north to see if the society could be revived. Longuemare found people who were interested in such a revival, and they organized a new version of the society known as the Order of American Knights and dedicated their support to the Democratic party. The new organization had all of the trappings of the normal secret society—oaths, ritual, strict security regulations, and an "inner ring," the Sons of Liberty.[14] As a recognition device, members used a copper coin or token with a head on one side; thus, the members of the society became known as "Copperheads."

It is frequently difficult to understand the goings-on of such secret political movements because these organizations tell many different stories—one to encourage recruits, one to appeal to a broad constituency in the populace, one for members of the organization at large, one for selected members who could be trusted to be discreet, and yet another for the opposition. Another factor confusing the record of the Copperhead movement is that the Copperheads, the Confederates, and the Union each had reasons for projecting a view of the activities of the Order of American Knights and the peace movement. The Copperheads pictured themselves as strong in order to make themselves respected and as determined to take armed action if necessary in order to impress the pro-Lincoln forces and the Confederates. The Confederacy promoted the peace movement as strong and determined to take armed action in order to encourage others to join it and to give it increased political influence. The Union portrayed the movement as a threatening revolt to discredit the Democrats, who the Copperheads claimed to support. All sides tended to exaggerate the strength of the movement.

The report of the Copperhead trial in Indianapolis and Judge Advocate Gen. Joseph Holt's October 1864 report on the Order of American Knights were sensational and conveyed the feeling that the Copperhead movement was a serious threat to the Union, a threat narrowly averted by decisive action on the part of the administration.[15] The Union prosecutors at the Indianapolis and Cincinnati trials of various Copperheads in 1864 and 1865 failed to understand the nature of the clandestine organization that they were combating and gave all of these cover stories some credence. The result was a caricature of reality.[16] In spite of the confusion in the Copperhead cover stories, modern scholars have been able to put the Copperhead menace in much better perspective.[17]

The consensus of modern scholars is that the Copperheads were not as numerous as previously believed, that most of them did not have a serious intention to secede from the Union, and that their threat was exaggerated by the Republican administration in its efforts to discredit the Democratic opposition. Unfortunately, not all of the revisionist historians stopped at this point. Some have gone so far as to suggest that the stories of Copperhead preparations for armed action were little more than Republican propaganda designed to scare the electorate into voting for the Lincoln administration that was saving the country from treason and rebellion.[18]

Apart from this extreme school who would categorize the whole Copperhead threat as a Republican myth, the revisionist historians have generally been on target. The Copperheads never did threaten to become a majority of the electorate. On the other hand, some Copperheads armed themselves and prepared for military action; some tried to interfere with Union recruitment and circulated antiwar and anti-administration propaganda; and some cooperated with Confederate agents in planning antigovernment action.[19] Current analysis indicates that the Order of American Knights, like any secret political movement searching for power, was not as strong as it wanted people to believe it was. But it was not toothless. Modern historians need to recognize that the Copperhead movement held the seeds of a threat that in slightly different circumstances could have flourished.

While a secret organization can have political influence, it cannot exercise full power and still remain secret. To have full political power people must know that the organization exists, and they must think that it has power. Secrecy may add the attraction of mystery and protect its members from their enemies, but its primary purpose is to hide the real strength of the organization.

Thus the principal objectives of the Confederate political action campaign in the North must have been to create a "secret" organization of people who could take advantage of opportunities to work for peace, to cause the Northern electorate to interpret events on the battlefield as signs that the war was going badly for the Union, and to promote the election of candidates who would seek a peaceful end to the war. In addition, however, the Confederates had a number of objectives more directly related to military aspects of the war, including such actions to interfere with the Northern war effort as sabotage of military and transportation facilities, raids to force the Union to withhold troops from the front in order to protect areas in the rear, and release of Confederate prisoners of war, which would have the same effect as a raid and might also relieve the Southern shortage of manpower.

In order to achieve these objectives, the Confederates needed to carry out a number of different activities. They would have to maintain liaison with the Order of American Knights at several different levels in that organization—at one level to discuss policy matters and at other levels to carry out specific clandestine operations. They would need to generate propaganda themes favorable to Confederate objectives and to work with selected correspondents and editors. They would also have to establish a way of handling money that could support the clandestine activity of many people over a very large area. (One could hardly expect Jacob Thompson to keep his million dollars in gold in a bag under his bed.) This would include expense money for the operatives as well as money for bribes, for purchase of weapons and explosives, for manipulating the market for U.S. currency, and for the purchase of real estate, ships, and other items needed for operational use. And since the Confederate plan foresaw the possible need for force, there had to be an element responsible for recruiting, training, and commanding military personnel and for planning and carrying out military operations. With personnel engaged in clandestine armed action not necessarily members of an armed service, such activities are sometimes referred to as "paramilitary" activities, which implies the need for an element to train selected Copperhead personnel in clandestine tradecraft and to help train the paramilitary personnel.

The bases for the clandestine operation in the North could only be in Canada, where both geography and operating conditions were favorable. There travel was possible by ship or rail from Windsor, opposite Detroit, to Montreal, which had rail connections to Boston and New York. In the center was Niagara Falls with its cluster of tourist hotels on both sides of the border; and from Niagara there was easy access to New York, Pittsburgh, or Cleveland. Furthermore, the British/Canadian authorities were lenient—clandestine operations could be carried out without too much official interference. There was a strong element in England that would like to see the United States permanently divided, that would be only too glad to cooperate with the Confederacy.

In examining the people who later played some part in the Confederate operation in Canada and the nature of their activities, it appears that central to the operation's strategy was George Nicholas Sanders. And he was probably the man who made John Wilkes Booth believe that political assassination was a permissible action. Sanders was also a key player in defeating the Union effort to pin responsibility for the assassination on the Confederacy. Though a number of historians have written about Sanders, he remains a mystery.[20]

Sanders was born on February 21, 1812, in Lexington, Kentucky.[21] Later his family moved to Carroll County, on the Ohio River, where his father became a successful breeder of fine cattle. Their home, Grass Hills, was near the town of Ghent, Kentucky, which lies a few miles up river from Madison, Indiana. George's father, Lewis Sanders, was a strong believer in the principles of democracy and kept himself and the family well informed on public affairs. One of his subscriptions was to a small political journal called *Passion Flower*, which was published in New York by Samuel C. Reid, a former naval officer, and edited by his daughter, Anna Reid. George was impressed with the writing and began a correspondence with the editor—which led to their marriage on November 29, 1836. George and Anna returned to live at Grass Hills, where George eventually took over the cattle business from his father.[22]

The Sanders family was action oriented. John Sanders, George's older brother, graduated from West Point in 1834, a few years after Robert E. Lee. Like Lee, John became an officer in the Army Engineers and served with Lee in several assignments before his untimely death in 1858.[23] A younger brother was executed by the Mexicans while fighting for the Texas Republic in 1836. At first George Sanders was

A democratic politician and ardent supporter of republican revolutions against European monarchy, George Nicholas Sanders (1812–73) was a leading Confederate political agent. In addition to having influenced John Wilkes Booth, Sanders is largely responsible for convincing the world that the Confederacy had nothing to do with the assassination of Lincoln. Courtesy of the Library of Congress.

interested in cattle and horse racing, but in 1843 he became interested in the value to the United States of a canal across the Isthmus of Panama, and this led him to urge the annexation of Texas. Thereafter he became active in the Democratic party as a manipulator and propagandist. He moved his family to New York City to engage in business and to be closer to the center of political activity. In 1848, at age thirty-six, he visited Europe and was reported to be involved in furnishing arms to the revolutionaries in the great uprisings of that year. In the course of his European visit he became friendly with a number of the revolutionary leaders.

Sanders became associated with a group in the Democratic party known as the "Young America" movement. The men in this coterie believed that democracy was the ideal form of government and that as a young country, the United States was destined to expand, bringing the benefits of republican government to people currently ruled by monarchies and dictatorships. In keeping with these goals, they felt that the dispute over slavery should be put aside in favor of a realistic development of the national power needed to support their broader objectives.[24] In 1851 Sanders allied himself with John Louis O'Sullivan, the founder of the *Democratic Review,* who had lost control of the publication. Sanders managed to recover control of the paper and put Devin Reilly, an Irish revolutionary of 1848, in charge.

The *Review* considered republicanism the ultimate society and advocated American intervention in Europe to assist the revolutionary movements there. Freeing Cuba was also one of the top priorities because of that nation's proximity to the United States and because of its strategic importance.[25]

Eighteen forty-eight saw a series of revolutions begin in the monarchies of Europe. The revolts were put down, but hundreds of the most active revolutionaries fled into exile. By 1852 London had become a refuge for these people, who found much in common in their opposition to monarchy and their desire to continue their revolutionary movements.[26]

In 1852 Sanders supported the election of Franklin Pierce and as a reward was appointed consul general in London. Other members of Young America were similarly rewarded: August Belmont became minister to the Netherlands, Senator Pierre Soule of Louisiana became minister to Spain, and Sanders's associate, John L. O'Sullivan, became minister to Portugal. Sanders left for London in late 1853, before being confirmed in his new post, and began a vigorous campaign to arrange support for his revolutionary friends. He was host to a famous dinner in February 1854 attended by Lajos Kossuth of Hungary, Giuseppe Mazzini and Guiseppe Garibaldi of Italy, Alexandre-Auguste Ledru-Rollin of France, and Alexandr Herzen of Russia as well as James Buchanan, the American minister in London, and a number of British political figures, including Joshua Walmsley, the organizer of the Liverpool Police.[27] The dinner made it appear that the United States was supporting the revolutionary movement throughout Europe. Such a position might have pleased the Young America movement, but it offended many powerful people in both the Whig and Democratic parties.

In the meantime, Pierre Soule, the new minister to Spain, was trying to persuade the Spanish to sell Cuba to the United States. Soule, son of one of Napoleon's generals, and a French revolutionary in his youth, came to the United States in 1825 to escape imprisonment for his political offenses. He became a successful lawyer and politician in Louisiana and then won a seat in the U.S. Senate, where he collaborated with Jefferson Davis in defending the Southern position against the Compromise of 1850. Soule may have been an effective politician in America, but he was not a good diplomat. He quarreled with Louis Napoleon, fought a duel with the French ambassador to Spain, offended nearly every faction on the Spanish political scene, and, in the summer of 1854, supported an abortive revolt against the Spanish throne. During all of these events, Soule kept in close touch with Sanders (who also got himself into trouble by urging the assassination of Napoleon and issuing a passport to Victor Fronde, a French revolutionary who was trying to kill Louis Napoleon).

On October 4, 1854, Sanders wrote a letter addressed to the "People of France!" in which he urged them to rid themselves of Napoleon and restore democracy. While the letter does not specifically advocate assassination, certainly violent overthrow and assassination are implications that could be drawn from the language.

Wisely do the perpetrators of these deeds fear there tributive hour, and strive with increased energy daily, to keep down the people. Well may Napoleon the Last! dread the expansive force

so fearfully compressed! . . . Let us but see that you have still the
virtue and the courage to strike once more for the Republic, and
one universal acclamation from America shall cheer you on.
Europe—America, expects it of you. Strike! and though you fail
a hundred times, we will applaud you at every fresh trial!

In 1878 a biographical article about Sanders believed to have been
written by William Corry, a Sanders friend and collaborator, said that
the letter "advised the killing of Louis Napoleon." The comment may
have reflected Corry's knowledge of Sanders's true intentions. It seems
clear that Sanders was not afraid of assassination as a political tool.[28]

Sanders created a big stir in support of republicanism, but he also
stirred up those at home who were afraid of his radical leanings. When
his nomination as consul general was submitted to the U.S. Senate,
confirmation was denied. A successor to the post not having been appointed, Sanders stayed on in London for nearly a year, continuing to
work with his European republican friends.

These Young America members' machinations in Europe led in October 1854 to the issuance of the very undiplomatic Ostend Manifesto,
in which Soule, Buchanan, and John Y. Mason, the American minister
to France, expressed the determination of the United States to free
Cuba from Spanish rule.[29]

When Sanders and Soule returned to the United States, Soule set
up a law practice in Louisiana and resumed his activity in the state's
politics, and Sanders became Naval Agent in New York City. Sanders
returned to Kentucky in 1859 to organize a meeting to acquaint the
people of Kentucky and the neighboring states with the issues involved
in state rights and free trade. This was the beginning of a political
theme called the "New Mississippi Valley Movement," which was intended to show the common interests of all those who lived in the
Mississippi Valley, regardless of their attitude toward slavery. He also
worked hard for Stephen A. Douglas, the mainline Democratic candidate in the election of 1860. When Lincoln was elected, Sanders sided
with the Confederacy.[30]

Sanders submitted several proposed projects to the Confederate
government, including the sale of weapons, the building of iron ships
in England, and the organization of a courier system between Europe
and the Confederacy, but they all fell through. While he was engaged

in the presentation of these various projects, he continued to operate in the political arena. In early 1862, showing his political agenda, he wrote an article addressed to the "Democratic Masses of the Mississippi Valley North." To those who hear an echo of Karl Marx in those words, it is worth remembering that Sanders was in London when Marx was resident there and that both Sanders and Marx associated with the revolutionaries of 1848. It is likely that they at least met during this time, and it is certain that they were subjected to some of the same radical ideas from mutual acquaintances. Appealing to its readers as allies of the South, Sanders's letter said:

> The capitalists and self-styled conservatives of your great Atlantic cities, have betrayed the confidence your generosity reposed in their direction of your interests in the Presidential Canvas. These mere money-making machines never had any sympathy with, or any appreciation of, republican liberty, and it is not surprising that they rejoiced at the first gleam of a sword government. . . . You have but to open your eyes to see that this is a war of a capital against labor. . . . It will, however, soon be in the power of the people of the Ohio Valley by bold revolutionary acts to tear themselves from the Lincoln iniquity. Organize! Organize for revolution! Form clubs in every neighborhood, whether you have associated action or not. Let your first object be to prevent enlistments and contributions to the army of the usurpers, to elect one of your number to all of the municipal, State and Federal offices within your gift. . . . The southern slopes of Illinois, Indiana, and Ohio, fighting side by side with Kentucky, Missouri, Arkansas, Mississippi and Louisiana, all of the Valley of the Mississippi for the right will re-establish much that has been lost by trading leaders and the madness of the hour. . . .The independence of the State is the only safeguard against the centralizing and despotic instincts of the general government.[31]

In 1863, while negotiating with Secretary of State Benjamin concerning a courier system, Sanders also broached to Jefferson Davis the idea of establishing in Canada an operation to work with the Northern peace democrats.[32] Davis did not approve the idea at the time, but he did take it under advisement. (He may already have been considering such an action.) Sanders left for Europe in pursuit of other projects, but his uncle by marriage, Richard Hawes, the provisional governor of Kentucky, was in Virginia and could continue to lobby for the proposal. It was probably Hawes who in June 1863 approached Cleary with the possibility of Cleary's going to Canada.

Sanders and Hawes may have had help from another quarter. From late 1863 through the first half of 1864, Pierre Soule was in Richmond and involved in some mysterious project of supposed interest to Jefferson Davis. It was even suggested that he had the rank of brigadier general. Aside from these vague hints, there is very little that can be firmly established—only that he lobbied in Richmond on behalf of General Beauregard and served as attorney for a man seeking reimbursement for planting torpedoes for the Confederacy.[33] So there is no way of proving Soule's involvement with the planning for the Canada operation. But as a long-time associate of Sanders and with similar leanings toward revolutionary activity, it would not be surprising if Soule had thought about supporting the peace movement in the North and presented arguments to Davis in its favor.

Preparations for the Canada operation continued. Cassius F. Lee settled in Hamilton, Ontario, where he acted as a coordinating center for Confederate clandestine correspondence. Beverly Tucker, former U.S. consul in Liverpool but now a Confederate agent, arrived in Canada from the Confederacy in February 1864 ostensibly to arrange for the shipment of supplies to the South.[34] At that season of the year, with the St. Lawrence frozen over, Tucker's trip would have involved avoiding arrest while traveling through the North, or an arduous cross-country trip from Halifax to Quebec after running the blockade out of Wilmington, North Carolina. In either case, it would have meant a high-priority effort on the part of Tucker.

On March 23, 1864, Jefferson Davis signed a request for $46,512 in secret service gold for a "Mr. Tucker." This might have been Beverly Tucker, or it might have been Joseph W. Tucker who was interested in organizing a boat-burning project behind Union lines. The request cited "Necessities and Exigencies," however, which suggests that the money may have been intended for Beverly Tucker, since a request for money for boat burning should have cited "Secret Service."

Other operatives sent to Canada included two Episcopal priests familiar with clandestine operations, Kensey Johns Stewart and

Stephen F. Cameron, Nashville banker John Porterfield, and an expert in money exchange named Davis. The latter established an office across the street from St. Lawrence Hall, the large hotel in Montreal used by the Confederates as an informal headquarters. Thus, the Confederates had available a financial adviser and somebody to actually handle money.[35]

Also in early 1864, George P. Kane, former marshal of police in Baltimore, arrived in Richmond. Kane had been in Canada since 1862 and had worked with P. C. Martin, one of the leaders of Confederate secret service operations there.[36] Kane was now in Richmond to serve as an adviser on Confederate operations in Canada. There was a "serenade" on February 15 to welcome him to Richmond, and William Cleary attended it.[37]

On March 14, 1864, on the heels of the Dahlgren raid, Thomas H. Hines, a captain in the 9th Kentucky Cavalry, was ordered to go to Canada to begin operations with the Confederacy's friends in the North. Hines had previously contacted friendly parties in Indiana while working with General Morgan in anticipation of Morgan's raid into Indiana and Ohio in June and July 1863. Captured with Morgan in Ohio, Hines played a key role in helping Morgan and others escape from an Ohio prison in late 1863. (Inasmuch as the prison was a civilian prison and under joint civilian and military jurisdiction, it is interesting to speculate that the Confederates may have had Copperhead assistance in obtaining their freedom.[38]) On March 18[39] the department gave him CS$5,000 to buy cotton to sell behind Union lines in order to get the greenbacks needed for operations in the North.[40] Davis had not yet approved the Canada project, but the War Department seemed to think that the idea was a good one.

Other people seemed to be active in the Canada project. On March 16, 1864, William Cleary wrote to Governor Hawes asking to be part of the mission to Canada. On March 24 Cleary was interviewed by "Colonel ———," an interview that discouraged Cleary; on April 7, however, he had "another interview with Col. S——" on the same matter and felt more encouraged about his "prospects with Gov. Hawes." [41]

During this build-up of Confederate personnel in Canada, Benjamin had been hunting for the senior statesman to be the head of the operation. Governor Hawes may have thought of himself as heading the enterprise, but Davis and Benjamin felt otherwise. On March 25, 1864, Benjamin wrote to Alexander Hugh Holmes Stuart, secretary of the Interior from 1850 to 1853 and a former member of the U.S. Congress, asking him to come to Richmond on a confidential matter of great importance. Later, Stuart recalled that Benjamin advised him that he and Davis had decided to send a team of secret service operatives to Canada to foster the peace sentiment that was believed to be strong in the Northwest. Congress had deposited £3 million in London to finance the operation, and Davis and Benjamin had decided that Stuart should head the enterprize.[42] Stuart, however, declined the appointment, and Benjamin had to search for another candidate.

While Benjamin was searching for a head for the Canada operation, William Cleary went to Nelson County, south of Charlottesville, on April 11, 1864, where he visited the home of Governor Hawes's cousin and brother-in-law, John Jay Coleman (with whom Hawes stayed when not in Richmond). Cleary stayed at Coleman's for a week and then returned to Richmond with Hawes, who promptly visited Jefferson Davis. Davis informed Hawes that the Canada project was now approved. On April 20 Cleary saw Benjamin, who confirmed that Cleary was to go to Canada as part of the project.[43]

Two other things must have happened at about this same time, but because there is no direct information it is necessary to interpolate: someone wrote to George Sanders telling him that the project was approved, because Sanders received word in time to leave Paris, catch a ship, and reach Montreal on June 1, 1864; Jacob Thompson was selected to fill the position first offered to Stuart. Thompson, who had served as U.S. secretary of the Interior from 1857 to 1861 and had a long career in Mississippi politics, was well known to Jefferson Davis. He may have been selected as late as mid-April, because he left Richmond in a great hurry; also, financial arrangements were incomplete, and it is clear that he had not been filled in on all of the work that had been done by the Kentuckians.

On April 25, 1864, the Confederate State Department filled out a form requesting $1 million in gold for secret service purposes. At first the clerk filled in the blanks citing "Necessities and Exigencies," as he had been doing habitually for secret service funds. Davis signed it. Someone, however, possibly Davis, noticed that the Canadian

Executive Office
Department of State,
Richmond, Apl. 25, 1864

TO THE SECRETARY OF THE TREASURY,

Sir:

Please cause a WARRANT for the sum of One million dollars

payable out of the Appropriation for "Secret Service", Act of 15 Feb. 1864.

to be issued in favor of Hon. J. P. Benjamin Secretary of State

Payable in foreign Countries.

£ 206,185. 11. 4

Exchange on England requested

Jefferson Davis
President C.S.A.

Secretary of State.

Appropriation for "Secret Service" $1,000,000

This is a photograph of the file copy of Request No. 32 signed in the original by Jefferson Davis, directing the Confederate treasury to make available one million dollars in gold for covert action. This was the money used by Jacob Thompson to finance the Confederate operation in Canada aimed at supporting the antiwar party in the North. Courtesy of the Library of Congress.

operation was going to involve more than conventional espionage or political agitation. Furthermore, there was not $1 million in that fund. Thus, because of its broader scope, it was decided that the operation in Canada should be funded from the new appropriation (February 15, 1864) of $5 million for secret service. As a result, "cancelled" and "see next page" were written on the record copy of the completed form and a new one was prepared citing "Secret Service" as the source of the funds. The clerk later wrote "Thompson" on this new form. It apparently took the treasury some time to prepare the documents implementing the request. Thompson left Richmond with a draft dated April 27, 1864, for $100,000 in gold. He did not receive the remaining nine $100,000 drafts dated April 29, 1864, until he reached Wilmington on his way to Canada.[44]

Davis and Benjamin chose former U.S. senator Clement C. Clay as Thompson's associate. Both carried the title of commissioner, but Thompson carried the money. On the basis of subsequent events, it appears that Clay represented the interests of the Confederate War Department in the operation while Thompson, being in charge and responsible for everything, spent much of his time looking after the high-level political contacts that the mission required. Clay was given his own $1,500 in secret service gold to finance his trip to Canada, but on the whole, he had to obtain money for his operations from Thompson.

To the team of Thompson and Clay, Benjamin added James P. Holcombe, a professor of law at the University of Virginia. Holcombe had been sent to Canada in late February to investigate the case of a ship claimed to have been captured by Confederate privateers but retaken by the United States in Canadian waters. Finding that the Confederate case was a weak one, Holcombe had been given the extra task of trying to repatriate several hundred escaped Confederate soldiers believed to be in Canada. Since the escaped soldiers might also be good recruits for secret service operations, Holcombe and his tasks were assigned to Thompson and the Canadian operation.

Thompson and Clay left Richmond without adequate briefing on the situation in Canada and without a clear plan or operational doctrine. They traveled together as far as Halifax, but there Clay fell sick and stayed behind for several weeks. Clay's stay in Halifax was followed by the exploitation of the trickle of escaped Southern soldiers returning to the Confederacy to recruit an action team and organize a raid against the town of Calais, Maine. The plans of the action party were leaked to the Union, and the town was warned in time to frustrate the raid. Several of the raiders were captured on July 16 when they arrived at Calais.

Thompson arrived in Montreal on May 27, 1864, and sent William Cleary on to Toronto, the city that was to be their permanent headquarters. Thompson stayed on in Montreal for two weeks, waiting for Clay, but he finally gave up and went to Windsor for his first meeting with potential leaders of the peace movement. The chief representative of the Confederates in Windsor was a Colonel Steele from Kentucky. Unfortunately, there were several men who met this description, and the correct one has not been identified.

After more than two weeks of conferring with the friends of the Confederacy, Thompson wrote his first report to Judah Benjamin on July 7, 1864. Discussing his actions while in Montreal, he commented, "I have . . . arranged an interview with a reliable and sensible gentleman from New York City. After the fullest and freest conversation with him I became aware that nothing could be done in the Eastern States because of the profit that they think they are deriving from its [the war's] prosecution." Thompson's description of his activities at Windsor was much longer and more positive.

> Here I met with Mr. Bennett, the Grand ———— of the Secret Order in the Western States, and its President, Mr. V–.[45] They had the right to admit members, and I became at once a member. This gave me an insight into their principles and strength. I was much pleased with it, and there was nothing in it, so far as I was permitted to go, which did not meet my hearty approbation, and I took three degrees. I think they are in fair working order. All they need now is an "occasion," as they style it, to rise and assert their rights. . . . it is now fixed that this movement shall take place on the 20th [of August].

Further on in the report he wrote about specific details:

> The enrolled strength of the Order in Illinois is 85,000. In Indiana 56,000 and in Ohio 40,000, in Kentucky unknown, repre-

sented as large. This investigation was made four weeks ago and the numbers are increasing daily. The plan is this. Instantaneously a movement will be made at Chicago, Rock Island and Springfield. These places will be seized and held, the prisoners released, armed and mounted, 7000 at Chicago, 9000 at Rock Island. A man has visited me from Chicago who asserts he has two regiments in that place eager and organized and armed. They complain that they have been cramped heretofore for lack of money, with which they have been supplied. Efforts are now making to communicate with the Indiana patriots, to induce them to initiate proceedings on the same day, and by a bold movement seize and hold Indianapolis and release the 6000 prisoners there. If they are successful in Illinois they expect to seize the Governor and Lieutenant-Governor and the Speaker of the Senate.[46] A friend will be duly and legitimately the governor. If Indiana and Ohio will move they will constitute themselves a Western Confederacy and demand peace (and if peace is not wanted, then it shall be war, and war to the knife). . . . If a movement could be made by our troops into Kentucky and Missouri by the latter part of the month it would greatly facilitate movements in the West. They would occupy all the organized troops in this quarter and leave the Western States no excuse, and the whole movement could be made without firing a gun. . . . The people of the North are growing weary of the War, but the violent Abolitionists and the preachers of all denominations save the Catholics are so rigorous in their advocacy of an entire extermination. The people of Canada generally sympathize with us. . . . [U]nless we have great success in Richmond and in Georgia, there is no hope of defeating a War-man at the ballot-box. At least I have none. I fear the leading politicians of the North will favor peace. They think if the Federal arms are defeated a Peace man can carry the ballot-box. I do not think so. The military power is too large and will be drawn too actively in to the contest. In short, in my opinion, nothing but violence can terminate the War. . . . Captain Hines is with us, and is acting with great discretion, and he possesses my entire confidence. I greatly rely upon his courage and sagacity. We have here about sixty escaped prisoners who are ready for any enterprise. Many of the men of first-rate intelligence.[47]

Several comments need to be made about Thompson's report. On December 6, 1864, Benjamin wrote to Thompson saying, "I have never heard from you since your arrival in Canada," indicating that he had not received the original of this document. Other documents quoted in the source manuscript appear to be genuine, the information given by Thompson is supported by Hines's papers in the University of Kentucky, and the content of the report sounds plausible. The unevenness of the language can be attributed to Thompson hand writing the report without the assistance of a secretary and without benefit of a redrafting. He may have sent a copy to Benjamin that was lost en route, but it is more likely that he intended to smooth out the language before transmission and never got around to doing so.[48] Furthermore, Thompson was wise to get an independent reading on the situation in the "old" North. It led him to write off the possibility of profitable action in the northeastern part of the country.

It is apparent that the efforts of Longuemare, Hines, and others to stimulate the formation of an antiwar secret society was successful. The numbers of members of the secret society cited by Thompson may have been reasonably accurate insofar as nominal members were concerned, but it would be surprising if 5 percent of the members would actually have been willing to risk life, limb, or property to achieve a political objective. Still, 4,250 dedicated men in Illinois, 2,800 in Indiana, and 2,000 in Ohio could have done much on behalf of Confederate aims if properly organized and led.

Thompson, having given a fairly euphoric report, felt compelled to throw cold water on the situation by saying that, in effect, even if successful the peace movement could not bring an end to the war by itself. The major influence still lay in the battlefield. The people of the North were tired of the war. If the war was going well, the war party was so strong that it could not be unseated; if it went badly, the peace party might be able to overthrow the war party, but doing so might require force.

Thompson's emphasis on freeing the Confederate prisoners reflected both the Confederate need for manpower and the recognition that the act of releasing the prisoners could be presented as a great blow to the Northern war effort. If the Union army could not keep their prisoners locked up, how could the army protect the country at large? Free the Confederate prisoners, and both the political and the military situations would be affected favorably for the South. If the opening of the Democratic convention had been accompanied by a street revolt that freed Rebel prisoners in Chicago, the convention might well have been influenced to adopt a position calling for an immediate end to the war.

When George Sanders arrived in Montreal on June 1, 1864, Thompson was not aware of the extent of Sanders's involvement in the planning for the Canada operation and did not know how to use him in his action-oriented effort with the Copperheads. Sanders, on the other hand, was interested in political results, had no doubts about what should be done, and proceeded to do it. While Thompson was concentrating on the members of the secret society in the northwest, Sanders was after bigger game: he was out to discredit the war party and Lincoln himself.

Many people think of Pickett's charge at Gettysburg as the high tide of the Confederacy. But, more meaningfully, the real high point of the Confederacy came in July 1864. Grant was stuck in the trenches outside Richmond and Petersburg after having been defeated repeatedly in the Wilderness campaign. The Army of Tennessee stood between Sherman and Atlanta, and Gen. Jubal A. Early's foray into Maryland was forcing Lincoln to pull troops away from Grant to protect Washington. Union forces in the lower Mississippi valley were still recovering from an embarrassing defeat in the Red River valley; the siege of Charleston was not making significant progress; and the flow of Confederate war supplies through the blockade to Wilmington, Charleston, and Mobile was well organized. The Confederacy was no longer organizing and improvising; it was operating well with experience gained and was confident that it could continue to do so indefinitely.

In the face of war-weariness in the North, this was the best opportunity that the Confederacy had to negotiate an end to the war. Sanders seized this opportunity to put Lincoln on the spot. He wanted to show that Lincoln was either in a weak position or was not seriously interested in a reasonable end to the war. With the Democratic party convention only a few weeks away, either result would be beneficial to the Confederacy. Either result could be used to discredit Lincoln and the war party and encourage the peace democrats among the electorate in the North.

Sanders used William Cornell Jewett, a peace activist with ties to both North and South, to pass word through Horace Greeley, publisher

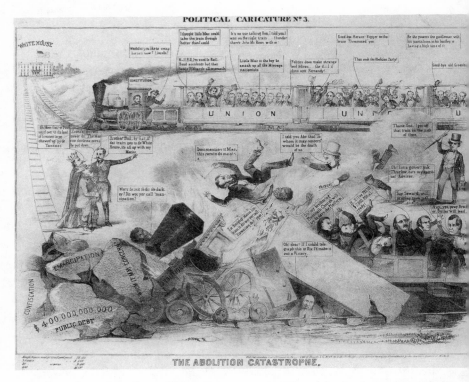

This unsigned cartoon shows how the pro-peace Democrats presented their case after the breakup of the Niagara conference in July 1864. The leadership of abolitionists and Republican radicals was predicted to lead to disaster at the polls in November 1864. Courtesy of the Library of Congress.

of the *New York Tribune,* that the South was interested in negotiating peace with the North. When Jewett reported that Greeley had responded favorably, Sanders wrote to Greeley on July 12 and offered Clay, Holcombe, and himself as negotiators to go to Washington. Jewett and Greeley managed, however, in their enthusiasm for peace, to handle the information about the positions of North and South in such a way as to mislead both parties about the possibilities of mutually acceptable terms. The upshot was that the Confederates appeared to be eager for an honorable peace, but Lincoln's secretary, John Hay, together with Greeley, arrived at Niagara to meet Sanders on July 20 with a letter, addressed "To Whom it May Concern," in which Lincoln re-stated the Union position in completely unacceptable terms to the South. The outcome was a situation that could be used by the Confederates to paint themselves as the peace-loving, injured party.[49]

Throughout the negotiations Jacob Thompson was silent. He had just spent several weeks working with Copperheads who intended to launch a revolt with Confederate help and here the Confederates were talking peace! Thompson must have feared that the negotiation would make him look insincere and discourage the Copperheads from taking their promised action. From that point of view, it is no small wonder that Thompson disapproved of what he felt was meddling on the part of Sanders.[50]

When the dust settled after the conclusion of Greeley's visit, the posture of the Confederate secret service in Canada was as follows:

- At Toronto: Jacob Thompson and William Cleary as his secretary; William L. (Larry) Macdonald and a number of associates who had been involved in Confederate secret service work before Thompson's arrival.
- At Hamilton: Cassius F. Lee, who served as a cut-out[51] for communications with various secret service agents.
- At St. Catharines: Clement C. Clay, Beverly Tucker, and Robert Edwin Coxe. This was a headquarters for operations with a regular system for clandestine contacts at the Niagara Falls Museum a few miles away.
- At Windsor: Col. [first name unknown] Steele, who maintained contact with Copperheads living in the old Northwest Territory.
- At Montreal: Patrick Charles Martin, the leading agent of the Confederate secret service in Canada as it existed before the arrival of Thompson, Clay, and Sanders; George N. Sanders and his twenty-one-year-old son, Lewis Sanders; John Porterfield, the Nashville banker; "Mr." Davis, the money exchange expert; and a number of other Confederate agents and couriers. Montreal had good rail connections with Boston and New York, and people associated with the Confederate secret service agents here appear to have done a lot of traveling between Montreal and various points in the North as well as to Richmond.

While Thompson was planning for an uprising in Chicago in August, a supporting activity was under way. One of the several Confederates arrested in the attempted raid on Calais, Maine, in July was Francis X. Jones, formerly of the 1st Missouri Regiment. Shortly after his arrest, Jones informed his jailers that he knew that the Confederacy was planning raids against the coast of New England. His story was so convincing that Judge Advocate General Joseph Holt traveled to Maine to interview him. On September 16, Holt reported that he was convinced Jones was telling the truth, but in retrospect it is obvious that Jones's story was disinformation.[52]

Holt was particularly impressed by Jones's knowledge of the activities of the Confederate raider *Tallahassee,* which raided off the New England coast in August. In Holt's view, Jones had been held incommunicado and therefore must have known about the *Tallahassee* and other Confederate plans *before* he was captured in July.[53] In fact, the *Tallahassee* did not exist until July 23—after Jones had been captured— when the blockade runner *Atlanta* was renamed and armed for her raid along the Atlantic coast. Furthermore, the scale of operations contemplated in Jones's story is ludicrous when compared with the Confederate assets available for such an enterprise.

Jones must have been coached on his story by Confederate agents after he had been put into prison. One Confederate agent, Robert Edwin Coxe of St. Catharine's, Ontario, was in Maine during the summer of 1864 and was probably involved in the operation. But more importantly, the operation must have been started by the Confederates while they were preparing for the Chicago uprising: the story of threatened action in New England would have been beneficial in diverting attention from events in the old Northwest Territory.

In the meantime, while Clay, Holcombe, and Sanders were trying to negotiate through Greeley, John Wilkes Booth was spending a vigorous summer at his oil well in western Pennsylvania. In 1863 Booth had reestablished an acquaintance, established originally by his father, with John Adam Ellsler, who operated the leading theater in Cleveland. Young Booth and Ellsler struck up a personal friendship and became partners in the new petroleum industry. After the theaters closed for the summer in 1864, the two men met at the site of their well near Franklin, Pennsylvania, to familiarize themselves with their property. They spent most of July living in spartan conditions near the well site.[54]

Something, however, prompted Booth to go to Boston, where on July 26 he registered at the Parker House in the company of three men from Canada and one from Baltimore.[55] An exhaustive search has failed to identify these individuals, although a man using one of the names, H. V. Clinton, registered at the St. Lawrence Hall in Montreal on May 28, 1864, and again on the following August 24. There is no way of knowing what was discussed in Boston, but before this date Booth was interested in oil; after this date he was interested in putting together a team to capture Lincoln as a hostage. Thus the elusiveness of Booth's companions at Boston is compatible with the behavior that one would expect from secret service agents engaged in recruiting a new and important member of their organization. A reasonable hypothesis is that Booth was meeting with representatives of the Confederate secret service group in Montreal who were traveling under assumed identities.

One countertheory suggests that the men were more likely obscure actors whom Booth knew. The chief problem with that theory is that the identities of most actors successful enough to afford a ticket to Boston are well established, and the list does not include the names registered at Boston. Another objection sometimes raised to the idea of Booth being recruited as an agent of the Confederate secret service is that Booth, because of his sometimes frivolous behavior, would have made a poor agent. In my view, the recruitment of Booth would have been a great coup for the Confederacy.

Booth was an intelligent man with well-established leanings to the Southern cause. According to his sister, he had established his *bona fides* by smuggling quinine into the Confederacy and serving as an informant.[56] He had independent means, had no immediate family ties to limit his activity, and was engaged in a profession that allowed him to move about without being accountable to anybody for his time. In addition, he was athletic, a good shot, and skilled at playing a role— something an agent must do on occasion. Furthermore, he was so well known to the public that he could gain access almost anywhere and, if recognized, attract adulation instead of suspicion. In other words, Booth could do and get away with almost anything. From the Confederate standpoint, he must have seemed like an ideal addition to the ranks of their secret service operatives. George P. Kane, the former police commissioner of Baltimore, who had been in Canada until early 1864, knew the Booth family in Baltimore and could have been the one who

This picture of a pensive young John Wilkes Booth (1838–65) was taken by an unknown photographer and exists today only as a rare *carte de visite*. Booth appears to be wearing a coat and tie similar to those he wore in pictures taken in Chicago in 1862 or 1863. Courtesy of the Lincoln Collection, Brown University Library, Providence, Rhode Island.

suggested to Confederate authorities that John Wilkes Booth might be recruited as an action agent for the operation to capture Lincoln.[57]

Also during July 1864, Capt. Thomas Hines was busy delivering secret service funds from Thompson to the leading Copperheads. First, August 20, and then August 29, had been picked as the day on which to launch the uprising by the Order of American Knights. August 29 was the opening day of the Democratic convention in Chicago, and the presence of crowds attending and observing the Convention would obscure the presence of additional friends of the Confederacy. Weapons were shipped under various subterfuges to selected Copperheads for distribution, and other preparations were under way. Unfortunately for Thompson's plans, however, in early August an event unknown to the Confederates took place, ruining the entire idea of a Copperhead revolt.

On August 5, 1864, a group of leading Indiana democrats, under the leadership of Joseph J. Bingham, editor of the *Indiana Sentinel,* met with the heads of the Order of American Knights in Indiana and extracted from them a promise not to take part in an uprising. Since the Knights' political legitimacy stemmed from their alleged support of the Democratic party, members could not take action if it was opposed by the party's leaders. The Indiana Knights could not back out of the agreement with the other Copperheads without losing face, but they could think of numerous excuses to avoid action without altering their professed opposition to the war. Without the Indiana contingent, however, there was no way that the Knights from Illinois and Ohio could carry off the uprising.[58]

John W. Headley, formerly of the 1st Kentucky Cavalry and later assigned to the Confederate secret service in Canada, described the outcome of the planned uprising on the basis of information that he said he had received from Captain Hines,[59] and he was able to add some documentation to Hines's version of events. According to Headley, Thompson decided to augment the Copperhead effort in Chicago with a group of Confederate soldiers who would be armed in Canada and infiltrated into the United States under the command of Captain Hines. On August 24, Capt. John B. Castleman, formerly of the 2d Kentucky Cavalry, was assigned as second in command under Hines. According to a list printed by Headley, sixty-two men, including Hines and Castleman, were issued weapons that had been obtained by William Cleary. Headley described what happened next:

On the 27th and 28th of August the Confederates detailed for this important service proceeded to Chicago, travelling in small parties and assuming the appearance and conduct of men attracted there by the political interest of the occasion. . . . Men commended to us by Mr. [Clement Laird] Vallandigham had been entrusted with the necessary funds for perfecting the county organizations; arms had been purchased in the North by the aid of our professed friends in New York; alliances offensive and defensive had been made with peace organizations, and though we were not misled by the sanguine promises of our friends, we were confident that with any sort of cooperation on their part success was reasonably possible. . . . We felt . . . that we could move with promptness and effect upon Camp Douglas. With nearly five thousand prisoners there, and over seven thousand at Springfield, joined by the dissatisfied elements in Chicago and through Illinois, we believed that at once we would have a formidable force, which might be the nucleus for much more important movements.

Headley went on to point out that Chicago was thronged with people from all sections of the country, and in this crowd were many of the officers of the Order of American Knights. In order to establish definitely what armed forces were available, a meeting was held in the rooms of Hines and Castleman at the Richmond House on the night before the convention.

The reinforcement sent by the [Lincoln] Administration to strengthen the Chicago garrison had been vastly exaggerated, and seven thousand men was the number rumor brought to the ear of the Sons of Liberty.[60] Care had been taken to keep informed as to what troops came to Camp Douglas, but the statement made by Hines and Castleman, to the effect that only three thousand were present, did not counteract the effect produced by the rumor that the Federal forces there numbered more than double that number. When, therefore, a count was taken of the number of the Sons of Liberty on whom we could rely, it seemed worse than folly to attempt to use them.[61]

August 29, 1864, came and went without action by the Copperheads. The Democratic convention nominated General McClellan as its candidate for president on August 31, but on September 8 he disavowed the "peace" plank in the Democratic platform. The Confederates had failed to get a candidate committed to a position favorable to the South. Short of that, they had failed to bring about an open revolt. And even more disturbing, they had failed to release the Confederate prisoners in Chicago. The entire operation had been a failure.

On top of this turn of affairs, Sanders's oldest son, Maj. Reid Sanders, a prisoner of war at Ft. Warren in Boston harbor, died in early September. Thereafter, Sanders had a deep personal reason to hate the Yankees in addition to his already strong political and philosophical opposition.

On September 12, Clay wrote to Benjamin discussing the political results of the Greeley episode and the nomination of McClellan. In this letter he said, "Mr. Thompson has, since Mr. Sanders was started to Richmond, put in my hands all the funds I asked for."[62] Whether Clay was referring to George Sanders or his son, Lewis Sanders, is not clear. Lewis Sanders traveled to Richmond in August 1864 in a well-documented trip, but it does not seem likely that Clay would refer to the son without clearly distinguishing him from his father. There is no independent reference to George Sanders being in Richmond at this time, but from September 12 to 15 there was a series of meetings involving both Benjamin and Secretary of War James A. Seddon, which resulted in the launch of Thomas Nelson Conrad and a small team of associates on a mission to investigate the activities of President Lincoln with a view to his abduction. In view of Sanders's later association with John Wilkes Booth, it would not be surprising for Sanders to have traveled to Richmond incognito, participate in the meetings, and slip back to Canada before anyone knew where he had been.[63]

In the meantime, Thompson had started another operation that could have made a useful complement or follow-on action to a successful Copperhead revolt. This operation, a reprise of the 1863 attempt to release the Confederate prisoners on Johnson's Island, involved the capture of the only Union ship on Lake Erie, the USS *Michigan*. The *Michigan* had been stationed at Buffalo, but in view of rumors of an attempt to free the Confederate prisoners, it had been moved to Sandusky, Ohio, and was anchored near Johnson's Island. The operation involved Charles H. Cole, an agent who lived on shore and had made friends among the naval officers. Cole was to cause a surprise diversion on board the *Michigan* to coincide with a Confederate attack. John Yates Beall, a former associate of Edwin Grey Lee in his irregular naval operations in the Chesapeake, was assigned to charter or capture a civilian vessel and bring a boarding party of armed Confederates alongside the *Michigan*. This was a technique that had already been used successfully in the Chesapeake, and with Cole's help it could be made to work in Lake Erie.

Beall was successful in capturing the *Philo Parsons,* a small vessel that operated between Detroit and Sandusky. Cole, however, had been arrested on the basis of information obtained from Confederate sympathizers in Detroit. When Beall approached the Michigan, on September 19, he discovered that she was on alert.

Beall's crew was mostly made up of men provided on short notice by Confederates in Windsor, and there were fewer of them than had been promised. They were not well known to Beall, and there had been no opportunity to train together or develop a unit discipline. When the men learned of the ready condition of the *Michigan,* they refused to continue with the mission, and Beall was compelled to retreat, scuttle his ship, and disperse his crew. The capture of the *Philo Parsons* caused widespread alarm in the North, but nothing more useful than that was gained.[64]

Shortly thereafter, in early October, Sanders persuaded Thompson and Clay to call on Governor General Lord Charles Stanley Monck in Quebec. The exact nature of this maneuver has never been fully explained, but the upshot was that Lord Monck refused to receive the two Confederates, who left Quebec in considerable embarrassment. Sanders had many high-level contacts among Democrats in the North and among British politicians, and it is possible he thought he had arranged a situation in which Monck might be willing to establish an informal dialogue with the senior Confederates.

While this diplomatic maneuver was under way, action was also taking place in the operation to capture Lincoln. On October 16 John Wilkes Booth was seen in Newburgh, New York, a few miles from Poughkeepsie, where Confederate agent Robert Edwin Coxe was staying

St. Lawrence Hall, Montreal. This picture was made long after the Civil War (ca. 1909), but the only significant change in the hotel's appearance since the 1860s was the addition of window awnings. Courtesy of the Blackader-Lauterman Library of Architecture and Art, Montreal.

with his in-laws, and on October 18 Booth arrived in Montreal and registered at the St. Lawrence Hall. Clay and Thompson passed through Montreal on their return from Quebec shortly before Booth's arrival. It seems clear that Clay could not have met Booth on this trip, but several days of Thompson's time are not accounted for, and it is possible that he met Booth during the first day or two of Booth's Montreal visit.[65]

During his stay in Montreal, Booth was given $300 in gold by "Mr. Davis," the Confederate money-handler.[66] There are two known outcomes of Booth's association with Martin: he arranged with Martin to ship Booth's dramatic wardrobe to the Confederacy; and Martin gave Booth a letter of introduction to Dr. William Queen, a prominent Southern sympathizer in southern Maryland.[67]

Booth also spent some time with George Sanders. His meetings with Sanders were interrupted, however, when on October 19 a group of Confederates under the command of Lt. Bennett H. Young raided St. Albans, Vermont. The raiders were successful in escaping to Canada, but several of them were arrested by Canadian authorities and jailed at St. Johns, Quebec, not far from Montreal. Caleb Wallace, one of those arrested, immediately sent a telegram to Sanders asking for his help. Sanders went off to visit the captives on October 23, but on his return to Montreal on October 25 he checked into St. Lawrence Hall and was given a room near Booth's. Booth must have spent considerable time with Sanders, because Federal detectives later found three reliable witnesses who reported seeing the two together at the St. Lawrence.[68]

The Sanders that Booth met was a man who believed in strong action to achieve a republican form of government. He was an idealist willing to encourage assassination of political tyrants. Sanders had much prior experience working with political radicals in clandestine operations and believed in the radical cliché that chaos and disorder could be used to topple governments. He was the sort of idealist who felt that he was right and that his righteousness entitled him to impose his views on others. In the twentieth century George Sanders would have found the communist idea of "vanguard of the proletariat" to be a comfortable philosophy. Given his age, experience, and glib tongue, he must have made a favorable impression on Booth.

Two other men later reported meeting Booth during this period. One was Col. Robert M. Martin, another Kentuckian, who was sent by Benjamin to report to Thompson with John W. Headley in late

September 1864.[69] It is not clear, however, whether Martin met Booth during his October trip to Montreal or on some later trip not independently documented. The second man to meet Booth was Lt. Col. James Gordon, married to Thompson's niece, who later wrote that he had been involved in planning the abduction of Lincoln and had met John Wilkes Booth in the process. Gordon did not arrive in Canada until March 8, 1865, and it is not clear whether he met Booth in Canada or in the United States before he went to Canada.[70]

Booth left Montreal and was in New York again on October 29, but he did not stay long. He returned to Washington and began to explore southern Maryland, armed with the letter of introduction from P. C. Martin.

After Booth's departure from Canada, three more major Confederate operations from Canada caused considerable stir but accomplished little. A team of armed men was sent back to Chicago in a reprise of the August venture. They were to release the prisoners at Camp Douglas on the eve of the election, but the operation was penetrated by Union agents and the leaders arrested on November 6, 1864.

In frustration over their inability to get the Copperheads to take concrete action, the Confederates in the action wing of the secret service decided to launch an operation on their own. On November 25 a team headed by Colonel Martin and Lieutenant Headley tried to set fire to New York City. The team rented hotel rooms in a number of strategically placed hotels and, equipped with "Greek fire," set fire to the rooms at an agreed time, expecting the fires to spread and overwhelm the city fire department. However, they made an important miscalculation: after setting the fires, they closed the doors and transoms to the rooms to avoid having the fires discovered prematurely. This had the effect of closing off the supply of oxygen, and the fires went out, leaving scorched rooms but little other damage.[71]

In December, the Confederates received word that a group of Confederate general officer prisoners was to be transferred by rail through upstate New York. A team was hurriedly assembled in an attempt to stop the train and release the prisoners. The operation was a failure, and on December 16 John Yates Beall (of *Philo Parsons* fame) was arrested as a suspected Confederate in Buffalo on his way back to Canada. The Confederates tried to bring influence to bear to save him, but Beall was hanged for piracy and espionage on February 24, 1865.[72]

There is a badly garbled story that has been repeated several times to the effect that Beall and John Wilkes Booth had been to school together and that Booth had appealed to Lincoln to save his friend. Lincoln had refused to intervene, the story goes, and Booth decided to kill Lincoln in revenge.[73] There are many problems with this story. While there is a possibility that Booth and Beall could have met at Charles Town, Virginia, in 1859, where they both participated in the militia guarding John Brown, Beall and Booth did not go to school together. Nor is there any record that Booth ever had an interview with Lincoln, and the assassination was obviously generated by a completely different series of events. There is, however, a possible explanation for the origin of the story. Booth had to be trained in clandestine tradecraft, and it is possible that Beall was the man assigned to provide the training and that they developed a friendship during their brief "schooling." After Beall's death, Booth might well have talked about Beall enough for somebody to associate the idea of "school" and Booth's anger and later remember the connection to form the basis for an explanation of the assassination.

Another glimpse at the status of Confederate operations was provided at the trial of Booth's associates on May 26, 1865, when one Henry Finnegass—born in Ireland, a resident of Boston, a former officer in a Massachusetts regiment, and a former commander of the 3d Louisiana Native Guards Regiment (a black regiment)[74]—testified. He said that he had been in the St. Lawrence Hall in Montreal on February 14 or 15, 1865, and that he had overheard a conversation between George Sanders and William Cleary in which Cleary said, "I suppose they are getting ready for the inauguration of Lincoln next month." Sanders replied, "Yes: if the boys only have luck, Lincoln won't trouble them much longer." Cleary then asked, "Is every thing well?" Sanders then said, "Oh, yes! Booth is bossing the job."[75] Finnegass went on to say that he had been in Montreal for eleven days and that he had left on February 17, 1865. He had not met either Cleary or Sanders but knew both of them by sight; Sanders had been pointed out to him by the clerk of the hotel, and he had seen both testify at the trial of the St. Albans raiders. He overheard the conversation from a distance of about ten feet.[76]

In dealing with witnesses, one must always be prepared for the frailties of human memory. It is perfectly possible that Finnegass wanted

This picture, taken several years after the war ended, shows the St. Lawrence Hall lounge, in which Henry Finnegass overheard George Sanders and William Cleary talk about John Wilkes Booth. Courtesy of Notman Photographic Archives, McCord Museum of Canadian History, Montreal.

to remember the conversation the way that he reported it but that in fact it was somewhat different. On the other hand, it is also possible that he was reporting the matter correctly.

Although Finnegass's character was later attacked, there are several pieces of information that support some elements of his story. The trial of several of the St. Albans raiders was under way during February 1865. An "H. Finnegass" did register at the St. Lawrence Hall in Montreal on February 6, 1865. William Cleary, the secretary to the Confederate mission and stationed in Toronto, registered at the St. Lawrence on

February 10, 1865. George Sanders, of course, was normally in Montreal. Thus, there is independent proof that all the players in Finnegass's testimony were present in Montreal at about the time he claimed to have overheard the conversation.[77]

The prosecutors at the trial presented Finnegass's testimony as relating to preparations for the assassination, but it is more likely that, if quoted correctly, the remarks referred to the plan to take Lincoln hostage.

If the alleged conversation between Sanders and Cleary is approximately correct, it supports the view that Sanders had a major interest in Booth's operation. It also indicates that Cleary, and doubtless his chief, Thompson, were aware of Booth's role as a Confederate agent but that they did not know the details of the project. For Sanders to know as much as his remarks indicated, there had to be a means by which reports of operational progress were passed from Washington to Montreal. Part of this could have been done by carefully worded letters to letter-drop addresses, and part of it could have been carried out by periodic meetings of representatives from the Washington and Canadian ends of the organization. This last function could account for some of Booth's visits to New York and Boston as well as his well-documented trip to Montreal in October 1864. There is also the possibility that Booth made at least one other trip to Canada that has not been documented.

Little other information has turned up regarding Sanders's operations during the final months of the war. Near the end of March 1865, the Confederacy decided to attack leaders of the government in Washington in order to disrupt the coordination of Union armies in the field. It is not known whether this idea originated in Richmond or among the Confederates in Canada, but its eventual outcome was for Booth to decide to carry out the intent by attacking the president and other key officials simultaneously on April 14, 1865.[78]

In the aftermath of the defeat of the Confederate armies and the assassination of Lincoln, the Federal government sought to prove that the Confederate government and its agents in Canada were responsible for the assassination. Such proof, and the imposition of punitive measures, would have had a devastating effect on the South. The Federal prosecutors were not successful in establishing the case, however, and George N. Sanders was the principal architect of their defeat. It was the most important and most successful clandestine operation under-taken by the Confederate secret service apparatus in Canada.

One of the chief Union witnesses used to implicate the Confeder-ates in Canada in the "assassination plot" was Charles A. Dunham, alias "Sanford Conover," "James Watson Wallace," and a string of other false names. In 1864 and 1865 Dunham had spent several months in Canada, met a number of the Confederates, and testified on behalf of the St. Albans raiders. Now, as Conover, he appeared in Washing-ton in mid-May willing to swear to a number of stories about Con-federate plotting in Canada. Later, at the congressional hearings in 1866, he introduced a number of other witnesses who told similar tales. Dunham and his witnesses were exposed as liars, and their expo-sure destroyed the credibility of the case against the Confederate government.[79]

A similar case was Dr. James B. Merritt, who had also spent some time in Canada and generally supported Dunham's line. He too was discredited as a witness. The effects of the exposure of Merritt and Dunham also spread to other witnesses who were not perjurers. Finnegass's testimony, for example, may have been ignored because at the time nobody could distinguish it from the stories told by Merritt and Conover.

Another witness against the Confederates in Canada was Richard Montgomery, the son of a customs official in New York City. Mont-gomery had convinced the Confederates that he was friendly to their cause and was employed by them as a courier between Canada and Richmond. The only hitch was that he stopped off in Washington and allowed the Union authorities to copy the dispatches that he was carry-ing. Some of the Confederates became suspicious of his loyalty, and his employment dwindled away.[80] In their effort to discredit the wit-nesses at the conspiracy trial, the Confederates managed successfully to treat Dunham, Merritt, and Montgomery in their posttrial propa-ganda as a trio of perjurers. But there remains a serious possibility that Montgomery may have been telling the truth. If he did, it would indi-cate that the Confederates in Canada were well aware that if the abduction plan did not work it might be necessary to attack Lincoln directly.

The details of the Confederate operation to discredit the Union effort will probably never be fully known. But there are several shreds of evidence. On May 29, 1865, W. W. Daniels[81] wrote to Secretary of War Stanton from Hamilton, saying that he had been in Montreal a few days previously and there had met George Sanders. He had found Sanders fully informed of developments in the military commission investigating the assassination, and Sanders had told Daniels that he had sent witnesses to Washington for the purpose of testifying in the trial of the conspirators.[82]

To understand the possibilities in this situation it is necessary to review some of Dunham's (Conover's) background. He was born in Croton, New York, about 1832, the son of a successful tanner. He went to New York in 1852 or 1853 to study law but did not succeed in passing the examination for the bar. By 1856 he was deeply involved in a swindle involving the search for heirs to a mythical fortune in England.[83] This project lasted for several years and was followed by another similar swindle involving heirs of another alleged fortune in England.

Very early in his career Dunham developed a talent for adopting various false identities and writing fictitious letters under assumed names. He plied this talent so diligently that it is extremely difficult to sort out the confusing trail that he made through the events following the Lincoln assassination. Similarly, it is difficult to establish exactly what happened to him in early life because his own descriptions of his life history are so full of false statements that it is almost impossible to determine if any of them are true. For example, he hinted that he took part in William Walker's expedition in Nicaragua and visited England on another occasion, but neither of these stories has been confirmed.[84] In 1861 his activities are better documented. He applied for and received approval to raise a regiment of infantry in New York City, with himself as colonel of the regiment. After glowing claims of progress in organizing his 400 or 600 recruits, but no action, his authority was cancelled and his men (about thirty-two in number) were incorporated into another regiment.[85]

Dunham held a number of short-term positions and wrote articles under various assumed names. In 1863 he crossed the lines and spent several months in Richmond, where he spun a number of lies for the Confederate War Department. Part of the time in Richmond he was confined to Castle Thunder, the Confederate prison for disloyal and suspicious characters. His time in Richmond enabled him to acquire a lot of background information on the Confederacy and provided him an opportunity to get copies of letterhead stationery, which he later used to advantage. Based on what he had learned while in Richmond, he later claimed (falsely) to have served as a clerk in the Confederate War Department.[86]

In 1864 Dunham was in Niagara reporting on the peace conference organized by George Sanders. In August 1864 he was in Washington where he generated a number of stories using his familiarity with details in the Confederacy to lend authenticity. He then spent some time in Baltimore and returned to Canada about the time of the St. Albans raid of October 19. He was arrested by the Canadians near the American border south of Montreal on suspicion of being one of the St. Albans raiders and put into the same Montreal jail that held the genuine Confederates. George Sanders visited him in prison and offered to help him. Dunham was released shortly afterward, when it became clear that he was not one of the raiders.[87]

In 1864, Dunham had begun to submit articles and letters to Sidney Howard Gay, editor of the *New York Tribune*, under the name of "Sanford Conover." In one of his letters he claimed to be on "intimate and confidential terms" with the Confederates in Canada as a result of his friendship with Sanders. When the St. Albans raiders were put on trial, he testified on February 14 under the name of James Watson Wallace, claiming to have personal knowledge of the signature of James A. Seddon, the Confederate secretary of war, and swearing that Seddon's signature on defense documents was authentic. Sanders also testified for the defendants on the same day.[88]

In April, after the assassination, Dunham was in Canada for several weeks. While there, he wrote letters using aliases and made a number of false claims. Drafts of similar letters in Dunham's handwriting were later found in his trunk and turned over to the U.S. consul in Montreal, who sent them to Judge Holt, the judge advocate in charge of the trial of Booth's associates.[89] Several of the draft letters were addressed to George Sanders, and Sanders appears to have recognized Dunham's talent for generating creative falsehoods to suit any occasion. Confederate propaganda later used some of the ideas that Dunham had been exploring in his other drafts, and Sanders probably developed with Dunham the idea of feeding bogus information to the Union prosecutors.

On May 20, 1865, Dunham, using the name of Sanford Conover, testified at the trial of the conspirators in Washington and alleged to have heard conversations conclusively proving that the Confederates were behind the assassination of Lincoln. His testimony did demonstrate his considerable knowledge about the Confederate personnel in Canada involved in clandestine operations, even if his allegations about what they said were later demonstrated to be false.[90] He returned to Canada immediately after his May testimony and conferred with George and Lewis Sanders. He may, therefore, have been a source of some of the information on the trial that Sanders mentioned to W. W. Daniels. While Dunham was in Montreal, the essential part of his Washington testimony was leaked to the press and published in Canada on June 5 and 6. On June 8 some of his Confederate friends (who did not know of his cooperation with Sanders) chastised him for making such false allegations. Dunham responded that some villain had used his name and slandered him by telling those awful lies. When he was asked if he would swear that he had not said such things, he agreed. As Dunham was preparing to write his statement, George Sanders turned up, and the two went off by themselves for fifteen or twenty minutes. Sanders and Dunham thus had an opportunity to finalize the strategy that Dunham was to follow in regard to the prosecutors in Washington. Dunham, as James Watson Wallace, then returned to the group and said that he was ready to make his statement.[91] As Wallace he then swore:

> I never gave any testimony whatsoever before the said court-martial at Washington City. . . . That I never went under the name of Sanford Conover. That I never had any confidential communication with Mr. George N. Sanders, Beverly Tucker, Hon. Jacob Thompson, General Carroll of Tennessee. . . . [T]he evidence of the said Sanford Conover personating me is false, untrue and unfounded in fact.[92]

As soon as Dunham (as Conover) returned to Washington in late June, he said that the Confederates had forced him to make this statement at gunpoint. This so incensed William Henry Carroll, a retired Confederate general (not a member of the Confederate secret service) who was present at the June 8 affair, that he published a pamphlet describing the incident in great detail. In its indignation and innocence, General Carroll's description is most convincing. He was telling the events just as he remembered them, but he did not realize the significance of what he was saying. He did not realize that he was revealing a collaboration between Sanders and Dunham.[93]

The fifteen or twenty minutes that Dunham and Sanders had alone together may have marked the beginning of a long-term campaign on the part of Dunham to provide invaluable assistance to the memory of the Confederacy. Nearly everything that Dunham did from that point forward helped to destroy the case that the Federal prosecutors were developing against Jefferson Davis and key persons in the Confederate secret service. Why Dunham should have engaged in such determined support of the Confederates is not clear. One can only surmise that he may have been given a lifetime annuity in return for his continued cooperation.

As soon as the Confederates had Dunham's sworn affidavit, they published a strong statement in the *Montreal Evening Telegraph,* accompanied by the text of Dunham's (J. Watson Wallace's) affidavit. The statement attacked the testimonies of Sanford Conover, Dr. Merritt, and Richard Montgomery.

Notwithstanding their apparent truthfulness, the depositions nevertheless contain unmistakable internal evidence going to show that they were cooked to order. Matters which, if specifically stated might readily be refuted are set forth in generalities in which all mention of precise dates is purposely omitted, and special clues to the speedy detection of the falsehoods carefully left out, while at the same time circumstances and conversations alluded to are couched in artfully concocted phraseology. All three of the witnesses in this regard committed the error false witnesses so often fall into of swearing to too much and of swearing too much alike. . . . The testimony of one of these witnesses, Sanford Conover, is given its quietus by the affidavit of James Watson Wallace, which has been handed to us by that person for publication. We are informed that other affidavits corroborative of his testimony will be published hereafter, and also depositions disproving the statements made by Merritt and Montgomery. . . . The Federal prosecutors of these charges may possibly strive to avoid the effect

of this affidavit of Wallace's by urging that they have been egre-
giously imposed upon by Sanford Conover and will perhaps allege
that the whole affair is the result of an ingenious and deep laid
conspiracy by Mr. Sanders and his confreres to deceive, mislead,
and entrap, gull and then expose them. . . . Conover, Meritt,
Montgomery, Hyams, and some others examined before the Commission, will not be credited either in Europe or America after the
exposure of what Mr. Sanders calls their "sample witnesses."

One can visualize a gleeful Sanders unable to resist the opportunity to
hint that the pro-Confederate outcome of this affair was his doing.[94]

The Confederate statement was later reprinted and circulated as a
handbill. It was followed by several pamphlets that examined the testimony of each of the major witnesses against the Confederates,
refuting them point by point.[95] The effect of this campaign was over-
whelming. The Federal government did not abandon its positions, but
Dunham was tried and convicted of perjury, and the country at large
has accepted the Sanders version of history: the Confederates had
nothing to do with Booth and his associates.

Sanders "feeding" Dunham and Merritt to the Union authorities
would have been very much in keeping with his reputation. He kept
himself informed on the most important political activity of the
moment—the trial. He was not going to let the trial take place without trying to influence it, and he was successful in shaping the way the
country thought about the assassination—even to this day.

Sanders may not have been in formal command in Canada, and he
may not have had control of any substantial sums of money; but he
did pay attention to operations, and he made things happen. After Appomattox he stayed on in Canada, helping with the Confederate
campaign to avoid blame for the assassination. In November 1865 he
returned to Europe. In 1870 he supported the Paris commune and
then returned to the United States in 1872. He died in New York on
August 13, 1873.

Throughout this long recital of Confederate operations in Canada run
five major themes. Of primary importance was influencing the election of November 1864. Before the election, the defeat of Lincoln had
top priority, and most of the Confederate activity was in some way re-

lated to it; after the election, there was no immediate point in continuing the same activities, and they dwindled in importance.

Another theme was the freeing of Confederate prisoners from Federal prison camps. The South was desperate for manpower, and the camps were inviting targets for Confederate planners. The attempts to free the prisoners at Camp Douglas in Chicago failed through the involvement of too many outsiders. The 1864 attempt to free the prisoners at Johnson's Island failed because the operation depended too much on makeshift arrangements.[96] Using a crew that had never worked together to attack a Union warship was asking for the kind of trouble that Beall encountered.

By accident, however, the Confederates in Camp Morton in Indianapolis showed how freeing the prisoners could be carried out. In November 1864 the prisoners there independently planned a breakout. The camp covered a large area on the outskirts of Indianapolis on the banks of a large creek. A group of forty-six prisoners secretly prepared a number of ladders and collected piles of stones at strategic points near the walls. On November 14, at a signal, they ran at the wall, simultaneously throwing rocks at the guards, and planted the ladders against the walls. The guards fired their rifles but had no chance to reload before they were overwhelmed. A large number of men got over the wall, including many who had not been among the planners. Some escapees got into the creek bottom where they could hide in the undergrowth. But since the men were unarmed, they could not hold off pursuit, and many of them were recaptured. When order had been restored, a total of forty-three men remained unaccounted for.[97] Troops guarding prisoner-of-war camps were not first-line troops trained in tactical operations. It seemed obvious to the Confederates that if there had been a small number of armed men on the outside to delay the pursuit, many more prisoners could have escaped.

News of the escape from Camp Morton must have arrived in Richmond shortly after Sgt. Berry Benson became the hero of the hour by escaping from the prisoner-of-war camp at Elmira, New York. He reached Confederate-controlled territory in Virginia on October 27, 1864, and arrived in Richmond a few days later. The coincidental arrival of information about the camp at Elmira and a technique by which it could be relieved of its prisoners doubtless influenced Confederate plans for operations from Canada.

After the election in November, the Confederates in Richmond assumed that Thompson would not be interested in continuing in his mission in Canada and decided to replace him with an officer who could ensure the proper attention to military details in organizing breakouts from other Northern prisons. The man selected was Edwin Grey Lee, son of a first cousin of Robert E. Lee. Although suffering from tuberculosis, E. G. Lee had considerable combat experience, including some irregular warfare in 1863. He was a brigadier general commanding reserve forces in Virginia and was stationed at Staunton when he was ordered to report to Richmond on December 6, 1864, for his final instructions.[98]

The third theme running through Confederate operations was that of destructive raids and sabotage designed to distract the Union from its operations in the Confederacy and to pay the North back for some of the destruction it had caused in the South. The only secret service raids actually carried out that appear to have primarily represented this theme were the aborted Calais raid, the raid on St. Albans, and the attempt to set fire to New York City. Sabotage efforts were more successful in the destruction of shipping on the Ohio and Mississippi rivers. The question of whether to raid or not to raid had been an issue between Thompson and Clay throughout their time in Canada. In frustration, Clay decided to give up the effort and began to arrange his travel plans to return to the Confederacy in October 1864. He finally left Montreal on December 10, 1864, but through the misadventures of travel he did not reach Richmond until April 2, 1865, the day the Confederate government left town.

The fourth theme was the operation to capture Lincoln. Booth appears to have been recruited initially by Confederates from Montreal. Though it is not known if they had the abduction in mind as an assignment for Booth, it is clear that by September 1864 the abduction was the mission for which he was preparing. It is also clear that the Confederates in Richmond were working on the same idea at the same time, because Thomas Nelson Conrad was sent to Washington in mid-September to observe Lincoln's movements.

What probably happened was that several people had been urging the capture of Lincoln, and, after Dahlgren's raid in March 1864, the Confederate government was willing to consider such an operation. In July the secret service people in Montreal presented Richmond with an unexpected opportunity—a new agent, Booth, who had unusual talents and an unusual opportunity to take action in the Washington area. The outcome of the Greeley negotiations at Niagara must have made it clear to all that Lincoln would never consent to Southern independence. Yet without Lincoln, there might be politicians who would be willing to compromise with the South to bring the war to an end. Both the secret service people in Canada and the senior element of the government in Richmond could agree that an attempt to capture Lincoln was worth the effort. Thus, in September 1864 desire, motive, and opportunity coincided in the launching of a clandestine operation to capture Lincoln. Sanders, certainly, would have been strongly in favor of such a move; Clay might well have supported it because it represented action; and Thompson might have favored it as a backup because he recognized that it would be difficult to assure a victory for the peace party at the polls in November.

At the beginning, the operation would have been considered a faint possibility. There was much organizing to do, and Booth had to have some training in the tradecraft of clandestine operations. As time went by, other clandestine ventures failed, and Booth, by recruiting a team of agents and beginning to arrange an escape route through southern Maryland, began to demonstrate some concrete results. By November Thompson apparently decided that both the Lincoln operation and the effort to free Confederate prisoners had enough probability of success to make it worth his while to continue with the mission in Canada.

The other aspect of the Confederate secret service in Canada was a peace agreement. Sanders had given it a big boost at Niagara in July 1864, and, knowing his penchant for dealing with highly placed politicians, he must have continued to work this theme. Clay and Thompson's Quebec trip reflects some such effort, and by January Sanders had engaged the attention of Union loyalist Robert James Walker, a former senator from Mississippi and governor of the Kansas Territory. Walker, who had been serving as an anti-Confederacy propagandist and political agent in Europe, returned to the United States in late 1864. Sanders persuaded him to come to Canada in January 1865, intending to use him as a channel for ideas for a peace agreement. It would have been classic Sanders to try to maneuver Lincoln politically on the one hand and haul him off to Richmond as a captive with the other.

The principal knowledge of this phase of Sanders's activity comes from a letter that he wrote to selected Northern newspaper editors on February 27, 1865, and from a letter to Jefferson Davis on March 7, 1865. In addition, however, the St. Lawrence Hall register shows that George Francis Train, the wealthy, eccentric former devotee of "Young America," had arrived in Montreal on January 17, 1865. It is possible that Sanders had even more going on than his letters indicate.[99] A supporter of the "Young America" idea, Train had provided funds to the Italian and Irish revolutionaries and may have assisted Sanders and others as well. He had a habit of turning up in the company of radical activists. He had lived in Liverpool while Confederate agent Beverly Tucker was serving as U.S. consul there during the 1850s and claimed to have a high regard for Tucker. Sanders and Train had doubtless met at some point during the 1850s, and Sanders may have sought Train's assistance in some political action scheme at this late date in the war.[100]

The Confederate clandestine operation in Canada, undertaken with the active participation of many Kentuckians and headed by Jacob Thompson, was based on a recognition of the importance of public support to the Northern war effort. In general, the Confederacy recognized the nature of the target population and adopted tactics appropriate to that population. The operation failed for several reasons, any one of which alone might have been enough to cause the failure, but, together, there was no chance that the Confederates could succeed.

One factor was the Confederates' inability to gain adequate control of the Copperhead movement. They established a good liaison with the peace Democrats at several levels, but they did not have adequate penetration of the Order of American Knights to know what was actually going on inside the various elements of that organization. Thus they had no way of knowing how true a picture of Copperhead strength and determination they were being presented by the Copperhead leaders. A good case in point is the defection of the Indiana organization. The Confederates should have known of the change in objective forced on the Indiana organization by the state's Democratic party; if they had learned of it, the Confederates might have been able to work around the problem, but as it was they went ahead thinking that the Indiana organization was fully collaborating in the Confederate plans. They did not recognize that current demographic trends in their target area were against them. Related to this is the fact that many of the Copperhead leaders were great on talk and poor on action. In particular, they were great on talk as long as the talk led to money, but past that point there was not much real determination to act.

Another matter that plagued the Confederates was the lack of policy agreement and coordination within their own ranks. While the Kentucky element might have been turned into a more effective force by judicious organization and training, the decentralized control element of Thompson, Clay, et al., did not have enough cohesion or agreed-upon operational doctrine to enable the operation to function efficiently. In addition, Jacob Thompson did not have enough experience at clandestine operations to recognize some of the standard pitfalls, such as accepting too readily an agent's assessment of the likelihood of success. And while the million dollars in gold allocated to the project by the Confederacy was probably enough to do the job, what was missing was the trained manpower to use it effectively.

But the main factor contributing to the failure of the Confederate operation was the negative turn of Confederate fortunes on the battlefield. After the fall of Atlanta, it would have taken a tremendous Confederate victory to convince the majority in the North that the war was going badly.[101]

In spite of these shortcomings, however, the Confederates managed to create a stir in Northern politics and succeeded in interferring with the smooth flow of reinforcements to the combat zone. If events on the battlefield *had* turned in Confederate favor, there was an organization in existence to help turn the political consequences in Confederate favor as well. But the main contribution of the Confederate secret service organization in Canada came after the fighting was over when it successfully defended the reputation of the Confederacy in a battle of ideas that could have cost the South dearly.

Chapter 6

APRIL '65

In 1865, the Confederates made one last desperate attempt to use their covert action capability to help bring about the success of Southern arms: they sought to attack Union leadership with the intent of disrupting the coordination between Grant and Sherman in conjunction with Lee's evacuation of Richmond. When the plan was frustrated, John Wilkes Booth took it upon himself to organize a makeshift attack on a series of Union officials to approximate the damage that would have been caused by blowing up a meeting of Lincoln and his advisers.

From the perspective of the Confederates who were trying to manage the operation and its consequences—in this particular case John Singleton Mosby, who showed great skill, ingenuity, flexibility, and dedication to his cause—we are only now beginning to understand what great efforts were going on behind the scenes in April 1865.

The Confederate army's Torpedo Bureau made it a practice to keep their trained personnel actively employed at the front or behind enemy lines. Men might be detailed in the Richmond area to perform specific tasks such as maintaining the mine fields in the James River and planting subterra torpedoes in front of the trenches, but the bureau itself kept only a small cadre of skilled personnel available for emergency assignments. In May and June 1864 the group included:

Thomas F. Harney, operator
Frank M. Blackwell, operator
Frank H. Elmore, operator
John B. Smith, electrician
John B. Syphrit, mechanic
Perry P. Clanton, mechanic
William R. Hammond, clerk[1]

In July 1864, Thomas F. Harney was reported to be at Charleston in command of a special detachment of forty men armed with hand grenades, but apparently after that assignment he returned to Richmond. The cadre as listed was substantially intact in early 1865.

In November 1864 General Rains asked that Capt. Samuel G. Leitch, who had been an ordnance officer in Pickett's division, be assigned to the Torpedo Bureau. The secretary of war approved the transfer, and Captain Leitch was put in charge of the torpedoes in the James River below Richmond. Later he became the adjutant of the bureau.[2]

In January, in the scramble to meet Sherman's march north from Savannah, Rains was ordered to South Carolina to use his subterra torpedoes to delay the Federal advance, though he and his explosives arrived in the Carolinas too late to accomplish the mission. On leaving Richmond, Rains had left Leitch in charge of the remnant of the Torpedo Bureau. Shortly thereafter Leitch arranged for the assignment of Pvt. William H. Snyder to the bureau.[3]

On March 30, 1865, Leitch reported that Hammond and Elmore had deserted, leaving the bureau with only two "operators" present for duty—Harney and Blackwell. Harney, a former schoolteacher, had served as a lieutenant in a Missouri regiment. In 1863, after being exchanged as a prisoner of war, he became a sergeant in the Torpedo Bureau and served on a "strategic corps" in Mississippi before returning to join the cadre at the bureau's headquarters in Richmond. Blackwell had served in Company F of the 43d Georgia Infantry and was detailed to the bureau in 1863. He had helped plant torpedoes at Mobile Bay and, like Harney, had been stationed in Richmond for almost a year.

On March 27, Rains was reported to be in Raleigh, North Carolina. On March 31, however, just four days later, he sent a memorandum from the bureau's headquarters to the secretary of war reporting on recent successes of Confederate torpedoes against Union shipping.[4] He may have arrived in Richmond just in time to participate in a critical decision.

On about April 1, 1865, during the same time that John Harrison Surratt, John Wilkes Booth's principal associate, was in Richmond reporting on the status of the project to capture Lincoln, Sergeant Harney was assigned to report to Colonel Mosby with a supply of "ordnance," presumably fuses and detonators. Based on his actions following Harney's arrival, it would appear that Mosby was directed to arrange for Harney's entry into Washington with some of Mosby's troopers to provide disciplined muscle to help Harney.[5]

On March 31, before Surratt left Richmond to return to Washington, Confederate Secretary of State Benjamin gave him $200 in gold. From an account made up by the Confederate State Department disbursing clerk, we know that on April 1, 1865, Benjamin had on hand $1,000 in gold from a fund cited as "Foreign Intercourse" and $480.66 for incidental and contingent expenses. Benjamin also had under his care a secret service fund cited as "Necessities and Exigencies," and this may be what the clerk meant by "Incidental and Contingent" expenses. This "Necessities and Exigencies" fund was used to cover conventional secret service expenditures, but if covert action were involved, the funds had to come from another fund, cited only as "Secret Service." The $200 may have been what Benjamin had left from previous requisitions for "Secret Service" gold, or Benjamin may have advanced Surratt the money from another account intending to replace it with a new requisition on the treasury.

We know from a surviving treasury warrant that Benjamin drew $1,500 in gold from the treasury on April 1 using the "Secret Service" citation reserved for covert action. According to Confederate procedure, the issuance of the treasury warrant meant that the State Department clerk had to fill out a request form for the money and then get Jefferson Davis to sign it. (Normally this would have had to happen on March 31 in order for the treasury to issue the warrant on the April 1.) Although Benjamin had access to $1,480.66 in gold, these funds were not authorized for covert action purposes. He needed $1,500 in gold for an action project, and Davis approved the purpose for which the $1,500 was requested.

This treasury warrant for gold was issued to Confederate secretary of state Judah P. Benjamin on April 1, 1865, from the covert action "Secret Service" account. Benjamin already had a substantial amount of gold available from appropriations authorized for other purposes. Courtesy of Special Collections Library, Duke University.

Harney and Surratt are the only agents that we know of in the Richmond area at that time who would have required money from the covert action account. It is likely, therefore, that when Harney left Richmond he too was supplied with "Secret Service" gold to finance his new assignment.

Come Retribution told how John Wilkes Booth and his associates tried to capture Lincoln on 17 March 1865, and, the enterprise having failed, how John Surratt went to Richmond where the Confederates decided to give up the abduction plan and to attack the top echelon of the Federal government instead. A number of reviewers have taken the position that we had advanced a plausible case but that we had not proved that the Confederate government in the person of Jefferson Davis had made the critical decision which indirectly led to the assassination. Now there is an additional chain of evidence to support the thesis.

This is probably as close to the "smoking gun" as one will ever get. It is impossible to prove that events occurred in a specific way or that Benjamin did not lie to Davis to get the secret service money (or some other notion to avoid pinning final responsibility on Davis). What has been established, however, is a network of documented facts that logically coincide with the information that would have had to exist if Davis did decide to attack the leaders of the Federal government. One can refute the logic only by a bizarre distortion of reason. The probability that all of these facts were true and that Davis did not make the critical decision is very slight indeed.

It is not known for sure whether Harney had any company on this trip, but it is likely that he would have taken at least one other person to help transport the ordnance items that he brought with him. It is possible to reconstruct what must have happened in the next few days on the basis of subsequent events. If Harney left Richmond on Saturday, April 1, 1865, he would have arrived by train at Gordonsville, Virginia, the same day. The post commander at Gordonsville was Maj. Cornelius Boyle, who relayed messages between Richmond and Mosby (whose principal headquarters was near Upperville, approximately seventy-five miles north of Gordonsville) and would have been responsible for forwarding Harney on his mission. Boyle would have had to supply one or more horses and a guide to get Harney to Mosby, but horses were scarce at this stage of the war. If he were alerted he could have gotten ready to send Harney immediately; if not alerted,

Harney would have had to wait while horses were arranged. He would probably have been alerted by telegraph from Richmond and thus have been expecting his visitors.

If Harney left Gordonsville early on the morning of Sunday, April 2, he would have had a hard day and a half or two days' ride ahead of him, but he should have reached Mosby by late Monday, April 3, leaving Tuesday, April 4, free for Mosby to discuss the mission with Harney and with any others whose advice he sought.

Without any military training when the war began, Mosby came to the Confederate army with a good education and a logical mind. He was able to think about the real issue of warfare—winning—rather than the artificial issues sometimes generated by military tradition or conventional wisdom. In his own words, "The military value of a par-tisans's work is not measured by the amount of property destroyed, or the number of men killed or captured, but by the number he keeps watching. Every soldier withdrawn from the front to guard the rear of an army is so much taken from its fighting strength."[6]

He also stated that his purpose was "to weaken the armies invading Virginia, by harassing their rear. As a line is only as strong as its weak-est point, it was necessary for it to be stronger than I was at every point, in order to resist my attacks.[7] Elsewhere he said, "The operation should be in cooperation with, but independent of, an army."[8] He clearly recognized that his mission was not merely to raise cain in the enemy's rear, but to take actions that would help his army win. Throughout his independent command, Mosby reported directly to General Stuart or, after Stuart's death, General Lee. His attitude throughout the duration of his command was thoroughly professional. He knew that his job was to help Lee win.

Some writers have been so bemused by the romantic image of Mosby as the gallant guerrilla and the "grey ghost" of northern Vir-ginia that they have overlooked his tactical genius as a cavalryman. In a period in which cavalry around the world was armed with sabres as the preferred weapon, Mosby had the ability to keep his mind on the objective rather than the method. He made no secret of his original ideas: "I had no faith in the sabre as a weapon. I only made the men draw their sabres to prevent them from wasting their fire before they got to closer quarters."[9] His men habitually carried two pistols, which gave them twelve shots for close-range combat. It is no surprise that

This often-reprinted photograph of John Singleton Mosby (1833–1916) was recorded on a glass plate in Richmond in 1865, but in all probability it was not taken until after the war had ended. The colonel's uniform jacket has the wrong colors on the collar and sleeve and was most likely borrowed, as was the saber, a weapon that Mosby disliked. The scene is, of course, posed, but the haughty, intelligent, and determined face is certainly real. Courtesy of the Library of Congress.

Mosby's Rangers were consistently able to win over their conventionally equipped and led Union opponents.

Mosby was well aware that he was fighting a nasty war that involved traitors and ambushes and death. He appreciated courage and honor, but he was also prepared to do whatever it took to protect his men and their cause. He was willing to hang several captured Union soldiers in order to force the Federal troops to abandon a policy of hanging his men when captured. Clearly he would not have been upset at the thought of killing a number of high officials in Washington if it could lead to victory.

Mosby communicated with Richmond via a string of signal stations that ran down the mountains from the vicinity of Front Royal to Rockfish Gap, west of Charlottesville, where messages could be transferred to the telegraph. The main part of this system was installed to make communication possible between Richmond and Jubal Early during his defense of the Shenandoah Valley, but late in 1864 it was extended to provide Mosby with a linkage to that portion of his command that was sent to the Northern Neck. Longstreet's signal officer, Capt. Jacob Hite Manning, was assigned to Mosby's headquarters, and Lt. James Carey, a highly qualified signal officer, was assigned to the force in the Northern Neck.[10]

This signal system remained in operation until after Appomattox. Charles T. O'Ferrall, of the 23d Virginia Cavalry, later wrote, "On the 8th day of April (Saturday) I was encamped at a hamlet called Paintertown, not far from Edenburg. About two o'clock on that day I received a message from the signal station at the point of Massanutten Mountain at Strasburg, eighteen or twenty miles below or north of me."[11] Therefore, on April 1 Mosby's unit could communicate with both Richmond and the units in the Northern Neck.

The signal system was not a fast or high-volume system. Messages had to be transmitted one letter at a time, and it might take half an hour to transmit a one-hundred-word message. Thus, if there were fifteen stations in the line (there is no firm information as to how many stations there were), the one-hundred-word message would eat up seven and a half hours in just the waving of signal flags, not including the time spent correcting errors or, when visibility was bad, the occasions when the signalmen were not at their posts. A Confederate deserter said that his station was normally manned from 8:00 A.M. to

3:00 P.M. So if a message did not get through the line before the signalmen went off duty, it might have to wait until the next day to be transmitted to the next station.[12]

Mosby may well have received a message about Harney. A meeting of the main body of the rangers had been called for April 2 at Quaker Church in London County, but contrary to expectations, no operation was ordered.[13] If Mosby had learned of Harney's mission on April 1 or 2, he could have formulated a general plan for its implementation by the time Harney arrived at Upperville.

One other piece of background information is important for an understanding of what was to follow. When Lee surrendered on April 9, Joseph E. Johnston was still in the field with an army in North Carolina and was facing Sherman, who was coming up from Savannah. After Lee's surrender, Grant turned his army south to move toward Johnston from the north. Johnston quickly saw that the cause was lost and opened negotiations with Sherman, which ultimately led to Johnston's surrender on April 26.

It was not until Grant was satisfied that Johnston was truly "in the bag" that he began to send forces to the Richmond area to widen Union control of the countryside. On April 21 the 1st New York Mounted Rifles moved into Ashland, just fifteen miles north of Richmond, to begin to gather up stray Confederates.[14] After Johnston's surrender, the victorious Union forces returned to the Petersburg/Richmond/City Point area and took ship for Washington. On May 23 the Army of the Potomac held a grand review in Washington, and its units were dispersed shortly thereafter.

Thus, when Lee surrendered, there were Union forces in the Winchester area, in Fairfax County outside of Washington, and in the immediate Richmond environs. Between those locations and the James River, there were no Union troops until April 21, and many places were not occupied until early May.[15] Mosby's regiment, the signal line down the Blue Ridge Mountains, the various Confederate posts (such as Gordonsville), the reserve units, special headquarters (like the little unit at Taylorsville), and the Confederate civilian apparatus—all were left intact for several weeks and were under very little Union pressure. In effect, throughout most of April 1865, the Confederates were still in command in central Virginia, and Mosby was the principal Confederate field commander.

On March 27, Mosby had received orders from the Army of Northern Virginia to recall his outlying detachments and move his command to the south to operate in the area west of Gordonsville.[16] On March 31, Mosby was at Leesburg, and about the same time he began to talk of organizing Company H, which he did on April 5. Presumably, between those two dates Mosby was within reach of his headquarters and in a position to respond to new developments.

Headquarters
March 27, 1865. (Received 8.20)

Col. J.S. Mosby:

(Care Major Boyle)

Collect your command and watch the country from front of Gordonsville to Blue Ridge and also Valley. Your command is all now in that section, and the general will rely on you to watch and protect the country. If any of your command is in Northern Neck call it to you.

W. H. Taylor,
Assistant Adjutant General

The language of the message is clearly telegraphic and supports the existence of an operational signal system. It is not likely that the message was sent as a written dispatch. The message's content would have been in keeping with Lee's plans to abandon Richmond and move his army to the vicinity of Danville. Mosby had actually begun to implement these instructions by ordering the companies in the Northern Neck to return to his normal operating area; but suddenly, however, he seems to have been given a new task that centered around Harney and his ordnance materiel and involved action in a different direction. Furthermore, the new action was clearly not in support of the Army of Northern Virginia.

On Wednesday, April 5, Mosby took some drastic action. He organized a new company—Company H—and railroaded the election of a young man named George Baylor as its commander. Baylor was a lieutenant in the 12th Virginia Cavalry, which was stationed near the north end of the Shenandoah valley and engaged in keeping an eye on Union activities in the area, and with such a position must have had to cooperate with Mosby on occasion. Baylor had a reputation as an aggressive fighter and Yankee-hater, and Mosby appears to have had a very high opinion of him.[17] Upon its formation, Mosby promptly sent Company H off on a scout to give it some experience in working as a team. On April 6 Baylor got wind of the location of the Loudoun Rangers, a Union partisan unit, and surprised them, capturing sixty-five men and effectively putting them out of business.[18]

As soon as the company returned from its success, Mosby created a task force comprised of Companies H and D with Capt. Alfred Glascock of Company D in command. (Glascock later withdrew from command.) The ostensible purpose of this task force was to raid a mule train near Burke, Virginia, between the Union troops at Fairfax and those at Alexandria. The actual purpose would have been to create a diversion while Harney and his escort would have remained behind to be infiltrated into Washington. In the meantime, the Confederates evacuated Richmond on the night of April 2–3, and the Union forces, members of a brigade of New Hampshire and Vermont troops under the command of Brig. Gen. Edward Hastings Ripley, moved in on the morning of the third.

Ripley recalled that after Lincoln had toured the captured city on the morning of April 4, a Confederate soldier had come to his headquarters asking for an interview on a "very important subject." This soldier was William H. Snyder, recruited for the Torpedo Bureau by Captain Leitch just two months earlier.

> He began by saying he was an enlisted man in [Gen. Gabriel R.] Rains' torpedo bureau, an organization of the Confederate secret service, which had among its duties such services as blowing up of our magazines and of our river steamers, raids on our rear like the St. Albans raid, firing of northern cities, like the simultaneous attempts on the Fifth Avenue and many other New York Hotels, the blowing up of the powder boats at City Point, distribution of small-pox clothes, etc., etc., in fact all kinds of deviltry and irregular warfare, calculated to create panic or discontent in the rear of the Union armies. Their method was to plan an expedition and detail certain men who never knew what they were to do until they arrived at a designated rendezvous and received their orders. He was particularly anxious to tell me that a party had just been dispatched from Rains' torpedo

bureau on a secret mission, which vaguely he understood was aimed at the head of the Yankee government and he wished to put Mr. Lincoln on his guard and have impressed upon him that just at this moment he believed him to be in great danger of violence and he should take the greater care of himself. He could not give names or facts, as the work of his department was secret, and no man knew what his comrade was sent to do, but of this he was convinced, that the President of the United States was in great danger. Upon expressing willingness to make a statement and swear to it, I called in Capt. [Rufus P.] Staniels, acting assistant adjutant general, who took down his statement under oath.[19]

The only mission that Snyder could have been describing was the one on which Harney had been dispatched.

The statement dictated to Staniels concerning Harney's mission has not been found, but another statement made by him on April 12, 1865, has been.[20] In this statement, Snyder described how he had been recruited by Captain Leitch and passed on a mixture of gossip and facts that he had learned about the Confederate secret service during his two-month service in the Torpedo Bureau. He mentioned that Leitch had told him that the Confederate Congress was in secret session considering a bill to create a secret bureau that would include a corps to carry on "a systematic crusade against the enemy's shipping, Arsenals, Magazines, Powder Mills, Hotels etc." He described several other Confederate operations as well as speculation about a raid on a seashore resort like Providence, Rhode Island.

Ripley took Snyder to see Lincoln on his boat in the James River on the morning of April 5, but the president refused to take the matter seriously and declined to hear Snyder's story. Clearly, Ripley had reasonably accurate information about the mission that Harney and Mosby were working on: Harney was to use explosives to attack the head of the Federal government; Harney was under orders to blow up the White House.

But neither Ripley nor Lincoln could foresee that Harney's mission would be aborted and that John Wilkes Booth would attempt to carry it out by personally attacking those who might have been Harney's targets.

The interpretation of Harney's mission as involving the demolition of the White House was based originally on the premise that such an unusual operation as that involving Mosby and Harney would only be aimed at a target of the utmost importance—and at that juncture of the war, the White House appeared to be the most important target available. The interpretation is further supported by a statement made by one of John Wilkes Booth's subordinates, George Atzerodt, during his imprisonment after the assassination: "Booth said he had met a party in New York who would get the prest. [president] certain. They were going to mine the end of the pres. [president's] House near the War Dept. [The west end of the White House] They knew an entrance to accomplish it through."[21]

Presumably, while Baylor and Company H were on their shake-down scout, Mosby would have had additional time to work with Glascock and Harney in planning the next phase of Harney's mission. Mosby would have been responsible not only for infiltrating Harney into Washington but also for seeing that there was a way out for the infiltrators: he would have had to organize security and reception parties at appropriate points to help Harney and his party escape after they had carried out their task. Both the infiltration and the escape task would have taken considerable planning effort. In addition, Mosby was doubtless gathering in his outlying detachments for eventual implementation of the order he had received on March 27.

Mosby's last opportunity for communication with Richmond would probably have been on Sunday, April 2. After that date, however, he would have remained in contact with his units in the Northern Neck, which not only had to arrange for their return to the Upperville area but also were involved in some of the planning for Harney's escape from Washington. Mosby's communication with these units would have followed the signal station route to Rockfish Gap and then, by telegraph, to the vicinity of Hanover Junction, where the messages would be retransmitted up the telegraph line to Milford Station in Caroline County. From that point the messages probably had to go by courier, but the system had experienced signal officers at each end of the route and doubtless functioned satisfactorily.

If Mosby had ordered the units in the Northern Neck to return to the main unit as soon as he received the April 27 order from the Army of Northern Virginia, they were delayed by preparations for

Harney's escape. They did not leave the Northern Neck until April 9 and were reported by the Union navy to be passing through the Fredericksburg area on April 11. According to Lt. Col. Chapman, they reached Warrenton on the April 12 and reported to Mosby that night or the next day.[22]

The guide for the operation to the Burke area was Lt. Edward F. Thomson of Company H. During March, before the formation of the new company, Thomson had led two scout missions to the Fairfax County area, one to Munson Hill and one to Occoquan, located on opposite sides of Burke, the current target. Munson Hill, about halfway between Baileys Crossroads and Falls Church (a short distance southeast of the present-day Seven Corners intersection), had been the advance Confederate fortification in 1861 after the First Battle at Manassas.[23] It was well sited for the observation of the Washington and Alexandria area. In 1896, Myron Munson recollected Munson Hill: "From the summit, which contains about one acre of table land, there is a good view of the capitol, Washington monument[24] and several miles of the Potomac River." There was a small signal detachment on nearby Upton Hill operating clandestinely "to contact Southern spies in Washington."[25] E. Pliny Bryan, who had a long career in both signal corps and torpedo corps activities, made an arrangement to rent a room in the Washington area with a window facing the Confederate position, intending to send information from Washington by signaling from his room. But his plan was frustrated when the Confederates suddenly retreated from their advance position on September 28, 1861.[26] Munson's Hill was incorporated by the Union army into the defenses of Washington by the construction of a battery to be occupied by field artillery in the case of an attack by the Confederates. The battery was usually unoccupied and thus available for Confederate clandestine use.

On the other hand, however, reference to Munson's Hill may refer to the area rather than to the hill specifically. One resident of the area recalled later that "Mosby and his men also stayed around quite a bit. There were many high hills that made splendid signal posts around here." Mosby's men were doubtless helping to keep in contact with Confederate agents inside the ring of forts, a duty formerly performed by Walter "Wat" Bowie, and Thomson had become a specialist in the task of contacting the Confederate underground in Washington.[27]

Occoquan, where as late as December 1864 the Confederates from Fredericksburg had maintained a picket, was near the Potomac at the southern edge of Fairfax County and served as a point where Confederates leaving Washington on clandestine trips south sometimes crossed from Maryland into Virginia. (Here was where the Confederates caught Congressman Henry S. Foote on December 12, 1864, while he was trying to defect to the North.[28]) It would appear that Mosby had more than one operation involving clandestine contact with the Confederate underground in Washington.

On April 8 the task force of Companies D and H left Upperville and crossed Fauquier County. The next morning, upon assembling the task force, Baylor learned that Glascock had withdrawn from the operation and that Baylor was now in command.[29] This withdrawal is puzzling and not in accordance with the normal behavior of Mosby's partisans. But Glascock could have had misgivings about raiding so close to Washington, for the enterprise clearly had numerous risks associated with it. The risk, the mission's incompatibility with Mosby's orders from the Army of Northern Virginia, and the lack of any obvious military justification for the raid, strongly suggest that Mosby must have believed that he was acting under a very powerful authority. Mosby's behavior in the entire Harney episode is in direct contradiction to the order issued him only a few days earlier by Lee's headquarters. This is particularly significant when recalling that Mosby reported directly to Lee as commander of the Army of Northern Virginia, and Lee's interest in moving Mosby south is indicated by a reference to Mosby's prospective move in a March 27, 1865, letter from Lee to Early.[30]

Baylor and his task force proceeded to Fairfax County and spent the night of April 9–10 near a tavern known as Arundels' (in the vicinity of the present-day intersection of Ox and Burke Lake roads). Although the unit was less than fifteen miles from Alexandria, the surrender of Lee, which took place on the April 9 at Appomattox, was nothing more than an incredible rumor.[31]

Early on the tenth, the task force moved forward a few miles to Burke Station between Fairfax Station and Alexandria, but it found no mule train. Indeed, there may never have been a mule train at Burke; the story could have been contrived to explain the purpose of the raid to the participating rank and file. But even if there had been a mule train, the information on its expected presence would have been at least four or five days old, and it would not be surprising to find that circumstances had changed and that the mules were gone.

The Federal troops at Fairfax Station, the next station beyond Burke Station, were informed of the Confederate presence in the area, and a force from the 8th Illinois Cavalry set off in pursuit. In the meantime, Baylor had turned his rangers back toward Arundels' to rest and decide what to do next. The task force having made a showing, this was probably the point at which Harney and his escort were to separate from the main body. They would make their way into Washington while Baylor created a disturbance in another direction.

Before Harney could leave, however, the 8th Illinois caught up with the task force's rear guard. Baylor tried to organize resistance, but the Federal troops were reinforced and pushed the Confederates out of their position. A running fight ensued, and in the course of the fight Harney and several other Confederates were captured. Baylor and the rest of his men finally crossed the Occoquan River and escaped. J. Marshall Crawford of Company B wrote of the skirmish, "Baylor lost two men killed and five or six captured, including Lieutenant Harney, whose loss was irretrievable."[32] Crawford must have known something more about Harney's mission than he was saying! Harney was held in the Alexandria jail and then sent to the Old Capitol Prison in Washington, arriving there on April 12. (The skirmish at Burke was reported in the Washington papers, and the Confederates had most likely penetrated the Old Capitol Prison and were able to get information about who came and went.)

It was just about this time that John Wilkes Booth started serious planning for the assassinations. From the pattern of his targets, it would appear that Booth was trying to wreak the same havoc on the Union government that would have resulted if Harney had succeeded in blowing up the White House during a meeting of high-level officials. Booth targeted the president, vice president, secretary of state, and possibly the secretary of war to be attacked simultaneously at 10:00 P.M. on Friday, April 14.[33]

In his memoirs, Baylor said that the strength of his force in the fight at Arundels' was about seventy-five men from Company D and about forty from Company H. This creates a bit of a puzzle. James J. Williamson, a Mosby veteran, prints rosters of the Mosby companies in his book, and his roster for Company H lists forty-four names.[34] The compiled service records of the men in Mosby's unit in the U.S. National Archives show that forty-three men from Company H were paroled at Winchester during the latter part of April. The same records also show, however, that sixteen men from Company H were paroled in Fairfax County during the same period. Thus the records show at least sixty men in Company H. What caused the discrepancy?

Consider the task facing Mosby when he became involved in the Harney mission. He not only had to get Harney into Washington, presumably accompanied by some of Mosby's own soldiers, but he also had to get them *out* of Washington. If Harney's mission proved successful, the Federal army and other authorities would be hot on the heels of any Confederates who could get away. Mosby had no way of knowing what route would be most feasible for Harney's group to use for their escape. He had to prepare for all eventualities.

There were three main escape routes: across the Potomac River into Fairfax County; south through Prince George's, Charles, and St. Mary's counties, Maryland; or north through Montgomery County, Maryland. Each of these areas had a fairly large population of Southern sympathizers who would have formed some sort of underground organization to pass information and provide assistance. It makes sense that anybody in Mosby's position would have believed that, if he put a small, mobile team of armed men in each area, the local underground would be able to guide escaping Confederates to them. And it would have been a good idea for Mosby to have had a small mounted unit in each of the three areas, prepared to help Harney and his associates if they should escape in that direction.

The sixteen men from Company H might well have been part of the unit that Baylor was to leave behind in that area to act as a reception party if Harney were to escape through Fairfax County. The party in Montgomery County may be accounted for by information that the Union got from interrogating the prisoners captured at Arundels'. According to these prisoners' statements, a Mosby company had been sent to Maryland, presumably from the area around Upperville, from which Company H had departed. Later the Union troops heard that the Mosby company was moving through Loudoun County toward the Potomac along the Montgomery County border.[35] There is no confirmation of this movement.

The story of the Mosby group in southern Maryland, however, has been sitting in the Official Records all of these years, but because a jurisdictional dispute involving a pair of young Union officers made the matter seem unimportant, the story has been ignored. The evidence is complex, but the incident is so important to an understanding of Mosby's role that it is worth the effort to unravel it. It illustrates Mosby's preparations for assisting Harney and his party and reveals the situation that Booth was trying to exploit on his escape after shooting Lincoln.

On April 14, the day of Lincoln's assassination, Gen. Christopher C. Augur's Twenty-second Corps headquarters at Washington sent Maj. John M. Waite, an officer of the 8th Illinois who was serving as the corps's acting assistant inspector general, to the Union force at Fairfax with a supply of blank parole forms. The Federal forces were trying hard to get Mosby's troops to surrender, and they were being offered parole on the same basis as the troops who had been surrendered by General Lee.

On the day after the assassination, April 15, Brig. Gen. James Barnes, commanding the Union forces around Point Lookout in St. Mary's County, Maryland (the site of a large camp for Confederate prisoners of war), reported that a scouting party commanded by a Lieutenant Davis had seen a group of Confederates—three officers and twenty-seven men—on the evening of April 12 in the area between Newport and Crookshank's store, in the northern part of St. Mary's County, moving in the direction of the store.[36] Also on April 15, Augur's headquarters informed Major Waite of the assassination and directed him to order the local Union forces to patrol the area between Fairfax and the Potomac.

In the meantime, reaction to the assassination was flowing through other channels in the Union army. James L. McPhail, the provost marshal at Baltimore, sent a message to one of his detectives, R. B. Hough, at St. Inigoes in St. Mary's County, informing him of the assassination and directing him to search for Booth who was reported to be heading toward St. Mary's and Calvert counties (on the west coast of Chesapeake Bay).[37] Hough promptly repeated to McPhail the information reported by Lieutenant Davis.[38]

On April 16, Capt. John Buckley reported to the Union post at Leonardtown in St. Mary's County that he had skirmished with a

Confederate force near Mechanicsville, Maryland, on the previous evening and lost one man. Buckley added that the enemy troops were commanded by Garland Smith and that one Confederate had been captured. Also on April 16, Lt. Edward F. O'Brien reported from the government farms in St. Mary's County that Buckley had arrived there on the night of April 15 and that Buckley had skirmished with "a portion of Mosby's men, under Captain Garland Smith, just on the edge of the farms."[39]

The geography involved in these events is significant. Living at The Plains on the Patuxent River just south of the town of Benedict (where Golden Beach is now located) was a prominent planter, Col. John H. Sothron (also spelled Sothoron), who had occupied a number of important positions in the community—headmaster of the Charlotte Hall Military Academy, president of the Maryland State Senate, and member of a committee organized in 1861 to provide arms to protect the pro-Southern citizens of St. Mary's County. On October 20, 1863, a party of black Union soldiers under the command of Lt. Eben White, a white officer of the 7th U.S. Colored Regiment, visited The Plains on a mission to recruit blacks for service in the U.S. army. Sothron and his son, Webster, a Confederate private on leave from his regiment, met the recruiting party and an altercation followed. When Webster was threatened, Colonel Sothron shot and killed Lieutenant White. The recruiters fled, and Sothron and his son hurriedly departed for Virginia.[40] Two weeks later The Plains was confiscated by the Union and became one of the "government farms" charged with growing vegetables for the prisoner-of-war camp at Point Lookout, Maryland. The other government farms were located about twenty miles further down the Patuxent. From the description of the movement of the Confederate cavalry under Garland Smith, it would appear that the unit was headed directly for The Plains, and the skirmish must have taken place at the edge of that farm rather than the two located on the lower Patuxent.[41]

In early December 1863 Fitzgerald Ross, a British visitor to the Confederacy, met Sothron in the office of Maj. William Norris, the head of the Signal and Secret Service Bureau. Sothron told the story of the killing of Lieutenant White, and Ross was duly impressed by the threat to young Sothron. What is significant, however, is that Sothron was in the hands of an element of the Confederate secret service. This suggests that The Plains, in spite of its confiscation by the Union government, may have been intended as a rendezvous point for Harney and his relief party. Sothron knew the geography of the area and could have described landmarks for those planning the operation. The neighborhood of The Plains would have been a good rendezvous spot: it offered options of escape by boat out of the mouth of the Patuxent or overland to several different crossing points over the Potomac.[42]

At the moment of the skirmish between Captain Buckley and the Confederates, John Wilkes Booth and David Herold were approaching the same area from the direction of Dr. Mudd's house in Charles County. Whatever his intended destination on the night of April 15, Booth did not reach it; instead he sought guidance to the home of Col. Samuel Cox in Charles County. It is possible that Buckley disrupted a prearranged escape plan for Harney that Booth was trying to use.

One or both of the April 16 reports concerning the Confederate cavalry appear to have been forwarded to General Augur's headquarters, because Major Waite later referred to the incident. But Waite was not present in the headquarters on April 15 and 16 and may not have seen all of the reports that came in during that period.

During the winter of 1864–65, Mosby had divided his force and sent several companies to the Northern Neck, where they were scattered across the countryside and quartered in small groups in farmhouses. Company G, of which W. Garland Smith was a second lieutenant, had been quartered in Lancaster and Northumberland counties, Virginia, at the eastern end of the Northern Neck. About the only way that Buckley could have learned Smith's name was from a prisoner.

Buckley's report was passed on to the War Department, which responded on April 17: "The murderers of the President and Mr. Seward are no doubt in the gang of rebels mentioned in your telegram. Have the navy vessels scour the coast, and spare no effort to arrest and hold them. Put your whole force on the work, as far as can be done with safety to your command."[43] On the same day, General Augur's headquarters issued orders to Major Waite to assume command of a battalion of the 8th Illinois Cavalry and proceed to the "lower Maryland Counties lying in this department." There he was to "capture and destroy" the band of guerrillas, arrest all suspicious persons, and allow no one to pass who could not explain his business. He was to assume command of all cavalry that he might meet and use them in his general operations.[44] On April 18, the newspapers were reporting from Baltimore that

> A gentleman who was at Point Lookout yesterday morning was informed by an officer of one of our gunboats that Booth and the other conspirators—about twenty in number—were in St. Mary's county, heavily armed, and endeavoring to make their way across the Potomac, which was strongly picketed and no one allowed to pass. . . . He also stated that on Sunday morning a small squad of our cavalry had a collision with them, and had been repulsed, and succeeded in capturing one of them. . . . In the meantime our cavalry were reinforced yesterday morning and were understood to have them completely surrounded, and their escape deemed impossible.[45]

In moving into southern Maryland, Waite split his force to cover different routes. On April 20 he reported that he had just arrived at Leonardtown with one company. He also promptly informed Augur's headquarters that the fight between Barnes's cavalry and the guerrillas was "all a humbug." But it is important to recognize that he had not yet "scoured" the area and could hardly have been familiar with the situation—he was making an assertion based on little evidence.[46] At the same time, Barnes was complaining to Augur about Waite's incursion into Barnes's jurisdiction. Augur replied with a mealymouthed apology.[47]

On April 23, Waite justified his "humbug" remark by saying that he was convinced that Captain Buckley was of no use—that a man reported lost by Buckley had fallen off his horse and had finally walked in, without his horse. He claimed that Buckley had admitted that he had not actually seen a single Rebel. Waite had not made much of an effort to see one, but he was now sure that there was no armed band in the area.[48]

Waite apparently was not aware of the specificity of the first report submitted by Lieutenant Davis. He did not like Buckley, could not find the force that he had been directed to destroy, and chose to interpret Buckley's remarks as proving that the enemy did not exist. Buckley could well have had the skirmish without actually seeing a

Confederate soldier; southern Maryland is heavily wooded. Moreover, the size of the enemy force could have been estimated from the number and location of the shots fired; or the size could have been extracted from his prisoner, who seems to have been ignored by Waite. In short, there is no evidence that Waite knew all of the pertinent facts, and there is evidence of friction between Waite and people in Barnes's command.

In support of the existence of the Confederate force, there is the logic of geography and two independent reports of the Confederate group in St. Mary's County. Each report has several believable details, and each reinforces the other. The first report specifies three officers and twenty-seven men; the second estimates the enemy at about thirty-five men. The first report gives specific location and direction of movement; the second gives a compatible location and the name of the Confederate commander, who was proven to have been just across the Potomac shortly before the date of this episode. Furthermore, Waite was sufficiently behind the events for the Confederates to have left the area before he even arrived: they were seen on April 12 and 15, but Waite did not reach the area until April 20. The stir of Union activity in the aftermath of the assassination would have encouraged the Confederates to leave as quickly as they could.

This incident shows that while Booth was making his way through Charles County, Maryland, on April 15, 1865, after leaving Dr. Mudd's house, a mounted Confederate force was less than five miles away. If Union cavalry had not accidentally encountered the Confederates, they might well have met Booth and helped him to get to Virginia days before he finally crossed the Potomac.

There is further confirmation of the incident in the records of the Union prisoner-of-war camp at Point Lookout. The master list of prisoners in the camp shows that a Francis Donohum of the Virginia reserves was captured at Mechanicsville, Maryland, on April 15, 1865, and turned over to the prison from St. Mary's County on April 21.[49] In other words, the prisoner was held locally by his captors, presumably for interrogation, for six days after his capture and then turned over to the prison. So it is hard to see how Waite could not have known of this prisoner. In the compiled service records in the National Archives, Donohum, spelled "Donohyon," is listed as being a member of the 1st Virginia Reserves, which was organized in Richmond in mid-1864, and is described as having a florid complexion, dark-brown hair, and grey eyes and being five-feet-five-inches tall.

The compiled service records of the 1st First Virginia Reserves show some interesting facts. Many of the men in that unit were captured at or near the Battle of Sayler's Creek on April 6, 1865. That is to be expected of a reserve unit that was part of Custis Lee's division. A substantial number of the men from the same unit, however, were paroled in May 1865 at Charlottesville, Gordonsville, Louisa Courthouse, or Beaver Dam—all points on the Virginia Central Railroad north and west of Richmond. It looks as if many men in the unit, possibly a fourth of them, were not with the Army of Northern Virginia when it evacuated Richmond, were not captured in the weeks after Appomattox, and did not seek parole until well into May—nearly a month after Lee's surrender. And when they did seek parole, they seem to have sought it at about the same time and in the same areas, which suggests that they had been together as a unit during the weeks after Appomattox.[50] The 1st Virginia's service records reveal one additional intriguing fact: 1st Lt. T. V. L. McKaig was paroled at Winchester, Virginia, on April 21, 1865—the same day that Mosby's unit was disbanded.

The fact that the majority of the men in the 1st Virginia Reserves were captured at Sayler's Creek or in Richmond is just what one would expect of a Richmond reserve unit made up of clerks, hospital orderlies, and convalescent soldiers. This is exactly the kind of unit found in Custis Lee's division. Some of the men doubtless were left behind in Richmond at the time of the evacuation, and the majority of the division was captured at Sayler's Creek. What is unusual is that so many of the men in this unit turned themselves in for parole a month later in a fairly small area not near Richmond and not on the route that Lee's division took on its way to Sayler's Creek. The pattern of paroles suggests that a large number of the men in the 1st Virginia Reserves were not with the division when it left Richmond and that they stayed together for several weeks after the surrender of the Army of Northern Virginia.

The presence of Donohum with a Mosby lieutenant in southern Maryland, a number of 1st Virginia reserves located along the route of Mosby's communication line, the association of an officer from the reserve unit with Mosby's main body of troops—all suggest that something more than coincidence may be involved in Donohum's association with Mosby's troops. When the Harney operation was launched on April 1, no one expected to have to evacuate Richmond the next day. It is possible that a detachment from the reserve unit had been sent off to provide extra bodies for the various tasks that Mosby would have to organize in support of the operation. They were not first-class soldiers and therefore would not detract from the defense of Richmond, but they would provide useful bodies where manpower was needed.

The Mosby units in the Northern Neck under the command of Lt. Col. William H. Chapman had several things to do in support of the Harney operation. They not only had to organize Garland Smith's unit and get it across the Potomac into Maryland, but they had to establish a scouting organization to provide information on what was happening tactically in southern Maryland. They also had to provide for a group to remain in the Northern Neck to help Smith and his group back across the Potomac and to maintain the signal connection to Mosby's headquarters.

An interesting result of all this activity by Mosby's troops is that it caused an ad hoc organization to be overlaid on the area that had already been organized by the secret service element that had been trying to capture Lincoln. Richmond had tried to simplify the organization by assigning Sergeant Weddell and the Signal Corps personnel in the Northern Neck to control by the Secretary of State, but now the Mosby troops had been given this new task without knowing enough (if anything) about the previous arrangements. Sufficient confusion must have been generated among Confederate ranks to make it understandable that scholars trying to piece together the story of April 1865 have pursued red herrings.

Very little is known about the Mosby "stay-behinds" in the Northern Neck, but some bits of information can be pieced together. Sixteen men of Mosby's command were paroled in Westmoreland County, Virginia, in May 1865; an additional seven were paroled just across the Rappahannock River at Bowling Green in Caroline County (through which Mosby's signal line ran); a couple of other rangers were paroled in the Northern Neck's King George and Northumberland counties. So a total of twenty-five men were paroled in or near the area in which a stay-behind group would have operated.[51]

It would appear that Mosby had organized his force specifically to support the infiltration and extraction of Harney and others, but instead he found himself responsible for handling the "hot potato" named John Wilkes Booth. It would have been logical for Mosby to send word to the Confederate apparatus in Washington as soon as he had made his plans for the Harney operation. The Confederates in Washington would have known that there would be reception parties waiting along the three main escape routes from Washington.

Late on the afternoon of April 15, 1865, Booth left the home of Dr. Mudd near Bryantown, Maryland, and made a wide swing to the east and south (most accounts of Booth's escape have Booth going west into Zekiah swamp, based on disinformation supplied by Dr. Mudd), eventually ending at the home of Samuel Cox in southern Charles County near midnight. While we do not know every place that Booth visited on this segment of his escape route, within an hour or two of the event he was at least within five miles of the location of Garland Smith's skirmish with Captain Buckley.

While Garland Smith was dodging Federal troops in southern Maryland, George Baylor and his task force were making their way back to Mosby to report the failure of their mission. The fight at Arundels' took place on April 10, which means that Baylor did not get back to Upperville until some time on April 12. And since Baylor had no rapid means of reporting the outcome, Mosby did not know of the failure of the project until Baylor's arrival. On that same day, however, he received a message from General Hancock, the commander of Union forces in the Shenandoah Valley, calling on him to surrender his command on the same terms that had been accorded General Lee.

Mosby was in a quandary. Lee had surrendered. Lt. Col. Chapman's battalion from the Northern Neck reached nearby Warrenton on April 12, but the stay-behind group in the Northern Neck and at least one party, Garland Smith's, were still on the Maryland side of the Potomac. Harney had been lost, but did that mean the end of the Harney operation? In an effort to get some advice on what to do next, Mosby stalled in replying to Hancock and sent his friend Capt. Robert S. Walker of Company B with a small party to Gordonsville "to learn the true state of affairs."[52]

Mosby must have considered Walker's mission to be of great importance. And, since Mosby could probably communicate with Gordonsville via the signal line down the mountains, the mission doubtless required more than a mere exchange of information. There must have been a need to discuss plans for future action, and such a discussion would have been sufficiently complex to require the participation of several of Mosby's men. Aside from Maj. Cornelius Boyle, who was surely involved, there is no information about the others at the meeting.

As noted previously, Boyle had been a successful physician in Washington, D.C., before the war. As the war approached, he was instrumental in organizing a unit of pro-Southern militia known as the National Rifles. When war finally broke out, most of the men in this unit crossed the Potomac and joined Alexandria's militia battalion, which eventually became the 6th Virginia Infantry Battalion. (One of the leaders in the unit was William N. Barker, who later became second in command of the Confederate Signal Corps.) Boyle was commissioned as a major of volunteers in Virginia's state forces on April 29, 1861.[53] After the Confederate forces took over the defense of Virginia, General Beauregard put Boyle on detached duty, which was continued after Gen. Joseph E. Johnston took over the command. In 1862, Lt. Col. George W. Lay of Johnston's staff, who took over Colonel Jordan's duties in maintaining contact with the Greenhow espionage group in Washington, wrote, "Major Boyle's duties have to a great extent been performed in connection with this office. . . . His peculiar duties at Manassas covered a great deal of ground."

In 1863, Gen. A. R. Lawton, the quartermaster, tried to have Boyle reassigned to the quartermaster corps. But Boyle, who by that time had become provost marshal and post commander at Gordonsville, protested the proposed transfer, saying that he was assigned to "*special duty*" for General Johnston and General Lee. The matter was referred to General Lee, who denied the transfer saying, "Major Boyle was commissioned specially for the service on which he is now engaged. I know of no one who can take his place."[54] Boyle clearly was a man who was trusted at the highest levels in the Confederate army and who played some special role in the conduct of clandestine operations. Moreover, Gordonsville was one of the routes by which people passed through Confederate lines on their way to and from Canada and various Northern destinations.

When the Confederate government evacuated Richmond on the afternoon of April 2, 1865, it left a problem for its clandestine operators. There were agents in the North, such as Frank Stringfellow, who were expecting to return to Richmond. There were couriers from the

Secret Line who had mail and information to deliver. There were couriers en route from overseas Confederate agents whose arrivals could not be predicted. And there was the Harney mission, which when it was dispatched doubtless had a high priority, and a number of actions had been set in motion to support the operation. But now, suddenly, there was no government in Richmond to whom these agents could report.

Those responsible for overseeing the various clandestine operations must have made some sort of provision for a party to meet the arriving agents and steer them to safety. There was a small headquarters at Taylorsville, near Hanover Junction, that was charged with the Confederate defenses south of the Rappahannock, and it may also have had some responsibility for the soldiers on security duty in the Northern Neck in connection with the aborted scheme to capture Lincoln. Moreover, this element at Taylorsville was in a position to intercept and guide those traveling down the Secret Line. And for arrivals from the north or west, Boyle and his small force at Gordonsville could have played a similar role. It is even possible that these two groups had been organized to operate under one commander.

Given this background, it is conceivable that the meeting at Gordonsville involved more than just Major Boyle, and it is even possible that one or more senior operators from the Confederate clandestine apparatus who had made their way south from Canada, New York, or Washington were present. In the absence of concrete information, this is speculation, but one should keep the possibility in mind in evaluating subsequent events.

If Walker left the Upperville area on April 12, he would probably have arrived at Gordonsville on April 14, the day of Lincoln's assassination. At about 5 P.M. on April 15, news of the assassination had reached Richmond.[55] It is probable that by April 16 Boyle had news of the event via the telegraph from Hanover Junction. It is also possible that he might have received the same news at about the same time via the Secret Line. Regardless of where it originated, the news would have caused a drastic revision of the group's strategic thinking.

To complicate matters further, John Wilkes Booth was firmly in the hands of Samuel Cox in Charles County, Maryland, by the morning of April 16, and this news could have been communicated down the Secret Line by April 17. The Northern reaction to the assassination was doubtless apparent from the dismay of the Union troops in Richmond and possibly from reports passed down the Secret Line. It must have been clear that if Booth were to be kept out of Union hands, Mosby's Rangers would have to do it; there was no other unit with the force and the ability to act in the area between the Potomac and James rivers.

Although not all of the participants in the meeting at Gordonsville are known (nor is it known what they talked about), it is possible to make some deductions about what might have been discussed. Mosby received General Hancock's request for the rangers' surrender on April 12. He sent Lt. Col. Chapman and a small delegation under a flag of truce to deliver his reply, which said in part:

> As yet I have no notice, through any other source, of the facts concerning the surrender of the Army of Northern Virginia, nor in my opinion has the emergency yet arisen which would justify the surrender of my command. With no disposition, however, to cause the useless effusion of blood, or to inflict on a war-worn population any unnecessary distress, I am ready to agree to a suspension of hostilities for a short time, in order to enable me to communicate with my own authorities, or until I can obtain sufficient intelligence to determine my future action. Should you accede to this proposition, I am ready to meet any person you may designate to arrange the terms of an armistice.[56]

General Hancock reported on this meeting with Chapman to General Halleck in Washington:

> Winchester, Va., April 16, 1865
> I have this day received a communication from Colonel Mosby and have had an interview with Lieutenant Colonel Chapman, of his command. I have no doubt but that Mosby will surrender his whole command on the terms given to General Lee. Arrangements have been made for a meeting at Millwood on Tuesday noon [April 18], when I expect to receive the surrender. Meanwhile Mosby agrees to refrain from any operations whatever, and I have directed no offensive operations against his command to be made. They are aware of the death of the President.[57]

At Millwood, Mosby asked for an extension of the truce in order to give him more time to communicate with Confederate authorities. Hancock agreed that the truce could be extended to noon on April 20. Meeting again on the twentieth, however, Mosby was informed that the Union would not extend the truce further. Just at that moment, one of Mosby's men dashed in to say that he had discovered Union cavalry hiding a short distance away. Doubtless, there was no underhanded intent, but that piece of information and the declared end of the truce sounded like a plausible scenario for treachery, and Mosby and his party beat a hasty retreat without any further negotiations.[58]

Obviously, Mosby was playing for time. He had not yet heard from Walker's meeting at Gordonsville, or, if he had heard, he had not yet decided what to do. It is unlikely that Walker, having arrived at Gordonsville on about April 14, would not have left before the news of Lincoln's assassination arrived, and such news would certainly have extended the conference to April 17, at which point the news of Booth's location and circumstances would probably have caused further delay. Thus, Walker may not have been able to leave Gordonsville with any well-considered advice until April 18, and leaving on that date would have brought him to Mosby's base area on April 20. So when Mosby left Millwood at noon on April 20, he may not yet have heard from Walker.

By the next day, April 21, however, Mosby appears to have known exactly what he wanted to do. He assembled the entire command— at least as many as could be collected from their scattered billets in the time available—at Salem (now Marshall, Virginia), near the center of Fauquier County, and read his farewell address to each of the units, which were then dismissed for the last time. It was announced that Lt. Col. Chapman would be going to Winchester on April 22 to seek parole, and a large number of the men stated their wish to accompany him.[59]

Indeed, from April 22 to 27, at Winchester several hundred of Mosby's men were given their paroles, including forty-two from Company H. But while this mass surrender was going on, Mosby was still at war. He had retained a group of rangers and was headed south with the explanation that he wanted to join General Johnston in North Carolina. Three memoirs give independent accounts of the affair and of how many men were involved. One account estimates the final head count at six, though somewhat larger initially; another estimates the number at thirty to forty; and a third lists the initial count at fifty men.[60] On the early afternoon of April 23, Mosby and at least some of his men were seen at the home of Capt. Alfred Glascock in Fauquier County, not far from Salem. Mosby stayed at Glascock's only a short while and then proceeded on his journey. From that point the unit had a seventy-mile ride to Fredericks Hall, a station on the Virginia Central Railroad, where he left the majority of his small force. They probably reached Frederick's Hall late on April 24 or early on April 25. With a select group of ten or twelve men, Mosby appears then to have gone to Taylorsville or some other place in that vicinity, arriving on April 25 or early on April 26.[61]

In the meantime, on April 21 John Wilkes Booth was moved out of his hidden camp in Charles County, Maryland, and put into a boat to cross the Potomac to the mouth of the upper Machodoc Creek in Virginia. The weather and the presence of a Union gun boat, however, forced him back to Maryland; he attempted a second try the next night. Booth and David Herold, his companion, finally reached the Virginia shore near their intended destination on April 23.[62] There they were met by an agent of the Confederate War Department, Thomas Harbin, and a young soldier from the local signal corps camp belonging to the Secret Line, Joseph Baden.

Apparently Booth did not like what Harbin and Baden told him about the plans for his future travel, and he left angrily.[63] With the help of a local farmer, Booth and Herold went to the house of Dr. Richard Henry Stuart, one of the prominent Confederate citizens of King George County. Dr. Stuart may well have been aware of the earlier plans to capture Lincoln, and Booth probably thought that Stuart would use his influence to make arrangements more suitable for Booth. In this he was mistaken. Stuart was not eager to be associated with an assassin, and, furthermore, the doctor had been visited earlier by people from Mosby's command and may have felt that whatever had been arranged for Booth had better not be changed by him.

In a subsequent interrogation, Dr. Stuart said that Booth had told him that he wanted to find his way to Mosby. Stuart answered by saying that Mosby had surrendered and was not available. That could have been an accurate description of what was said, but it may also have been a statement designed to diminish the interrogator's interest in exploring a possible Mosby connection. After all, Dr. Stuart was a loyal Confederate and was well informed concerning Confederate activity in his area. For example, the report of the inspector general on the Signal Corps shows that Stuart was aware of the activities of the soldiers manning the local station of the Secret Line. He could also have been aware of Mosby's involvement in the effort to keep Booth out of Union hands.

After spending the night in the cabin of a nearby black family, Booth and Herold hired a son of the family to take them in a wagon to Port Conway on the Rappahannock River. The two fugitives arrived at their destination in early afternoon of April 24 and, apparently by accident, were met by three Mosby soldiers. One of the three was Mortimer B. Ruggles, who had been second in command to Thomas Nelson Conrad, one of the key people involved in the plan to capture Lincoln, so it is more than likely that the three were sent deliberately to get Booth back under control.

While at Port Conway, Booth asked William Rollins, the Signal Corps agent at that point, about finding somebody to help him go to Orange Court-House. Since Orange Court-House is near Gordonsville, Booth may actually have been interested in making contact with Major Boyle. Rollins said that he did not know the way, and Herold asked if they could be guided to Bowling Green, just fifteen miles from their present location. The places mentioned are interesting because Bowling Green was on the way to Ashland, Taylorsville, and Hanover Junction, the area toward which Mosby was traveling, and was also one of the routes to Gordonsville.

Booth and his escort crossed the river to Port Royal in the company of T. Wellford Mason, a soldier who had just returned from Appomattox, where he had been paroled as a courier (which meant that he could keep his horse). Mason's home was in King George County, north of the Rappahannock, but he was south of the river on this trip for almost two days. It is possible that since returning home he had been acting as one of the couriers who connected the Northern Neck to the end of the telegraph at Milford Station, five miles beyond Bowling Green. On this trip, he could have gone on to the Hanover Junction area to deliver a message to Mosby in person.

After a certain amount of exploration, Ruggles and his group arranged for Booth to stay at the farm of Richard Garrett, located about three miles south of Port Royal on the Caroline County side of the Rappahannock. Thus, late on April 24 Booth and Mosby had moved within twenty-five miles of each other. While at Garrett's farm, Booth again talked of going to Orange Court House and spent some time poring over a map of Mexico. Other descriptions of Booth's stay at the Garrett farm tell of another Mosby soldier (unnamed) who rode up to the farm on the afternoon of April 25 to warn Booth of approaching Union cavalry. Again, this has been treated as mere coincidence, but it makes more sense to think that there was a security screen around Booth composed of men from Mosby's "stay-behind" group.

As an old man, W. D. Newbill, of Mosby's G Company (in the same company as Garland Smith), told how he and two other rangers had eaten supper at the Garrett farm with Booth and Herold.[64] Newbill had previously been a sergeant in Captain Sales's Company of Mounted Reserves stationed near Tappahannock, just south of the Rappahannock River, and apparently switched to Mosby's unit just a few weeks or months before April 1865.[65] He and his companions might have been part of this security screen around Booth.

After Lee surrendered, there were at least a thousand Confederate soldiers in the area between the Potomac River and Hanover Junction. Principally from Barton's brigade, these were men who had been sent home on leave to provide enhanced local security in the area through which the secret service expected to escort a captive Lincoln. After Booth's failed attempt to capture Lincoln on March 17, these men were ordered to return to their units. But because of poor communication and delays in spreading the word over such a large area, most of the soldiers were still at home when Richmond was evacuated. Some were coopted to help look after Booth and Herold, but the majority were no longer needed. So when the 1st New York Mounted Rifles moved into Ashland on April 21, the Confederates began to come in large numbers to sign their paroles.[66]

On the afternoon or evening of April 25, the Garrett household had another visitor. Allen Brockenbrough Bowie, a twenty-seven-year-old sergeant in Captain Thornton's Company, Lightfoot's Battalion, Virginia Light Artillery, came calling. Bowie was a resident of nearby Port Royal, and there were young ladies of marriageable age at the Garrett farm—a fact that alone might explain the visit. But there is another possibility. Bowie's unit had been stationed north of the James River during the final months of the war, and when Richmond was evacuated, Lightfoot's Battalion marched off with General Ewell's forces. Eventually twenty-nine men from the battalion were paroled at Appomattox. Bowie, however, was not paroled until he turned himself in to Union forces at Bowling Green on May 8, 1865. So when he visited the Garrett farm on April 25, he was still an uncaptured Confederate soldier.[67]

The situation is similar in many respects to the hundreds of men from other units stationed north of the James who were paroled near their homes in the Northern Neck in late April or early May. Twenty-seven men from Lightfoot's Battalion were paroled at Bowling Green during early May 1865, ten of them on May 8. Bowie, therefore, may have been one of the men from the area sent home on leave during early 1865.

These are tantalizing fragments of information. They do not, however, tell us much about the organization of Mosby's men. But if more than just multiple coincidences, they imply the existence of some central direction in the Northern Neck dedicated to the protection of John Wilkes Booth.

Union cavalry finally caught up with Booth at the Garrett farm early on the morning of April 26, most probably the day on which the Confederates planned to move Booth to his rendezvous with Mosby and his small group. Once in firm control of Booth, Mosby could then have joined the larger group at Fredericks Hall in preparation for a longer trip. But the meeting was not to be. Herold was captured and Booth was shot through the neck and paralyzed. He died at about seven o'clock that morning.

The shooting caused a great stir—a local doctor was called, arrangements were made to ship Booth's body, witnesses were questioned, and an escort was arranged for Herold. In the midst of this flurry of activity, William B. Lightfoot, an unparoled private in the 9th Virginia Cavalry, walked into the Garrett farm in the guise of a curious bystander. He was probably charged with ascertaining whether Booth was really dead and, before dying, whether he had said anything to incriminate anybody. Fortunately, the Yankee soldiers and detectives were too preoccupied to pay any attention to a stray Confederate soldier, and Lightfoot was able to leave without being questioned.[68]

Mosby must have heard of Booth's death quite promptly. Presumably the telegraph from Milford Station to Hanover Junction continued to operate, and the word might well have reached the area in which Mosby was located by the afternoon of April 26. There was no longer any point to Mosby's preparations. His mission to keep Booth out of Yankee hands was over.

Since several of the men who were most likely part of Mosby's traveling party—G. Coleman, A. C. Flippo, and J. D. Coghill—lived in the area, they chose to seek parole at Ashland. Paroles issued at Ashland on April 26 numbered from 403 to 473, and those issued to these three men all numbered in the 460s, indicating that they were paroled late in the day. Thomas E. Pixley was paroled on April 27, and W. P. Taylor signed in on April 28. Another soldier who sought parole on the April 26 was Lt. Charles Cawood, the commander of the signal corps station in King George County that belonged to the Secret Line.

The number of soldiers seeking parole at Ashland had peaked on April 25 with 207. The sharp fall-off on April 26 suggests that the presence of the Union cavalry near Bowling Green had interfered with the flow of parole seekers to the area.[69] That being the case, Cawood must have already been south of Bowling Green when the cavalry arrived. It may well be that he had gone south to meet Mosby to finalize plans for the meeting of Booth and Mosby. (Perhaps it was Cawood who was tending to the Northern Neck end of the communications line that connected to Gordonsville and Mosby.)

While his men were seeking their paroles at Ashland, Mosby and six others were on their way to Richmond. They cut across country and camped near the James River and Kanahwa Canal several miles west of the city. James A. Seddon, former Confederate secretary of war, lived close by. Seddon would have been familiar with Mosby's role in clandestine operations and would have seen Mosby as recently as December 1864–January 1865, and therefore Mosby doubtless consulted with him about the uncertain future. Lt. Channing Smith also had an interesting conversation with General Lee, which he describes as follows:

. . . Colonel Mosby called for volunteers to go into Richmond and, if possible, get some information as to what to do with his command. . . . Flanking the enemy's pickets, five of us entered the city the next night, and, putting up my horse at a livery stable, I went to the home of my uncle, General Chilton, who, at one time, was General Lee's Adjutant General, thinking that he might possibly give me some information upon the subject. The door at which I knocked was opened by Uncle Robert's oldest daughter Laura. The family were all sitting in the dark, the gas works having been destroyed, when some one knocked at the door, and it proved to be General Lee. . . . I told him that Colonel Mosby was anxious to know what to do and would be glad to receive any advice from him. His reply was this: "Give my regards to Colonel Mosby, and tell him that I am under parole, and cannot, for that reason, give him any advice." . . . "But General," I said, "What must I do?" His reply was: "Channing, go home, all you boys who fought with me, and help to build up the shattered fortunes of our dear old State." I never saw him again.[70]

On April 27 the *Richmond Whig* printed the story of the surrender of Gen. Joe Johnston's army in North Carolina. While Smith, Munson, and the others were in Richmond, Lt. Ben Palmer of Company E, who had stayed behind with Mosby, obtained a copy of the newspaper from the crew of a passing canal boat. That piece of news was the final straw. Mosby dismissed his companions and headed back toward the larger group that he had left behind at Fredericks Hall.

A few of the men at Fredericks Hall may have gone back to their old base area in Northern Virginia and eventually taken their parole in May 1865, but the majority appear to have sought parole nearby. A total of thirty-seven soldiers from Mosby's Rangers were paroled at Charlottesville, Louisa Court House, Ashland, and Mechanicsville during May. A soldier traveling in Virginia without a parole risked arrest and imprisonment. In most circumstances a soldier seeking parole would have signed up at the closest feasible location. These locations are all near the route leading from Fredericks Hall. Adding to these thirty-seven the six who left Mosby at Richmond and the five who sought an early parole at Ashland results in total of forty-eight possible members of the group that Mosby kept together after he dismissed the majority of his command. Assuming that some men went home before seeking parole, that others did not ask for parole, and that still others were paroled in this area who were not part of the hold-over group, these forty-eight are enough to support an estimate of forty to fifty men as the actual size of the group intended to keep Booth out of Union hands.

After disbanding the Fredericks Hall group, Mosby made his way toward his home territory. After some waiting and making strong efforts to assess the Union attitude toward him, Mosby finally turned himself in at Lynchburg, Virginia, on June 17, 1865. Booth was dead. The Lincoln operation and Mosby's hold-over group had been disbanded. The trial of the assassination "conspirators" was nearly over, and it looked as if Mosby's possible association with these operations had escaped discovery.

In later years, Mosby denied any connection to the Booth operation, but such denials can be discounted. There were many people who wanted to hang Mosby as a guerrilla and who suggested his connection with Booth, so any other statement on Mosby's part would have been most damaging, and possibly fatal. He clearly wanted to avoid any serious allegations of connection to the assassination, and in later years any admission on his part would have damaged the carefully crafted myths developed to protect the Southern explanation of the Confederacy's non-role in Lincoln's assassination.

While our knowledge of many of the details of the Confederate secret service organization is not complete, there can no longer be any doubt that the Confederates engaged in such activity—and that Jefferson Davis kept a measure of personal control over the operations.

In addition to "conventional" clandestine activities like espionage, the Confederates engaged in "action" projects that were based on both experience and on a logical, developed doctrine. Their sabotage and paramilitary projects were not all just random, impulsive ventures; they devised judicious, well-planned operations intended to make concrete contributions to the Confederate war effort.

The operation based in Canada was a serious effort to use secret operations in support of the Southern cause and was compatible with the clandestine action doctrine developed by Sage, Maury, Raines, and others. The plan to abduct Lincoln fitted both the doctrine and the personal inclinations of the Confederate supervisors in Canada. Furthermore, there were doubtless many Confederates, like Sanders, with whom Booth conversed, who knew perfectly well that abduction and death are never very far apart; many of them would have been perfectly happy to see Lincoln dead and may well have said so in Booth's presence.

The operation aimed at blowing up the White House was intended to make a critical contribution to a plan designed to snatch a Confederate victory from what seemed to be impossible odds—they were trying to use irregular warfare and skillful manuever to vanquish superior Union manpower and resources. When the operation failed and Lieutenant Harney was captured, Booth decided that he could approximate the mission by simultaneously attacking Lincoln and other high officials. Events elsewhere had moved so fast that Booth did not realize that Lee's surrender made his effort pointless. He thought that there were still Confederate armies in the field with enough strength to take advantage of the opportunity that confusion in the Washington high command would present.

Furthermore, there was no responsible Confederate secret service supervisor available who knew enough of the actual situation to tell him that he should hold his fire. So Booth decided to carry out a desperate clandestine action operation on the basis of his mission, the battlefield situation as he understood it, his training, and his determination to support his cause. His decision was not based on mental aberration or personal considerations. He may have hated Lincoln, but he was acting to accomplish what he thought the Confederacy wanted accomplished. The facts surrounding Colonel Mosby's involvement with Booth do not fit the romantic picture of the Grey Ghost, but they do fit the picture of a tough, talented, partisan leader who was willing to go to great effort to do his duty to his cause.

The story of George Sanders and his machinations to divest the Confederacy of blame for the assassination depicts a classic clandestine operation with layers of apparent truth concealing the true objective. The shade of the Confederacy owes an immense debt to the steadfastness of that most unsteadfast character, Wallace-Conover-Dunham, for he apparently never revealed the extent of his collaboration with Sanders.

Appendix A

TABLE OF REQUESTS FOR TREASURY WARRANTS FOR SECRET SERVICE MONEY

THE FOLLOWING table lists secret service money drawn from the Confederate treasury as shown in the remnant of a record book in the Chicago Historical Society and on copies of request forms signed by Jefferson Davis for the issuance of treasury warrants for secret service money.[1] The requests cite two separate funds: "Necessities and Exigencies," which covered conventional secret service activity such as espionage, and "Secret Service," which denoted covert action such as sabotage. Both funds are clearly labeled in the record book as involving secret service.

In the following table, the first nine entries in the first column are the dates of the transactions as given in the secret service record book. Request forms signed by Jefferson Davis begin with the item for August 9, 1862, and the date of the request is given in the first column with the serial number of the request in the second column. The third column gives the number of the resulting treasury warrant when known.

The fourth column gives the amount of the transaction as stated in the record book for the first nine items and as given on the request forms for the remainder (except for the last item for which no request has survived). The fifth column gives the value of the transaction in

[1]These copies are in the Pickett Papers, Confederate States of America Records, reel 19 Manuscript Collection, Library of Congress, Washington, D.C.

gold dollars when it could be determined. Beginning with the item for September 4, 1863, and thereafter, the Confederates used the ratio of three Confederate dollars to one gold dollar. Before that date the ratio varied, making it impossible in most cases to determine the exact gold value of the earlier transactions.

The sixth column gives the nature of the proceeds of the transaction as desired by the requester. The language in this column is taken directly from the request forms. Informal notes on the forms written by the clerks in the Confederate State Department are shown in the last column. This column also shows information supplied by the author in brackets. All information in the last column not enclosed in brackets is taken from the forms themselves.

In the table all citations are for "Necessities and Exigencies" except for those marked in the last column as "Secret Service."

Date of Request	Serial Number	Warrant Number	Amount Stated	Gold Value	Proceeds Specified	Notes
1861						
Apr. 10			40,000.00	*		
July 6			10,000.00	*		
Aug. 5			500.00	*		
Aug. 6			11,250.00	*		
Oct. 29		446	360.00	*		
Nov. 28		506	3,082.85	*		
1862						
Apr. 15		197	25,000.00	*		
Apr. 15		198	6,188.00	*		
July 30			3,000.00	*		[$2,500 to Rose Greenhow on Aug. 1, 1862 from secret service funds $500 to C. V. Baxley]
Aug. 9	1		3,000.00	*	In Exchange	
Aug. 11	2		2,333.33	*		

*No basis for calculation of gold value

Date of Request	Serial Number	Warrant Number	Amount Stated	Gold Value	Proceeds Specified	Notes
Oct. 24	3	920	2,912.00	*	Exchange on England Requested for 2,668.36 (230.18.6+)	[Indicates rate of CS $11.56 or CS $12.63 per £]
Oct. 30	4		5,000.00	*	Confederate Bonds Requested	
Nov. 11	5	966	2,680.76	*	Exchange on England Requested	

1863

Date of Request	Serial Number	Warrant Number	Amount Stated	Gold Value	Proceeds Specified	Notes
Jan. 14	6	1,227	13,333.33	4,850.00	Exchange on England Requested (£1,000)	[Indicates rate of CS$13.33 per £]
Jan. 14	7	1,228	13,333.33	4,850.00	Exchange on England Requested (£1,000)	
Apr. 27	8		22,726.20	6,201.70	Exchange on England Requested (£1,278.7)	
Sep. 4	9		3,637.50	1,212.50	1,212.50 in gold requested	
Sep. 7	10		60,375.00	20,125.00	20,125 in gold requested	
Sep. 18	11		29,100.00	9,700.00	Two drafts of £1,000 each Exchange on England requested	[Indicates rate of CS$1,455 per £]
Sep. 29	12		3,000.00	1,000.00	Order on Collector at Brownsville for $1,000 in gold requested	
Sep. 30	13		3,637.50	1,212.50	$1,212.50 gold requested	P. G. Coghlan [written in lower left corner]
Oct. 5	14		14,550.00	4,850.00	£1,000 Exchange on England requested	
Nov. 13	15		900.00	300.00	$300 in gold requested	
Dec. 20	16		760.00	*		

Date of Request	Serial Number	Warrant Number	Amount Stated	Gold Value	Proceeds Specified	Notes
Dec. 22	17	2,247	29,100.00	9,700.00	Exchange on England requested £2,000	[Draft 5571 on Frazer Trenholm for $9,700 dated Dec. 29, 1863]
1864						
Jan. 8	18		36,000.00	12,000.00	Requested: $12,000 in gold or Sterling Exchange on England	$4,000 in gold and £1,674.9.8 received for [illegible] Preston & Walker Fearn Esq.
Feb. 2	19		5,742.16	1,914.25	Exchange on England requested one bill for £206.3.81/2 and one for £188.9.31/2 [totaled as] £394.13.	Col. Lamar
Feb. 5	20		8,730.00	2,910.00	Exchange on England requested £600	For Mr. Heyliger
Feb. 19	21		24,000.00	8,000.00	$500 in gold requested and £1546.7.10 Exchange on England	Holcombe
Feb. 20	22		29,100.00	9,700.00	£2,000 Exchange on England requested	Hotze
Feb. 22	23		63,750.00	21,250.00		Stinson & Beale
Feb. 29	24		290.00	96.66		H. A. Parr
Mar. 5	25		48,000.00	16,000.00	$7,500 in gold requested and £1,752.11.61/2 in Exchange on England	
Mar. 23	26		60,000.00	20,000.00	$20,000 in gold requested	
Mar. 23	27		139,536.00	46,512.00	$46,512 in gold requested	Mr. Tucker

Date of Request	Serial Number	Warrant Number	Amount Stated	Gold Value	Proceeds Specified	Notes
Mar. 26	28		850.00	150.00 and 133.33	$150 in gold requested [times] 3 [=] 450 and 400 in C.S. Treasury notes [=] £850	
Apr. 1	29		709.50	236.50	$236.50 in gold requested [times] 3 [=] $709.50	Lancaster
Apr. 12	30		16,616.00	3,872.00 and 1,666.66	$3,872 in gold requested [times] 3 [=] 11,616 + 5,000 [=] $16,616	
Apr. 14	31		14,550.00	4,850.00	Two bills of Exchange on England requested, each for £500 £1,000 = $4850 x 3 [=] 14,550	Mason & Slidell [Draft 6064 to Mason Apr. 18, 1864]
Apr. 25	32	1,000,000	1,000,000	1,000,000	Payable in foreign countries. £206,185.11.4 Exchange on England requested	Cancelled see next page
Apr. 25	32	1,000,000	1,000,000	1,000,000	Payable in Foreign Countries £206,185.11.4 Exchange on England requested	Thompson [cites Secret Service
Apr. 26	33		9,728.85	3,242.95	$3,242.95 in gold requested [times] 3 [totals] $9,728.85	Lancaster for Greenbacks
Apr. 28	34		1,500.00	1,500.00	Payable in foreign countries Gold requested	Clay [cites Secret Service]

Date of Request	Serial Number	Warrant Number	Amount Stated	Gold Value	Proceeds Specified	Notes
May 3	35		240.00	80.00	$80 in gold requested	For 160 in Greenbacks
May 5	36		7,500.00	2,500.00	$2,500 in gold requested [times] 3 [totals] $7500	
May 25	37	6,265	29,100.00	9,700.00	£2,000 Exchange on England requested 4.85 [times] 2,000 [=] 9,700.00 [times] 3 [=] $29,100	[Henry Hotze receives Warrant for £2,000 dated May 27, 1864 on July 4]
June 16	38		3,600.00	1,200.00	$1,200 Gold requested	[Capt. George Dewson received on June 18, 1864]
July 2	39		1,000.00	333.33		
July 25	40		4,500.00	1,500.00	£309.5.7 = $1,500 [times] 3 [totals] 4,500 Exchange on England requested	
July 29	41		12,000.00	4,000.00	4,000 in gold requested [times] 3 [=] 12,000	
Aug. 1	42		2,640.00	880.00	$880 in gold requested [times] 3 [=] $2,640	
Aug. 4	43		450.00	150.00	$150 in gold requested	
Aug. 20	44		35,000.00	35,000.00	Gold requested	[cites Secret Service]
Aug. 31	45	2,980	242,500.00	242,500.00	£50,000 Exchange on England requested	Colin J. McRae [cites Secret Service]
Sep. 1	46			1,000.00	One thousand dollars in gold	[cites Secret Service]
Sep. 14	47		500.00	500.00	five hundred dollars in gold	[cites Secret Service; $400 in gold given to T. N. Conrad]

Date of Request	Serial Number	Warrant Number	Amount Stated	Gold Value	Proceeds Specified	Notes
Sep. 20	48		2,221.62	740.54	£458.1.4 Exchange on England requested	[Draft 6766 to Mason Sept. 20, 1864]
Oct. 6	49		1,200.00	400.00		
Oct. 6	50		4,850.00	4,850.00	four thousand eight hundred and fifty dollars in gold	[Apparently to replace similar amount advanced by State Department in Sept. 1864]
Oct. 24	51		2,700.00	400.00 and 766.67	four hundred dollars in gold and twenty-three hundred dollars in C.S. Treasury notes	[Form should have stated CS$3,500]
Dec. 6	52	3,178	1,500.00	1,500.00	fifteen hundred dollars in gold	[Probably travel money for E. G. Lee]
Dec. 7	53		9,700.00	9,700.00	£2,000 Exchange on England requested	
Dec. 8	54		15,000.00	15,000.00	fifteen thousand dollars in gold	$2,000 in Richmond and an order on Columbia S.C. for remainder
Dec. 26	55		100.00	100.00	one hundred dollars in gold	
Dec. 30	56		100.00	100.00	one hundred dollars in gold	
1865						
Jan. 7	57		200.00	200.00	two hundred dollars in gold	
Jan. 18	58		1,500.00	1,500.00	fifteen hundred dollars in gold	[Probably money for T. N. Conrad and General Hardee]

Date of Request	Serial Number	Warrant Number	Amount Stated	Gold Value	Proceeds Specified	Notes
Jan. 30	59		1,500.00	1,500.00	fifteen hundred dollars in gold	
Feb. 4	60		1,000.00	1,000.00	one thousand dollars in gold	
Feb. 23	61		9,700.00	9,700.00	£2,000 Exchange on England requested	
Feb. 25	62		2,500.00	2,500.00	twenty five hundred dollars in gold	
Mar. 1	63		9,700.00	9,700.00	nine thousand seven hundred dollars in gold	
Apr. 1		3,504		1,500.00	[Warrant dated Apr. 1, 1865, request not available]	[cites Secret Service]

Appendix B

ORGANIZATION
OF PRIVATE WARFARE

THIS PAMPHLET, *Organization of Private Warfare,* was written by Bernard Janin Sage in 1863. The original, from which this appendix was copied, was given to the U.S. Navy long after the war ended.[1]

---

[1]Confederate Navy Subject File, file VN, Record Group 45, National Archives, Washington, D.C.

ORGANIZATION OF PRIVATE WARFARE.

BUREAU OF DESTRUCTIVE MEANS AND MEASURES.

Bands of Destructionists and Captors.

Having proposed in the summer of 1861 the establishment of a Bureau or Board for the examination and testing of new inventions or contrivances for destruction, and the formation of operating bands of destructionists, to use or carry into effect the same, I have ever since had my mind on the matter, and have gathered many facts and considerations, some of which, with the above plans, I beg leave to present herein to the Government. I am the more moved to this by the approval of many persons of excellent judgment.

If our destructive means and measures of a novel or unusual character be made known, they may become possessed by the enemy, who, thereupon, is, in the first place, *put on his guard*, and secondly, *enabled to use them equally with us*. Hence every man who thinks he has made a discovery, should be encouraged to carry it to an examining and testing place of the Government, established and operating with a due degree of secrecy.

With such a bureau as proposed, it could be speedily and conveniently examined, tested, and either adopted or rejected, thus satisfying the proposer, stimulating—instead of discouraging—inventive genius, enterprise and patriotic aid, and securing to the Government, and to our cause, all meritorious inventions, contrivances, &c. And if the Government should not adopt such invention or contrivance for its own use, the approval of its excellence by such a board, would induce private capital and enterprise to take hold of it, with a view to the advantage or rewards offered by the Government, as well as to aid the cause of the country.

Instead of this, numerous inventions, plans, contrivances, &c., some of them quite meritorious, have, from the beginning of the war, been going about among State Legislatures, or individuals, for adoption or aid, till finally their owners have exhausted their means, and given up in despair, and the country lost, perhaps, some valuable implements of war and destruction; or, perhaps, some of these persons are still laboring painfully and disadvantageously on, wasting their energy and substance to reach success or failure, when such a Bureau or Board could settle the question with but little trouble in a single day, or, perhaps, an hour.

If the cases were few, the propriety and justice of such an institution might be questioned, but they are numbered by thousands, and scattered all over the country, and the only way of doing justice to those who devote themselves to such pursuits, and who are of the class of minds that make all the progress of a country, is for the Government to bring all such things into a common receptacle, and there separate the wheat from the chaff. All that is of value will be thus secured *to* the Government, and *from* the enemy.

Such a Bureau should, I presume, have for its chief a man of genius and large experience in such matters.[*] There should be a competent clerk, and both should be under obligations

---

[*] Such a man, for instance, as Gen. G. T. Rains, who, besides military training, and scientific acquirements, has given much special attention to such affairs, and been himself a successful inventor.

1

2

of secresy. Its repository should be secret, and it should have secret places of testing and construction, i. e., workshops, laboratory, &c. It might have a permanent Board, but probably, the best plan would be for the Chief to classify the inventions or devices offered, and periodically—say once a month—organize a Board, with the sanction of the President or Secretary of War, for the examination and testing of each class—in all cases allowing the inventor to be present to explain, &c.

The record of such Bureau and Boards, properly kept, would be very useful in future. It would show the progress of this kind of science and art, and be the starting point and magazine of such devices in future wars. Its description or models and drawings of inventions or contrivances for destruction, would naturally be in four classes. 1. Such as the Government should reward the inventor for, and take for its own use. 2. Such as should merely be approved as valuable, so that private capital and enterprise would take hold of and effectuate them, for such rewards as the Government might allow. 3. Such as could neither be approved or rejected, owing to imperfections, or for some other reasons. 4. Such as should be condemned or rejected.

At present all these new devices, or modifications of old ones, are presented to three, or more bureaux: 1. The Navy Ordnance Bureau. 2. The Army Ordnance Bureau. 3. The Engineer Bureau. 4. The Patent office. Each of these is already overtasked with various routine and incidental duties, and though, as I can bear witness, they try with alacrity to perform these additional ones, I am satisfied they prefer to be relieved of them: that in many instances they cannot do the cases presented full justice; and that the labor .senough to occupy exclusively one bureau.

The importance of these destructive means and measures—the above division of them—and the fact that the operators of them are separately organized, supplied, and sent out by both War and Navy Departments, shows the want of some general plan or organization, some one place for inventors and operators to apply to, some common receptacle or magazine for all such things, organized bands of operators everywhere, and some competent and efficient controlling authority for them all.

Such a Bureau would give us a magazine of destructive means—of knowledge and experience on this subject, and of plans for any enterprise either of Government or private parties. The hydrography of the country would be mapped out—showing what fields are occupied, and what are to be occupied; plans of operations would be furnished, information given, and necessary materials procured and provided. And as there should be some judgment passed upon the officers and men, as well as contrivances and plans of action to be employed, no authority would probably be more fit than this. Persons of peculiar bent and genius for such pursuits would be found, instructed, and put in service. And being devoted exclusively to these matters, such Bureau would, from the contrivances, plans, and ideas before it, often strike out something new and valuable, and suggest schemes highly important to the public welfare, and the success of our cause.

How far such Bureau should control this service in the field, I will not undertake to say. Perhaps some aid can be found in the analogy between this and the Engineer Bureau and service.

CASES ILLUSTRATING THE NEED OF THIS ORGANIZATION.

* * * * * * * * *

[For the purpose of illustration, I intended to present many cases, known and ascertained by myself, but space will not allow. There are hundreds of inventions in the land not presented. These, with those brought forward—the last, perhaps, the least meritorious—constitute a mountain that must be patiently delved and sifted to get a few gems and grains of gold from the mass of trash, and the numerous alleged inventions that are old, long since exploded, or violative of first principles. But it all must be done. The President and others must be relieved from the great draught on their valuable time; the genius and enterprise of the people must be developed, encouraged, and rewarded; justice must be done to inventors; and what is valuable must be found and put to the use of the country.]

* * * * * * * * *

Is it not obvious, from the above cases, that all such means and plans, and their effectuation, should be brought under some one proper investigating, organizing, and superintending authority?

I know of some plans and contrivances, which I am not permitted to mention, which promise tremendous results, and I believe some of these will be realized, if the proper course of encouragement and aid be pursued.

I could give many cases where the owner has either felt discouraged, and not brought forward his invention, or not finding proper facilities, has been compelled to incur great expense or loss of time; or has failed to engage attention, and get his contrivance tested, and (if valuable) brought into notice and use; so that the general result, for the want of some such organization as I suggest, has been to discourage inventive genius and enterprise, and, it may be, to cause the public interest to suffer.

Now, I cannot but think that all such schemes and contrivances should be brought into

3

a common repository or bureau, and, *if a competent Chief of Bureau deems necessary*, be examined, tested, and reported upon. The Government would thus be apprised of all valuable inventions, and could use them if it chose. If not, the favorable report of such a board would enlist private capital and enterprise. A fair examination, a favorable opinion and a full report would do the Government no harm, but would greatly aid the inventor, benefit the public, and, perhaps, be of special advantage to the Government, and "the cause," by inducing capital and enterprise to take hold of the plan in question.

Moreover, the impression which is abroad, that the Government does not favor such things, should be removed, for men are deterred from making, or presenting inventions, for this reason, and inventive genius and enterprise are discouraged. And it is generally supposed that some shrewd manager, or log-roller, or lawyer, must be feed with about one-half of the invention, or the value thereof, "to get it through," whereas, the way should be so straight, and blazed so plainly, that the simplest back-woodsman can follow it without direction or guide. I know the above impression prevails, because I have been offered considerable shares of a number of valuable inventions, or handsome fees if I would aid in "getting them through."

It must be remembered that inventors, as a class, not only are, or do become enthusiasts, but they are retiring and sensitive men, who are discouraged at mere adverse appearances, much more by rebuffs, sneers, or unapproving shrugs. They have not the necessary *savoir faire*, and perhaps, are doubtful of the merits of their inventions, and unless encouraged, or drawn out as it were, they will not bring them forward. I know cases in point. Moreover, what they have discovered or invented is as a dear child to them, or rather, a cherished treasure, which they gloat over as a miser does over hoarded gold. Fear of loss of the coinage of their brain, often keeps them back, for it is much easier stolen than material wealth, and the wrong is harder to detect and redress. And officers who have regular and arduous duties to perform, and can only attend to these others incidentally, begin all such examinations with a presumption against the invention, (which sometimes causes rejection before the merits are reached,) founded on the well known fact that nine out of ten inventions are failures, or not new,—forgetting that a large part of the duties of this life, particularly official ones, consists of separating wheat from chaff, and that the one in ten may be gunpowder, printing, Fulton's steamboat, or Morse's telegraph, and destined to revolutionize the affairs of men, or materially change the modes of war.

For these and other reasons, and because this is a patriotic class of men, desiring to serve the country, I invoke for them the liberal and facilitating policy of the Government as indicated above, and believe that their services will be highly advantageous to our cause.

I have been informed that European Governments have institutions similar to the one proposed.

BANDS OF DESTRUCTIONISTS AND CAPTORS.

Acting under regulations of the War Department, or perhaps connected with the aforesaid Bureau, corps or bands of destructionists and capturers, should be organized, or allowed to organize themselves, for destructive purposes, &c., in view of large rewards for success; such, for instance, as indicated in the act of 21st of April, 1862, (which gives 50 per cent for destroying the enemy's war vessels by any new contrivance,) or with a view to prize money; which, as well as protection to such men, should be provided for by law, as is done in the case of privateers. The band could be small or large, as the exigency might require. It should be under a leader who would act more or less under the immediate authority and protection of the commander of the military district where his operations are to be. This leader would generally be the inventor, who, with his artizans, assistants or partners, would form the operating corps. Seldom would be required more men. But if more should be wanted for aid or protection, they could be obtained as volunteers from the nearest troops, with the consent of their commander. Such bands having governmental authority for any expedition, would be protected from any penalty for irregular warfare.

Being always ready, on the watch, and stimulated by the mingled and powerful motives of great gain and bitter hatred to the enemy, as well as by patriotism, such bands would, besides destroying men-of-war and armed transports, capture war-vessels, merchant-vessels, river-steamers, transports, flat boats, barges, and all sorts of craft, and what they could not capture, they would destroy, if able.

These bands of ingenious and daring men would not only operate all destructive contrivances, but, like privateers, would make captures, and enrich themselves at the enemy's expense; "all along shore," on our 3,000 miles of coast, and in our bays and rivers, for the enemy is pressing upon us wherever we have navigation, particularly in the Mississippi and its tributaries, tempting and provoking destruction and capture. Men organized for the purpose, with the necessary means at command, lying in wait, or moving with great celerity, would improve these numerous opportunities, and do the enemy great damage. And this would be an excellent mode of preventing the navigation of the

4

Mississippi, should all other means fail. They would also, to some extent, defend the country, watch the enemy, give signals, convey or send information, &c., &c.

Since this plan was proposed, probably many scores of sea-going vessels, to say nothing of river craft, might have been destroyed or captured, with little or no risk.

To show what can be, by what has been done, see the following

CASES IN ILLUSTRATION.

The capture of the steamer St. Nicholas and other vessels by Com. Hollins and Col. Thomas. That of the steamer Fox by Capt. Andrews, and 16 daring men from Mobile. That of the steam tug Boston, and the burning of two barks by Capt. Duke and 12 men from same place. That of the Sea Bird near North Carolina coast. The blowing up of the large gun boat Cairo on the Yazoo by torpedoes. Various captures and destructions of boats and vessels in the Mississippi and other rivers, and along our coast, which all must have seen mentioned in the papers.[*]

AID TO OUR CAUSE, OTHERWISE QUIESCENT.

By adopting and organizing this style of warfare, we shall largely *increase our fighting force*. The many driven south, owing to their sympathy with us, the Marylanders and Delawarians, foreigners, many of our own people who have kept and will keep out of regular service, men over age, &c., &c., will all be brought to our aid by the inducements presented; and though somewhat actuated by cupidity, will be restrained from excesses by military authority and regulations. Moreover, I have reason to hope that *capital for these purposes* will come in from unexpected sources.

Such bands would work every variety of approved destructive expedient of the class held in view herein, known to warfare, or that may be invented and sanctioned—every variety of torpedoes, and modes of working them defensively and offensively, submarine boats, armor and other contrivances of that kind.

They would dash on vessels and steamboats in small boats, and capture them, or they might drench them with spirits of turpentine and other incendiary matter, and burn them. And as has been proposed, ambulating boat corps could be organized; the boats, howitzers, &c., on pontoon wagons. Such a corps could move quickly from bay to bay, or river to river, and make frequent surprises.

They could lie in wait at wood-yards and capture or destroy steamers, burn the wood at wood-yards, burn cotton, and destroy Yankee property generally.

Blow up railroad trains to prevent reinforcements and supplies during a battle or an attack on a place held by the enemy.

In short, they would effectuate their purposes by every variety of expedient and probably devise and carry out many not now conceived of. They merely want authority, and the encouragement of countenance, and the bounties hereafter proposed.

GOVERNMENTAL CONTROL OF SUCH MEANS.

The following considerations show why the Government ought to control, to a certain extent, the means and measures in question. Do they not also tend strongly to show that the system can only be perfected by having a bureau at the head of it?

1. They are properly a part of the means and enginery of war, and by being systematized, governed and directed by superior intellect and skill, instead of being left to individual, irregular, and ill prepared efforts, they will be prosecuted to a much wider extent, with more adequate means, and with vastly greater effect. There would necessarily be that command and application of means adequate to the end, which is the great *desideratum* in war.

2. Such operations could thus always be made to consist and not conflict with regular military operations, and not unfrequently to aid them. For instance, take the case of fireships and torpedoes in naval battles, and blowing up of railroad trains with torpedoes. to prevent the arrival of reinforcements and supplies of the enemy during a great battle.[†]

[*] Lately we have had the following: The destruction of the De Kalb, a large gun boat on the Yazoo, by a torpedo; the disabling of a gunboat in James river by the same means; the capture of two gun boats and other vessels in the Chesapeake, by a party under Lieut. Wood, of the Navy; the blowing up of several railroad trains by torpedoes; the destruction of the Ruth at Island No. 10, with 30 lives, $2,600,000 and 1,100 tons commissary and other stores; the capture of seven vessels on the Atlantic coast, by Acting Master Beall and 26 men; the burning of the six steamboats on the Mississippi river. The capture by Lieut. Wood and Acting Master Beall vindicate the suggestion about the boat corps.

Our crop in one-tenth of the field cultivated is so good we should at once put in the rest of the field.

[†] There are two inventions: one blows up the first train, doing more damage than can be repaired in a few hours, or perhaps, killing women, children and non-combatants, while the other infinitely preferable, blows up *given trains* for great strategic purposes. This shows how necessary is governmental investigation and control of these means.

5

3. The Government, through its officers, would be likely to know all vulnerable and unguarded points and places to strike; to know what auxiliary means are necessary, and be able to command them; and the Government could more readily concentrate means and men at a given point where a great blow could be struck.

4. All being regular, organized, and under a kind of military control, there is more likelihood of secresy—so frequently necessary—being observed.

5. Ill-advised and untimely demonstrations, and fruitless exposures of such means, would be less frequent.

6. *Tabooed* means, or such as the enemy could use with greater efficiency, would be withheld.

7. If thus organized and controlled, governmental sanction, in the eyes of the enemy, and of the world, would be more complete and efficient. The operators would have military *status*, and be protected in case of capture, or subsequent litigation.

Did space permit, I could give various circumstances to illustrate each of the above reasons, but I presume it to be unnecessary.

Now I submit, that to accomplish all the purposes proposed in this paper, several things are to be done by legislative power.

Such Bureau is to be established, its duties defined, and means placed at its disposal.

Such bands and the kind of warfare contemplated, must be authorized, so that persons engaged may have military status, and be protected by the Government.

Their captures should be secured to them as prizes.

They should have a handsome bonus or bounty for the destruction of war vessels and transports, (the bounty given now by act of April 19th, 1862, is only for destruction by *novel* means,) and, perhaps, a small one for destroying any other crafts and property of the enemy.

Richmond, April 25th, 1863.

———

NEED OF PROPER LEGISLATION DEMONSTRATED.

Since writing the foregoing, the want of proper legislation has been demonstrated in the repeated and earnest endeavors of the Secretary of War to form satisfactory organizations of such ingenious and daring men as sought authority, protection and aid in carrying out plans of destruction against the enemy. Acting for some of these parties, the undersigned had the honor to submit to him several propositions to choose from.

1. To let these men be attached to some company in the regular service in the department or district where they were to operate, and be detached for the special purpose.— Transportation, workshop aid, ordnance stores, &c., would be furnished at the discretion of the department or district commanders.

2. To organize them under the " act for local defence and special service," approved August 21st, 1861.

3. To form companies of not less than 20, under the " act for local defence," approved October 13th, 1862. The Secretary endeavored to accomplish the purpose under this act, but failed, owing to insuperable difficulties.

4. It was finally proposed on the plan of the first proposition, to organize them under the Engineer Bureau, according to act approved March 19th, 1863. This was adopted, and *the men were individually authorized to proceed to the department or district where they wished to operate, and be enlisted and organized with an engineer company; and then be detailed for their special purpose—the commanding General being requested or recommended to furnish them with transportation, workshop aid, ordnance stores, and military protection and assistance, at his discretion*.

Under this plan, some of the most ingenious, enterprising, daring and patriotic men in the Confederacy have gone to the South and South-west, who will form the *nuclei* of many organizations, of the progress of which, in the work of destruction, I hope we shall soon hear favorable and loud reports.

To get them into the field at once on the Mississippi and elsewhere, during the low water, and give them the necessary protection, facilities and aid, it was proper to contrive a temporary arrangement, as Congressional action could not be had

OBJECTIONS TO THIS PLAN.

But in this plan there are serious difficulties which can only be obviated by new and special legislative action, and a separate organization, as the following considerations will show:

1. Upon the assumption that their purpose is useful—nay, of the highest importance, (as evident from the blowing up of the Cairo, the DeKalb, &c , and from the wholesome fear manifested by, or delay caused to the enemy by torpedoes and other known and supposed means of destruction,) they ought to be peculiarly organized, and exclusively devoted to this service, and controlled only by a General commanding a department or

6

district, who would, of course, leave them with a wide discretion as to time, place and manner of action, and who could give them the aid required.

2. These bands should be multiplied and kept along our 3,000 miles of coast, and in our harbors, sounds and rivers, so that there will be no place to float the enemy's vessels, without ingenious, enterprising and brave men to destroy, or perchance capture them.— It is obvious then, that if they be attached to regular army organizations, they will be subject to the movements of the same—no matter how far, or great inconvenience, delay abuse, and unmilitary and illegal procedure will probably ensue.

3. An engineer company has its complement of officers, and if three, five, or ten destructionists be detached, there is no commissioned officer to command—as is indispensable—unless the company be destituted to that extent. Moreover, though the engineer officers be quite able in their proper duties, they may be utterly unfit for this service. Again, those who with their contrivances, are approved by the chief of their department of service—or by the General of a district—after due investigation, would be most proper for preparing and controlling the execution of their projects, and commanding the auxilliaries. Therefore, these ought to be commisioned.

4. The duties of the engineer corps and their officers are fixed by law, and do not include the ones in question.

5. This pursuit is amphibious, multiform and dangerous, and not of the nature of engineer duties as defined by law, and it requires peculiar organization and rules. And men will only follow it from choice—in their own way—and for prospects of great gain.— Such service require men of peculiar character and fitness, but they could not be induced to engage themselves for it. if put in an engineer or regular military organization for the war, and made liable to ordinary engineer or military duties. This is especially the case in regard to many of them who are entitled to exemption, or are over military age, and who are just so much addition to our military strength. To illustrate: one of these bands is composed of four men at present, one would be exempted at his desire, one from physical inability, one is fifty, and the last sixty years of age. The two last were formerly Attorney General and Secretary of State, of Texas.

6. Another seeming difficulty, showing the want of special enactment, is exhibited in the following case :

A Mr. McDaniel, of Kentucky, invented his ingenious contrivances, organized his bands, and was operating with a view to the reward of fifty per cent., offered by act of Congress, for destroying a war vessel by a new contrivance; when his agent obtained a commission for him, for the sole purpose of giving him the needed protection in case of capture. He destroyed the Cairo in the Yazoo, and now the Government seems to withhold the compensation on the serious doubt whether, being an officer of the Government, and under pay, he is entitled thereto. The same reason applied to officers and privates, particularly if they receive pay and rations. In the present organization, however, it is fair to say, that this, and other rewards, are expressly stipulated for by the parties.

Other considerations might be given, but these suffice to show that the present organization is quite defective, and that a new and peculiar one should be made.

As further showing the want of a general system and law, the Secretary of the Navy finds himself obliged to authorize parties with these self-same purposes, by giving the leader the warrant of an " acting master, without pay ;" which the Confederate Court at Mobile, has virtually decided to be no commission at all—these parties being therefore without legal warrant or protection.

THE CONGRESSIONAL ACTION REQUIRED.

In conclusion, I beg leave to state concisely *the points that ought to be covered* in the legislation of Congress on this subject.

I. Should not A PROPER BUREAU AND RECEPTACLE of inventions, plans and means for such ends, be established as heretofore suggested, and *proper boards* provided for, as well as *shops, testing places*, &c., all under a due degree of secrecy? Should not such bureau *organize and have general supervision, and some control of all the means, measures and men* employed in this kind of warfare, somewhat after the manner of the Engineer Bureau, in relation to engineers, engineering, &c :

II. AUTHORITY, ORGANIZATION and CONTROL *of these coast and river privateers* must be provided for. And as this kind of warfare is very important, and the field of operations very extensive, I submit that the general organization should be independent to some extent; and each band should be directed by the inventor or projector— *if he be a proper person*—or some specially fit leader; and should be bound to secrecy—having a system of signs, passwords, &c. The number, peculiar organization and mode of operating of each band, should be arranged by each leader according to exigencies, under the general authority and control of the department or district commander. Legal protection to operators in case of capture or litigation follows of course.

III. As to GOVERNMENTAL AID, the *transportation*, use of *workshops, ordnance stores* and *auxilliary men* that may be required, can be furnished by district commanders, under some provision or regulations just as they are to other troops. The convenient obtainment of ordnance stores is so indispensable to these bands, that they must be furnished by the Government from its depots, for otherwise they must be procured with the greatest expense, difficulty and delay, or perhaps not at all. If the Government cannot give them, let them be advanced, and the value reserved out of the bounties hereafter proposed, when they shall be paid.

IV. As to REWARD. But a small portion of this ground is now covered by law.

1. It is provided by act of Congress, of April 21st, 1862, that *if any person " shall invent or construct any new machine or engine, or contrive any new method for destroying the armed vessels of the enemy," he shall receive 50 per cent. of the value of the vessel sunk or destroyed by its means.* This is excellent, but it seems to require amendment to prevent the public good—in this crisis—from being limited to the movements—passive or active—or by the selfishness of the inventor, and the reward from being monopolized by him as against operators. Wherever patents or peculiar priviliges are granted for destructive inventions, it should be provided that all persons may use the same; and that the Government, which has the means of knowing the inventor, shall reserve a certain portion of the reward for him—the destroyer being required in making his proof to show what contrivance was used. Patents for war means which give exclusive right to use, are absurd and unpatriotic, while on the other hand, inventors must be rewarded.

2. A reward of *30 or 40 per cent. should be given for the destruction of such vessels by any means,* (for valor and enterprise and hazard by destroying war vessels, do the Government, or cause equal good with inventions,) and this would leave a margin of 10 or 20 per cent. to reward inventive genius.

3 *Should not a reward of—say 10 per cent., be given for the destruction of all commercial vessels and property on our coast and rivers?* If yea, some safe mode of ascertaining value should be provided. Such bounty ought also to be given to ships of the volunteer navy, and a smaller bounty to the ships of the regular navy. Smaller I say, because the Government owns the vessels, and pays all expenses, including full wages to officers and men.

4. *The vessels of every description, their freight, and all other property captured from the enemy,* all primarily belonging to the Government, *should be given or relinquished to the captors,* exactly as is done in case of privateers. The Executive Department is favorable to this, but Congressional action is necessary.

I feel sanguine that immense good would result from the proposed legislation. Such an organization, and the volunteer navy will constitute a species of volunteer or private warfare, thoroughly sanctioned by usage, and wisely regulated, *that will do vast harm to the enemy, while he pays the cost.* If these steps had been taken at the outset, ten vessels would have been taken or destroyed where there has been one, the enemy would have been much more impoverished, and his heart more strongly inclined to peace. His only success, and our greatest harm throughout the war have been, from mechanical contrivances and navigation, but for which he must, ere this, have retired from the contest; and hence we should bend every energy, and sharpen every faculty to meet him there with destruction and death. If we neglect this, he can do us incalculable harm, while he himself is in comparative safety, carrying on the war at such times, in such modes, and to such lengths as he chooses; and aiming to exhaust our energy, our war spirit, and our means of defence.

Henceforth, I trust our inventive genius and enterprise, and this kind of warfare will be encouraged: that we shall hold it in view; that damage to his material interests, is the most potent argument that can be addressed to the enemy in favor of peace; that in the mode proposed, we do the most harm with the least expense to ourselves; and finally, that instead of awaiting the judgment of Lincoln " ascertaining costs " against us, *our current judgment (and execution) shall be—"pay as you go!"*

Respectfully,

B. J. SAGE.

BILL TO ESTABLISH A BUREAU FOR SPECIAL AND SECRET SERVICE

THIS BILL to create a Special and Secret Service Bureau reflects much of the language and thinking contained in Sage's pamphlet *Organization of Private Warfare*. This bill was finally passed by the Confederate Congress in March 1865, but there is no record of its formal implementation.

[SECRET.]

[HOUSE OF REPRESENTATIVES, No. 361.]

HOUSE OF REPRESENTATIVES, January 30, 1865.—Read first and second times, made special order after pending special order and ordered to be printed.

[By Mr. CLARKE

A BILL

To provide for the establishment of a Bureau for Special and Secret Service.

1 WHEREAS, There is now no efficient system for the encourage-
2 ment, development or application of new inventions or secret
3 agencies for the defence of the country : and whereas, It has
4 been shown that, by individual exertion and private enterprise,
5 many useful inventions have been made which would be greatly
6 beneficial to the common defence, were they regularly and sys-
7 tematically applied ; and whereas, There is no w no department,
8 authorized under existing laws, to experiment upon and reduce
9 to system the operation of new and destructive modes of war-
10 fare, or for the efficient direction of secret agencies, and to pro-
11 vide for the perfection and application of the same :

1 The Congress of the Confederate States of America do enact,
2 That a bureau, in connection with the War Department, for
3 the examination, experiment and application of warlike inven-
4 tions and direction of secret agencies is hereby established, to

2

5 · consist of one chief of bureau and a board of examiners, to con-

6 sist of three members, to be composed of competent, scientific

7 and mechanical persons, whose attainments or experience may

8 qualify them for the duty. The rank of the chief of bureau and

9 of the board of examining officers to be determined by the Pres-

10 ident, who may assign officers now in service to those duties, or

11 make original appointments, as he may deem best.

1 Sec. 2. It shall be the duty of the bureau hereby organized,

2 to examine all inventions, plans and enterprises which may be of

3 value in offensive or defensive warfare, and to cause to be test-

4 ed, by actual experiment, such as may require it, and are so far

5 approved by the President or board of examining officers, as to

6 warrant the expenditure for such practical test; and whenever

7 any invention, plan or enterprise shall have been so examined

8 or approved, it shall be the duty of the bureau to provide for

9 its efficient application; and for that purpose it shall have power

10 and authority to make all necessary contracts for the construc-

11 tion or purchase of all necessary devices, materials and imple-

12 ments; and it shall be the duty of all other departments and bu-

13 reaus to answer all requisitions upon them, by the proper offi-

14 cers of the bureau of secret service, when it can be done with-

15 out serious detriment to other branches of the public service;

16 and to employ agents and experts in like manner as other depart-

17 ments and bureaus of the government; and the forms and regu-

3

18 lations of the engineer bureau, not inapplicable, shall be those
19 to be observed and conformed to by this bureau.

1   SEC. 3.   It shall be the duty of the board of examining offi-
2 cers, who shall be under the orders of the chief of bureau, to
3 examine and ascertain the merit and practicability of such in-
4 ventions, plans and secret enterprises, as may be submitted, as
5 specified in the second section, and to decide upon the qualifica-
6 tions of candidates for appointments, and the decision of a ma-
7 jority of their number shall determine the adoption or rejection,
8 subject to the approval of the President, if disapproved by the
9 chief of the bureau ; and the chief of the bureau will appoint the
10 proper persons and give the necessary orders for carrying into
11 effect the provisions of this section.   It is, however, *further*
12 *Provided*, That the President shall have the power to direct the
13 chief of bureau to carry into effect any plan or enterprise, or
14 secret service, which he may approve, and to apply, if necessary,
15 any of the secret service funds heretofore appropriated, or which
16 may be hereafter appropriated, for defraying the necessary ex-
17 penditures for carrying such plan or service into effect.

1   SEC. 4.   The chief of bureau shall have discretionary power,
2 subject to the approval of the President, when the service is un-
3 usually important, to employ secret agents for service either in
4 the Confederate States, or within the enemy's lines, or in any
5 foreign country ; and for this purpose is empowered, with the

4

6 approval of the President, to make use of any fund hereafter
7 appropriated, and, if necessary, to draw upon the secret service
8 fund already appropriated, to defray the expenses of such ser-
9 vice; and he is also authorized to organize such a system for the
10 application of the new means of warfare approved, and of secret
11 service agencies, as may tend best to secure the objects of the
12 establishment of the bureau herein provided for.

1 SEC. 5. There shall be organized, under, and in connection
2 with this bureau, a *polytechnic corps*, to consist of one chief of
3 corps, with the necessary number of commanders, captains, first
4 lieutenants and second lieutenants, to be appointed by the Pre-
5 sident, by and with the advice and consent of the Senate, or to
6 be assigned by him, and such number and grades of non-com-
7 missioned officers and men as may be necessary for the perfec-
8 tion and application of such plans and enterprises as may be ap-
9 proved, whose rations and pay shall be the same as in the cor-
10 responding grades of the engineer corps; and who shall be
11 under the control and act under the orders of the chief of bu-
12 reau, who shall receive his orders from and be under the control
13 and direction of the President.

1 SEC. 6. The officers and men of this corps shall be assigned
2 and detailed from other branches of service, upon the requisi-
3 tion of the chief of bureau, when this may be done without seri-
4 ous detriment to the service to which they belong, or recruited
5 in like manner as for other branches of the military or naval ser-
6 vice, reference being had in the assignment, detail or recruit-

5

7 ing of men, to their fitness for the particular service for which
8 they are assigned. *Provided*, that the number of commissioned
9 officers of all grades assigned, fit for duty in other branches of
10 service, shall not exceed twenty, and that the appointments of
11 officers from among persons now engaged in this service, and
12 from those not liable to, or who are unfit for active field duty,
13 shall not exceed a corresponding number; and that the number
14 of non-commissioned officers and men assigned from other ser-
15 vice, or from those liable to field duty, shall not exceed two
16 hundred.   This provision, however, shall not be construed to
17 prevent the temporary detail of men to this service, when deem-
18 ed necessary by commanders of departments; nor to prevent the
19 increase of the corps of non-commissioned officers and men by
20 the recruiting and employment of those not liable or equal to
21 field duty, or of persons outside of the limits of the Confeder-
22 ate States.
1 Sec. 7.   The chief of bureau shall be, and is hereby authorized
2 to make such contracts for the purchase of, or right to use, any
3 patented invention applicable to and valuable in this branch of
4 service, or to the Confederate States: *Provided*, That such con-
5 tract or purchase shall be subject to the approval of the Presi-
6 dent or board of examining officers, and that in the case of such
7 inventions as are intended to receive the benefits of the Act of
8 Congress, approved April 21st, 1862, giving one-half of the
9 armed vessels of the enemy which may be destroyed by any
10 new invention or contrivance, or the benefit of any Act which
11 may hereafter be passed, giving compensation for the destruction
12 of property of the enemy in similar cases, the cost of the con-
13 struction and application of such invention or contrivance in-
14 curred by the government, shall be deducted from the amount

6

15 authorized to be paid under said Act, or as authorized under
16 this Act.

1 SEC. 8. The bureau is hereby authorized to employ such clerks
2 draughtsmen and others, unfit for field duty, as may be necessary
3 for the business of the bureau, with the same pay as is received
4 by like employees of the engineer bureau, and to make such
5 other incidental disbursements as may be necessary to carry in-
6 to effect the objects of this Act; and the officers and men and
7 employees shall have the same rights and immunities and be
8 subject to the same penalties as those of other branches of ser-
9 vice in the army of the Confederate States.

1 SEC. 9. The companies and parties now irregularly organized
2 for the application of submerged or other defences, and known
3 as torpedo corps, and for the construction and use of new war-
4 like inventions or for secret service, shall be incorporated into
5 and form a part of the organization contemplated by this Act:
6 *Provided*, That in such incorporation, the terms and conditions
7 of persons heretofore organizing or joining such organizations
8 shall not be invalidated thereby: *Provided further*, That no
9 person shall be exempted from military service by reason of
10 being a member of any such organization, unless his personal
11 services are engaged in its duties.

1 SEC. 10. The valuation of public property, transportation, arms
2 and munitions of war of the enemy destroyed, and for which
3 compensation is provided in the Acts approved April 21, 1862,
4 or which may be provided in any Act which may hereafter be
5 passed, giving compensation in like cases, shall be made by the

7

6 board of examining officers, subject to the approval of the

7 President, and their award be immediately paid to the claimants

8 whose claims are approved; and the examining officers shall take

9 evidence as to the originality and priority of inventions, in

10 cases of claims for compensation, and also as to the claims of

11 different parties claiming the bounty for the same work per-

12 formed, the claimant being allowed a reasonable time to pro-

13 duce his evidence, and examination and valuation by experts be-

14 ing authorized when necessary, and the decision and award of

15 the examining board, when asked by the claimants, shall be

16 final and binding; and should it appear from the testimony that

17 the parties using any particular invention or device, in whole

18 or in part, were not the original inventors, a portion of the

19 award, to be determined by the board of examining officers,

20 shall be made to the party who shall prove his priority to the in-

21 vention; which rule shall also apply when an old invention is

22 successfully adapted to a new and valuable use. And for the

23 destruction of other property in the enemy's country, where

24 such destruction shall be considered serviceable to the cause

25 of the Confederate States, such compensation for the service

26 shall be allowed as may be adjudged equitable and just.

1 SEC. 11. When it shall be proven to the satisfaction of the

2 board of examining officers, by the evidence of patents or other-

3 wise, that the right of priority or ownership of any patented in-

4 vention is rightfully possessed, and the government has appro-

5 priated and is using such patented invention, a fair compensation

8

6   shall be awarded for such appropriation and use, the award to

7   be in proportion to the extent and value of its use to the gov-

8   ernment, such award to be determined by a majority of the

9   board of examining officers, and approved by the President.

1   SEC. 12. The operations of the corps hereby organized, shall

2   be, when in the limits of the Confederate States, under the con-

3   trol of the commander of the department where they may be

4   designed to act, as to the proper *time* and *place* for such action.

1   SEC. 13. All bounties and awards authorised to be paid under

2   the provisions of this Act, shall be paid in the currency of the

3   Confederate States, if the claimant shall so elect, in lieu of

4   bonds, as heretofore provided for in previous acts.

1   SEC. 14. It is hereby expressly declared that the right of

2   compensation for any new invention or contrivance, or the ap-

3   plication thereof, shall be in no wise invalidated by reason of

4   the inventor being in the service of the Confederate States.

1   SEC. 15. All the accounts and claims, settled and pending,

2   and all information necessary to the effective organization of

3   the bureau and service, in possession of the different depart-

4   ments, shall be turned over to the secret service bureau for

5   proper arrangement and classification, to afford the necessary

6   information for the settlement of claims and for the continu-

7   ance of the service which is now being performed; subject,

8   however, to the decision of the President, as to *what* service

9   and business of this character shall be placed under the control

10   of the secret service bureau.

NOTES

Preface

1. The research in which these men were engaged was supposedly incorporated into a book and motion picture. David Balsinger and Charles E. Sellier, Jr., *The Lincoln Conspiracy* (Los Angeles: Schick Sunn Classic Books, 1977). I am convinced that their story about Booth is not true.

2. Stanley Kimmel, *The Mad Booths of Maryland* (New York: Dover, 1969).

3. John Bakeless, *Spies of the Confederacy* (Philadelphia: Lippincott, 1970).

4. The story of Zarvona is told in more detail in William A. Tidwell, with James O. Hall and David Winfred Gaddy, *Come Retribution: The Confederate Secret Service and the Assassination of Lincoln* (Jackson: University Press of Mississippi, 1988), 134–35. It is also described in Letcher's biography by F. N. Boney, *John Letcher of Virginia* (Tuscaloosa: University of Alabama Press, 1966), but unfortunately the biography does not delve into some of Letcher's other clandestine activities.

5. Lee A. Wallace, Jr., *A Guide to Virginia Military Organizations 1861–1865* (Lynchburg: H. E. Howard, 1986), 124.

6. Men of the 47th Virginia Infantry Regiment, M-324, Compiled Service Records, Record Group 109, National Archives, Washington, D.C.

7. *Bulletin of the King and Queen County Historical Society* 24 (January 1968), unpaginated, Virginia Historical Society, Richmond.

8. J. Marshall Crawford, *Mosby and His Men* (New York: G. W. Carleton and Company, 1867), 359.

9. Otto Eisenschiml, ed., *Vermont General* (New York: The Devin-Adair Company, 1960), 305–8. See also chapter 6 for additional details.

10. In January 1992, I discussed the technical problem that the Confederates faced in trying to blow up the White House with several members of the Live Fire Division of the U.S. Army's Test and Evaluation facility at Aberdeen, Maryland. They all agreed

that, in the White House as it was constructed at that time, the task could have been accomplished by placing a charge of between twenty-five and fifty pounds of black powder inside the house.

11. Tidwell, *Come Retribution*, 416–18.

12. For authenticity of the papers, see James O. Hall, "The Dahlgren Papers," *Civil War Times Illustrated* 22 (November 1983): 30–39.

13. Since the publication of *Come Retribution*, Lincoln's personal involvement in the Dahlgren affair has been shown to be even deeper than we thought. See Joseph George, Jr., "Black Flag Warfare: Lincoln and the Raids against Richmond and Jefferson Davis," *The Pennsylvania Magazine of History and Biography* 115 (July 1991): 291–318.

Introduction: Come Retribution *Revisited*

1. See, for example, *Testimony of Sandford Conover, Dr. J. B. Merritt, and Richard Montgomery, before Military Court at Washington* (Toronto: Lovell and Gibson, 1865), a sixty-one page pamphlet probably printed at Confederate expense; and Stuart Robinson, *The Infamous Perjuries of the "Bureau of Military Justice" Exposed*, pamphlet, Rare Book Collection, Library of Congress.

2. For a modern summary of the trial of Booth's associates, see Roy Z. Chamlee, Jr., *Lincoln's Assassins* (Jefferson, N.C.: McFarland and Company, 1990).

3. Hall, "The Case of David E. George," 3–5.

4. Otto Eisenschiml, *Why Was Lincoln Murdered?* (New York: Halcyon House, 1937).

5. Allan Nevins, *The War for the Union: The Organized War to Victory 1864–1865* (New York: Charles Scribner's Sons, 1971), 326.

6. Thomas R. Turner, *Beware the People Weeping: Public Opinion and the Assassination of President Lincoln* (Baton Rouge: Louisiana State University Press, 1982); William Hanchett, *The Lincoln Murder Conspiracies* (Urbana: University of Illinois Press, 1983).

7. Hanchett, *The Lincoln Murder Conspiracies*, 181.

8. Tidwell, *Come Retribution*.

9. Frank Abial Flower, *Edwin McMasters Stanton* (1905; reprint, New York: AMS Press, 1973), 279; Ben: Perley Poore, ed., *The Conspiracy Trial for the Murder of the President*, 3 vols. (1865–66; reprint, New York: Arno Press, 1972), 1:143, 162; 2:196, 202, 206, 209, 213, 215, 216.

10. See, for example, Francis Dvornik, *Origins of Intelligence Services* (New Brunswick: Rutgers University Press, 1974); Bernard Porter, *Plots and Paranoia* (London: Unwin Hyman, 1989); David Kahn, *The Code Breakers* (London: Weidenfeld and Nicolson, 1967); Cecil B. Currey, *Code Number 72* (Englewood Cliffs, N.J.: Prentice-Hall, 1972); Bruce Norman, *Secret Warfare* (New York: Sterling, 1989); Edmund R. Thompson, ed., *Secret New England: Spies of the American Revolution* (Kennebunk, Maine: Association of Former Intelligence Officers, 1992); Alison Plowden, *The Elizabethan Secret Service* (New York: St. Martin's Press, 1991).

11. *New York Times*, December 10, 1870, reporting a speech by John Harrison Surratt delivered at the Cooper Institute on December 9, 1870, quoted in the *Surratt Society*

News, November 1979; *Record of the Trial of John H. Surratt* 2 vols. (Washington, D.C.: Government Printing Office, 1867), 2:793.

12. William Hanchett, "The Historian as Gamesman: Otto Eisenschiml, 1880–1963," *Civil War History* 36 (March 1990): 5–16.

13. William Hanchett, "Lincoln's Murder: The Simple Conspiracy Theory," *Civil War Times Illustrated* 30 (November/December 1991): 28–35, 70–71.

Chapter 1: Confederate Gold

1. The Confederate records were computed using three Confederate dollars as the value of one gold dollar.

2. Requisition Book, *Confederate States of America Records,* reel 19, Manuscript Collection, Library of Congress (hereafter cited as Pickett Papers).

3. Working with a microfilm copy, I originally read number 63 as number 65 and believed that numbers 63 and 64 were missing. The staff of the Library of Congress Manuscript Collection consulted the original document and informed me that the last form was number 63, dated March 1, 1865.

4. *Official Records of the Union and Confederate Navies in the War of the Rebellion,* 30 vols. (Washington, D.C.: Government Printing Office, 1894–1922), ser. 2, vol. 3:1090–91, 1162–63 (hereafter cited as ORN).

5. Tidwell, *Come Retribution,* 323.

6. J. P. Benjamin to J. P. Holcomb, February 24, 1864, *Southern Historical Society Papers,* 51 vols. (1879; reprint, Millwood, N.Y.: Kraus, 1977), 7:99.

7. Rev. Stephen F. Cameron, "Notes for 'A History of the Confederate Secret Service,'" Manuscript Collection, Museum of the Confederacy, Richmond.

8. This is not a particularly meaningful figure because it appears to contain some figures expressed in gold dollars and some in Confederate dollars with no indication of the difference.

9. Note, reel 18, Pickett Papers.

10. Ledger (listing vouchers submitted by persons in the Confederate War Department under various categories of expenditure, such as "Incidental and Contingent"), chap. 9, vol. 43:291–99, RG 109.

11. Charles W. Ramsdell, ed., *Laws and Joint Resolutions of the Last Session of the Confederate Congress (November 1864–March 18, 1865) Together With the Secret Acts of the Previous Congresses* (Durham: Duke University Press, 1941), 66–72.

12. *Register of Acts of the Confederate States of America,* George Washington Flowers Memorial Collection, William R. Perkins Library, Duke University, Durham, North Carolina.

13. James M. Matthews, ed., *Statutes at Large of the Provisional Government of the Confederate States of America* (Richmond, 1864) 65, found in the William R. Perkins Library.

14. Ibid., 124; James M. Matthews, ed., *Public Laws of the Confederate States of America Passed at First Session of Congress, 1863* (Richmond, 1863), 96, found in the William R. Perkins Library; Act 4, *Register of Acts CSA.*

15. Ledger, Pickett Papers, reel 19.

Chapter 2: The Organization of Secret Service

1. Telegrams Received by the U.S. War Department, M-473, reel 118, frame 0724, RG 107, National Archives.

2. Thomas A. Harris, Compiled Service Record, RG 109. See chapter 5 for additional information on the ship-burning operation.

3. Milligan to Davis, December 26, 1861, in Lynda Lasswell Crist and Mary Seaton Dix, eds., *The Papers of Jefferson Davis*, vol. 7 (Baton Rouge: Louisiana State University Press, 1992), 444.

4. Ledger, chap. 9, vol. 43:291–99, RG 109.

5. *The War of the Rebellion: A Compilation of the Official Records of the Union and Confederate Armies*, 128 vols. (Washington, D.C.: Government Printing Office, 1880–1901), ser. 4, vol. 3:741 (hereafter cited as *OR*).

6. "List of prisoners received at Old Capital Prison since the 1st of March 1861," *OR*, ser. 2, vol. 2:238; "List of Prisoners Confined in the Old Capital Prison, Washington, D.C., March 17, 1862, ibid., 272; Thomas Jordan to J. P. Benjamin, October 29, 1861, ibid., 564; "Copies of Intercepted Letters Sent Out of the Capitol Prison by Mrs. Augusta Hewitt Morris," February 27, 1862, ibid., 1348–51; Alfred Cridge to Baker, June 19, 1863, Office of the Judge Advocate General, Turner-Baker Papers, no. 1528, RG 94, National Archives.

7. Thomas H. Hines Papers, file 46M97, Manuscript Collection, University of Kentucky Library, Lexington.

8. John W. Headley, *Confederate Operations in Canada and New York* (New York: Neale Publishing Company, 1906), 210; Tidwell, *Come Retribution*, 335–36.

9. Beverly Kennon to J. A. Seddon, December 25, 1864, Telegrams Received by the Confederate Secretary of War, M-618, reel 19, frames 120–21, National Archives.

10. Thomas Nelson Conrad to General [Braxton Bragg], April 25, 1864, with endorsements, Jefferson Davis Papers, William R. Perkins Library.

11. Allan Pinkerton, *The Spy of the Rebellion* (New York: G. W. Carlton and Company, 1883), 414–28.

12. James Arthur Lyon Fremantle, *The Fremantle Diary*, ed. Walter Lord (Boston: Little Brown and Company, 1954), 157, 160.

13. A&IG Report on Confederate Signal Corps, December 21, 1864, Letters Received by the Confederate Secretary of War, M-437, reel 151, RG 109.

14. Paragraph xxx, Special Order 18, January 23, 1865, Letters Received by the Confederate Adjutant and Inspector General, 1861–65, M-474, reel 164, frame 0094, RG 109.

15. Receipt signed by Alexander W. Weddell, January 28, 1865, reel 18, Pickett Papers.

16. Henry Thomas Harrison, Compiled Service Record, RG 109.

17. David Winfred Gaddy, "John Williamson Palmer: Confederate Agent," *Maryland Historical Magazine* 83 (Summer 1988): 98–110.

18. Maury to Cooper, May 26, 1864; "Columbia 26" to Cooper, May 26, 1864; Smith to Cooper, March 26, 1865, Telegrams Received by the A&IG Office, RG 109.

19. In the Gilbert and Sullivan operetta *The Mikado*, the character PooBah holds all of the key jobs in the Mikado's court, including that of "Lord High Everything Else."

20. A recent biography of General Winder gives some useful detail on his early life but, unfortunately, has very little to say about his wartime responsibilities. Arch Frederic Blakey, *General John H. Winder C.S.A.* (Gainesville: University of Florida Press, 1990).

21. John H. Winder Papers, no. 915, Manuscript Department, University of North Carolina Library, Chapel Hill. Winder also held a commission as colonel in the Confederate regular army. Richard P. Weinert, Jr., *The Confederate Regular Army* (Shippensburg, Pa.: White Mane, 1991).

22. Rosters of personnel of Department of Henrico, Records of the Commissioner General of Prisons, vol. 54:27–65, RG 249, National Archives.

23. Account book of Maj. John H. Parkhill, Records of the Quartermaster General's Department, chap. 5, vol. 248½, RG 109.

24. W. Sidney Winder, Compiled Service Record, RG 109.

25. Tidwell, *Come Retribution*, 394–95.

26. Rives to Colonel Stevens, May 15, 1864, Files of Charles T. Mason, Manuscript Collection, Virginia Historical Society.

27. Copy of the Joint Resolution of Confederate Congress directing an award to McDaniel and Ewing for sinking USS *Cairo*, Manuscript No. 24335, Isaac Hammond Collection, Virginia State Library, Richmond; John C. Wideman, *The Sinking of the USS Cairo* (Jackson: University Press of Mississippi, 1993). The latter is an excellent account of McDaniel's relationship with the Confederate secret service.

28. J. Thomas Sharf, *History of the Confederate States Navy* (1887; reprint, Catasauqua, Pa.: The Fairfax Press, 1977).

29. "Company A, Secret Service," Compiled Service Records, RG 109.

30. Norris to Seddon, March 8, 1864, Letters Received by the Confederate Secretary of War, M-437, reel 105, RG 109.

31. *New York Times*, May 18, 1865. During World War II, the U.S. Office of Strategic Services published a manual on sabotage devices that included a detailed description of Courtney's bomb without using his name. The OSS also had a kit for issuance to agents that would enable the user to camouflage the bomb to match the particular kind of coal that it was to be mixed with. H. Keith Melton, *OSS Special Weapons and Equipment* (New York: Sterling, 1991), 70–71.

32. See, for example, Poore, *The Conspiracy Trial for the Murder of the President* 3:424–33.

33. Jerry O. Potter, *The Sultana Tragedy* (Gretna, La.: Pelican, 1992), 154.

34. Letcher's activities are reconstructed from receipts and notes in his papers. Letcher Papers, Marshall Research Foundation, Virginia Military Institute, Lexington; James I. Robertson, ed., *Proceedings of the Advisory Council of the State of Virginia* (Richmond: Virginia State Library, 1977), 65–66.

35. Rev. Stephen F. Cameron, manuscript notes for "History of the Confederate Secret Service," Museum of the Confederacy, Richmond, Virginia. Based on internal evidence, the manuscript was compiled at about the time of the trial of John H. Surratt in 1867. It is evident that at the time of writing the author was in correspondence with Jacob Thompson and other figures active in the Confederate operations in Canada.

Chapter 3: The Greenhow Organization

1. See, for example, Ishbel Ross, *Rebel Rose* (New York: Harper and Brothers, 1954); and Rose O'Neal Greenhow, *My Imprisonment and the First Year of Abolition Rule at Washington* (London: Richard Bentley, 1863), a copy in the Rare Book Collection, Library of Congress; and *Records Concerning the Conduct and Loyalty of Army Officers, War Department Employees, and Citizens During the Civil War*, box 1, RG 107.

2. Crist and Dix, eds., *The Papers of Jefferson Davis* 6:13–14.

3. Mallory to Mrs. Clay, October 28, 1864, Clement C. Clay Manuscripts, William R. Perkins Library.

4. Ross, *Rebel Rose*, 12–17; Henry Merritt Wriston, *Executive Agents in American Foreign Relations* (Gloucester, Mass.: Peter Smith, 1967), 835; Lynda Lasswell Crist and Mary Seaton Dix, eds., *The Papers of Jefferson Davis*, vol. 5 (Baton Rouge: Louisiana State Univ. Press, 1985), 358.

5. Letcher to Greenlee Davison, February 11, 1861, Letcher Papers; Robertson, ed., *Proceedings*, 65–66, 75; Jordan to Letcher, May 8, 1861, Letcher Papers.

6. Elizabeth Lindsay Lomax, *Leaves from an Old Washington Diary* (New York: E.P. Dutton and Company, 1943), 149–50.

7. Thomas Jordan to J. P. Benjamin, October 29, 1861, *OR*, ser. 2, vol. 2:564–65.

8. Greenhow, *My Imprisonment*.

9. Ibid., 42, 57.

10. Reports written by Rose Greenhow and turned over to the War Department by Allan Pinkerton, *Records Concerning the Conduct and Loyalty of Army Officers, War Department Employees, and Citizens During the Civil War*, box 1, RG 107.

11. James Chesnut, Jr., former senator from South Carolina and husband of diarist Mary Chesnut, joined General Beauregard's headquarters on June 13, 1861. He later served in South Carolina, as a colonel on Jefferson Davis's staff in Richmond and as a brigadier general commanding South Carolina reserve forces.

12. Alfred Roman, *The Military Operations of General Beauregard*, (New York: Harper and Brothers, 1884), 89. This book was apparently written with much direct help from General Beauregard.

13. This paper, which gives delivery instructions for Greenhow's message to General Beauregard, is in the possession of the author. It was acquired from a dealer who did not know its provenance.

14. Ruggles was appointed by Governor Letcher of Virginia to command the defenses of Virginia from Mount Vernon to the mouth of the Rappahannock. In a bureaucratic muddle, he was commissioned as a brigadier general, reduced to colonel, and then reinstated as a brigadier general. He took command on April 22, 1861, and continued in command until June 5, 1861, when Confederate brigadier general Theophilus H. Holmes was assigned by the Confederate authorities to take over the command of the lower Potomac area. Holmes took a number of troops from the area to join General Beauregard's force at Manassas while Ruggles continued to tend to the day-to-day operations in the Potomac area.

15. Meriwether Lewis, "The Military Orders of Daniel Ruggles: Department of Fredericksburg, April 22–June 5, 1861," *The Virginia Magazine of History and Biography* 69 (April 1961): 149–80.

16. *The R.O.T. C. Manual Cavalry* (Washington, D.C.: National Service Publishing Company, 1933), 361.

17. George Donnellan, Compiled Service Record, RG 109.

18. Confederate Correspondence captured with George Dent of Charles County, Maryland, in 1861, *Proceedings of the Commission Relating to Prisoners of State 1862,* RG 59, National Archives. Some reports were sent to the Confederate army in northern Virginia and relayed on to Richmond; other reports appear to have been sent to Richmond directly.

19. See, for example, Thomas A. Jones, *J. Wilkes Booth* (Chicago: Laird and Lee, 1893).

20. Bowie described his military career in several letters to Gen. Francis H. Smith, the superintendent of the Virginia Military Institute. See especially Bowie to Smith, September 11, 1863, Bowie file, Alumni Archives, Preston Library, Virginia Military Institute, Lexington. Lafayette C. Baker, *History of the United States Secret Service* (Philadelphia: L. C. Baker, 1867), 189–90. A&IG notes concerning charges against Walter Bowie, Confederate Adjutant and Inspector General Files, 236-B-1863, November 4, 1863, and 2324-S-1863, November 6, 1863, chap. 1, vol. 59, RG 109.

21. John W. Munson, *Reminiscences of a Mosby Guerrilla* (1906; reprint, Washington, D.C.: Zenger, 1983), 231–32.

22. *Allen Bowie Davis Papers,* MS 1755, Maryland Historical Society, Baltimore. This is a short diary kept by Walter Weems Bowie during January and February 1863.

23. Baker, *History of the Secret Service,* 181–85.

24. From the content of the letter it is clear that the intended recipient was General Lee. Unaddressed letter signed "B[owie]," April 27, 1864, Charles V. Venable Papers, Southern Historical Collection, University of North Carolina Library, Chapel Hill.

25. Maj. John Scott, *Partisan Life With Col. John S. Mosby* (New York: Harper and Brothers, 1867), 306.

26. Thomas Nelson Conrad, *Confederate Spy* (New York: J. S. Ogilvie Publishing Company, 1892), 70; idem, *Rebel Scout* (Washington, D.C.: National Publishing Company, 1904), 119.

27. Lieutenant Cawood was commander of the Secret Line camp in King George County on the banks of the Potomac River. Conrad to Seddon, September 16, 1864, Letters Received by the Confederate Secretary of War, 1861–65, M-437, reel 124, frame 275, RG 109.

28. William Gilmore Beymer, *On Hazardous Service* (New York: Harper and Brothers, 1912), 142.

29. *Come Retribution* discussed the development of the military doctrine of partisan warfare which charged the partisans "to provide security for the main army on the march, protect the main army's encampment or base area, reconnoiter the countryside and the enemy, raid enemy posts and convoys, and form ambushes" (132–33). Readers will recall that Mosby captured several Union generals during the war and will ask how that differs from capturing the governor of Maryland. The generals were captured in the theater of operations, and their absence would affect the command structure of the Union army in the field; the governor was not in the theater of operations, and his presence or absence would not affect the operations of the Union army.

30. James Wiltshire, *Baltimore American,* July 1, 1900.

31. This was a location on the Maryland side of the Potomac frequently used as a destination for clandestine crossings of the Potomac. It was probably near the home of Confederate Signal Corps agent Thomas A. Jones.

32. Unfortunately, most of the issues of the *Port Tobacco Times* are missing for this period; but the paper was usually published on Thursdays, and the most recent issue would have appeared on September 29, 1864.

33. James J. Williamson, *Mosby's Rangers* (1898; reprint, New York: Time-Life Books, 1981), 234.

34. John S. Mosby, *The Memoirs of Colonel John S. Mosby*, ed. Charles Wells Russell (1917; reprint, Millwood, N.Y.: Kraus, 1981), 374.

35. Williamson, *Mosby's Rangers*, 233.

36. Letter no. 11, to mother from Mary Dent Washington, September 27, 1864, Liberty Plantation, Historical Society of the Northern Neck of Virginia, Montross. This letter suggests that Bowie was a regular visitor during his pre-Mosby days.

37. Scott, *Partisan Life*, 310–11.

38. Bowie's decision to use only part of his force probably accounted for the failure of Mrs. Washington's boarders to show up for breakfast on September 27—they had either gone with Bowie or returned to Mosby's base area.

39. James Wiltshire, *Baltimore American*, July 1, 1900.

40. Scott, *Partisan Life*, 310–15.

Chapter 4: Sage and the Destructionists

1. Military Order of the Loyal Legion of the United States (MOLLUS), U.S. Army Military History Institute, Carlisle Barracks, Pennsylvania.

2. Robertson, ed., *Proceedings*, xi–xxiii.

3. Richard L. Maury, *A Brief Sketch of the Work of Mathew Fontaine Maury* (Richmond: Whittet and Shepperson, 1915), 6–8. The author was Maury's son, who took part in the experiment.

4. Joseph T. Durkin, S.J., *Confederate Navy Chief: Stephen R. Mallory* (Columbia: University of South Carolina Press, 1987), 63–64.

5. Ibid., 157–58.

6. Ibid., 192.

7. Much of the information about Sage comes from a series of documents that Sage turned over the United States Navy many years after the Civil War, when the navy was assembling historical documents pertaining to the war. B. J. Sage Papers, M-1091, reel 45, RG 45, National Archives.

8. Diary entry for August 15, 1864, Mathew Fontaine Maury Papers, Manuscript Collection, Library of Congress.

9. J. Thomas Scharf, *History of the Confederate States Navy*, 54–56; OR, ser. 1, vol. 5:796.

10. Scharf, *History of the Confederate States Navy*, 78–82, 92–93.

11. The Union government did put the first privateer crews captured into irons and accuse them of piracy, but after appropriate retaliation was threatened against Union prisoners of war, the policy was abandoned, and captured privateer crewmen were treated as prisoners of war.

12. Sage letter to "Government," July 22, 1861, B. J. Sage Papers, M-1091, reel 45, RG 45.

13. Paul H. Silverstone, *Warships of the Civil War Navies* (Annapolis: Naval Institute Press, 1989), 41.

14. Extract of notes on "Capture of Steamer St. Nicholas" by George N. Hollins, Letcher Papers; typescript draft of undated and unsigned article describing Zarvona's career and capture; John Letcher, "Col. Richard Thomas Zarvona," *Confederate Veteran* 22 (September 1914): 418.

15. William Morrison Robinson, Jr., *The Confederate Privateers* (1928; reprint, Columbia: University of South Carolina Press, 1990), 319–42.

16. S. A. Mallory to Jefferson Davis, January 6, 1862, *ORN*, ser. 2, vol. 2:124–25.

17. Robinson, *Confederate Privateers*, 322.

18. Note, January 1863, B. J. Sage Papers, M-1091, reel 45, RG 45.

19. James M. Mathews, ed., *Public Laws of the Confederate States of America Passed at First Session of Congress* (Richmond, 1863), Rare Book Room, Duke University Library, Durham, North Carolina.

20. Randolph endorsement of G. Moxley Sorrel to Rains, May 11, 1862, OR, ser. 1, vol. 4, 3:509–10.

21. W. Davis Waters, "Deception in the Art of War: Gabriel Rains, Torpedo Specialist of the Confederacy," *The North Carolina Historical Review* 66 (January 1989): 25–60.

22. Jefferson County, now part of West Virginia, lies in the Shenandoah Valley where the Shenandoah joins the Potomac. Harpers Ferry and Charles Town are in this county, and the Baltimore and Ohio Railroad ran through the county on the route between Wheeling and Baltimore.

23. J. Y. Beall to Maj. William S. Barton, April 24, 1864, Letters Received by the Confederate Secretary of War, RG 109.

24. War Department and Department of Henrico passes to E. G. Lee, April 3, 1863, William N. Pendleton Papers, no. 1466, Southern Historical Collection.

25. Ludwell Lee Montague, *Gloucester County in the Civil War* (Gloucester, Va.: De-Hardit Press, 1965), 34–35.

26. Robinson, *Confederate Privateers*, 330.

27. Silverstone, *Warships of the Civil War Navies*, 144.

28. Robinson, *Confederate Privateers*, 331–34.

29. Traveling abroad would include travel outside of the Confederate states into the territory of the Northern states.

30. John Yates Beall to William S. Barton, April 26, 1864, Letters Received by the Confederate Secretary of War, RG 109. In this letter Beall discussed irregular operations in the Chesapeake area and in the Great Lakes and said, "Recently Congress turned over all such enterprises to your Bureau." Beall also said that the secretary of state had told him that he did not need a Letter of Marque as "an order from your [Barton's] department to an officer [of] this command to seize by stratagem or force a vessel & use her to injure the enemy was all sufficient for my purpose."

31. A&IG Special Order 46½, February 26, 1864, Compilation of Special Orders, Library, Reading Room, National Archives.

32. Baker, *History of the United States Secret Service*, 185–90.

33. See chapter 3. The operations of Bowie's group may be the foundation for the incorrect stories that had Walter Bowie of Upper Marlboro engaged in guerrilla operations in southern Maryland.

34. B. J. Sage, *Organization of Private Warfare* (undated pamphlet), B. J. Sage Papers, reel 45, RG 45.

35. The Walter Bowie from V.M.I., for example, might have been one of those appointed as an acting master without pay.

36. An early date for the term "strategic corps" is established by a document concerning Thomas F. Harney, who was assigned to a "strategic corps" in Mississippi. He signed a receipt for a horse at Brandon, Mississippi, on July 16, 1863. Thomas F. Harney, unfiled slips, Compiled Service Record, RG 109.

37. A. L. Rives to Gen. E. K. Smith, March 20, 1863, *ORN*, ser. 1, vol. 26:191.

38. G. J. Rains to B. J. Sage, October 5, 1863, B. J. Sage Papers, M-1091, reel 45, frame 0823, RG 45.

39. Tidwell, *Come Retribution*, 178–81.

40. W. R. Boggs to Gen. Richard Taylor, December 12. 1863, *OR*, ser. 1, vol. 26, 2:501.

41. General Order 185, U.S. Mississippi Squadron, March 221, 1864, *ORN*, ser. 1, vol. 26:191–92.

42. Sage to Maury, September 11, 1864, B. J. Sage Papers, M-1091, reel 45, RG 45.

43. U.S. consul Halifax to secretary of state, December 13, 1864, Consular Despatches, T-469, reel 10, RG 59; Poore, ed., *The Conspiracy Trial for the Murder of the President* 1:405–7; Williamson D. Oldham to Jefferson Davis, February 11, 1865, Thomas A. Harris, Compiled Service Record, RG 109.

Chapter 5: The Confederate Secret Service in Canada

1. Robert E. Lee, *The Wartime Papers of R. E. Lee*, ed. Clifford Dowdey and Louis H. Manarin (New York: Bramhall House for the Virginia Civil War Commission, 1961), 410–12.

2. Ibid., 437–38.

3. This point is sometimes missed by readers of Lee's letters. Another classic example of a "position paper" is Lee's letter of January 11, 1865, to Andrew Hunter of the Virginia Senate in which Lee stated a position calculated to cause support for the enlistment of slaves in the Confederate army in return for their emancipation. The letter is carefully crafted to take account of the various negative views and prejudices held by Confederate legislators and to present the positive arguments in such a way as to answer expected objections. Lee may or may not have believed everything that he said, but the letter had a clear objective other than self-confession.

4. Lee, *Wartime Papers*, 507–9.

5. Tidwell, *Come Retribution*, 182.

6. Haskell M. Monroe, Jr., and James T. McIntosh, eds., *The Papers of Jefferson Davis*, vol. 1 (Baton Rouge: Louisiana State University Press, 1971), lxv.

7. Ibid. 2:142–59.

8. These family connections were pieced together from a number of genealogical sources such as Helen Hawes Hudgins, *The Richard Hawes Family of Kentucky* (Franklin, Tenn.: Privately printed, 1986); Charlotte Coleman Burt, *Coleman Lineage of Early America,* typescript, Kentucky Historical Society, Frankfort; U.S. Military Academy Archives, West Point; various census records; and other material in the University of Kentucky Library and in the Virginia Historical Society.

9. H. Levin, *The Lawyers and Lawmakers of Kentucky* (Chicago: Lewis Publishing Company, 1897), 754–57.

10. This and other information about Cleary's activities before going to Canada in 1864 is taken from Cleary's diary, which was microfilmed in June 1961 by the University of Kentucky. The current location of the original diary is not known.

11. Richard Hawes to J. A. Seddon, Confederate Secretary of War, December 22, 1862, requesting "passports" to facilitate movement of the members of the provisional government within Confederate lines. Letters Received by the Confederate Secretary of War, M-437, roll 97, frames 0567–70, RG 109.

12. The Flag of Truce boats traveled between Union-controlled Fort Monroe at the mouth of the James River and City Point on the south side of the James River and between Richmond and City Point. Prisoners of war and other personnel were exchanged via this route, which was under the jurisdiction of the commissioners on exchange of prisoners of war. Robert Ould was the Confederate commissioner. A limited amount of mail could be exchanged, more or less as a favor to the commissioners.

13. Albert G. Mackey, *Encyclopedia of Freemasonry* (Philadelphia: McClure Publishing Company, 1917).

14. Tidwell, *Come Retribution,* 182–84.

15. The Confederate commissioner in Canada, Jacob Thompson, commented on Holt's report, saying, "the number of [the Sons of Liberty] was large, but not so great as Mr. Holt, in his official report, represented it to be." J. Thompson to J. P. Benjamin, December 3, 1864, *OR,* ser. 1, vol. 43, 2:930.

16. Ben Pitman, *The Trials for Treason at Indianapolis* (Cincinnati: Moore, Wilstach and Baldwin, 1865). This volume contains a transcript of the testimony of the witnesses at the trial held in September 1864, the text of a number of documents describing the ritual of the Order of American Knights, the text of Judge Advocate General Joseph Holt's report on the order dated October 8, 1864, and other material.

17. See, for example, Robert H. Abzug, "The Copperheads: Historical Approaches to Civil War Dissent in the Midwest," *Indiana Magazine of History* 66, 1 (1970): 40–55; Mark Neely, Jr., ed., "Treason in Indiana," *Lincoln Lore* no. 1632 (February 1974); Emma Lou Thornbrough, *Indiana in the Civil War Era 1850–1880* (Indianapolis: Indiana Historical Bureau and Indiana Historical Society, 1965), 180–224.

18. Frank L. Klement, *Dark Lanterns* (Baton Rouge: Louisiana State University Press, 1984).

19. One of the best balanced statements of the modern historians is Gilbert R. Treadway, *Democratic Opposition to the Lincoln Administration in Indiana* (Indianapolis: Indiana Historical Bureau, 1973; vol. 48 of the Indiana Historical Collection). See especially "Critical Essay and Conclusions," 265–82.

20. See, for example, Meriwether Stuart, "Operation Sanders," *The Virginia Magazine of History and Biography* 81 (April 1973): 158–99; Randall A. Haines, "The Revolution-ist Charged with Complicity in Lincoln's Death," *Surratt Courier* 13 (September 1988): 5–8; Anna Virginia Parker, *The Sanders Family of Grass Hills* (Madison, Ind.: Coleman Printing Company, 1966).

21. Most authorities give Sanders's birthdate as February 27, 1812, but family infor-mation gives the date as February 21, and February 27 may have originated from a misprint of February 21.

22. Parker, *Sanders Family*, 37–44.

23. *Returns of the Corps of Engineers, April 1832–December 1916*, Department of the Army, Records of the Adjutant General's Office, 1780s–1917, M851, rolls 1 and 2, RG 94.

24. Allan Nevins, *Ordeal of the Union* (New York: Charles Scribner's Sons, 1947), 6.

25. Amos Aschback Ettinger, *The Mission to Spain of Pierre Soule 1853-1855* (New Haven: Yale University Press, 1932), 1–34, 171–73; William Ault, "Eisenschiml's Ques-tion" (unpublished manuscript), Illinois Historical Library, Springfield.

26. Robert C. Binkley, *Realism and Nationalism, 1852–1871* (New York: Harper and Brothers, 1935), 134–39.

27. Indicating the extent of Sanders's contacts in leading political circles in Britain, Walmsley later introduced Sanders to Richard Cobden, the political reformer. It is well to remember that in 1864 England still ruled in Canada and that Sanders's British con-nections may have been useful to him while he was operating in Canada. Much of the information on Soule's and Sanders's activities in Europe comes from Ettinger, *Mission to Spain*, 316–38; see also Binkley, 134–39.

28. George N. Sanders to "People of France," London, October 4, 1854, George N. Sanders Papers, RG 109; T. M. Armstrong, *The Biographical Encyclopedia of Kentucky* (Cincinnati: T. M. Armstrong, 1875), 2:538–41; Ettinger, *Mission to Spain*, 316–38.

29. Ettinger, *Mission to Spain*, 363–64.

30. Mary Ann Gentry, *A History of Carroll County, Kentucky* (Madison, Ind.: Coleman Printing Company, 1984), 24–25.

31. The article was reprinted in the Petersburg, Virginia, *Daily Express* on January 17, 1862.

32. George N. Sanders to Jefferson Davis, March 7, 1865, in *New York Herald*, July 8, 1865.

33. Roman, *The Military Operations of General Beauregard*, 176–79. Beauregard's pro-posal was to withdraw a number of troops from each army of the Confederacy to reinforce the army defending Atlanta, inasmuch as he regarded Atlanta as the main and most dangerous objective of the Union armies. Pierre Soule to Remy, March 31, 1864, Manuscript Collection, William R. Perkins Library.

34. Dispatches from U.S. Consuls in Halifax to Secretary of State, T-469, reel 1, RG 59. According to a letter Tucker wrote to Jefferson Davis on August 25, 1861, Davis had been friendly with Tucker in previous years. Crist and Dix, eds. *The Papers of Jefferson Davis* 7:309.

35. The existence of Davis is well established from testimony in the trial of Booth's as-sociates and from entries in the Montreal City Directory, but his first name was given in neither place. He remains unidentified. But in October 1864, when John Wilkes

Booth opened an account in a Montreal bank, he deposited $300 in gold received from Davis. *Mackay's Montreal Directory for 1864–65* (Montreal: John Lovell, 1864).

36. The Confederates had other interests in Canada besides the operation with the Copperheads and had developed a secret service apparatus to take care of those interests.

37. Cleary diary entry, February 22, 1864.

38. James S. Ramage's *Rebel Raider, the Life of General John Hunt Morgan* (Lexington: University Press of Kentucky, 1986) devotes a chapter to Morgan's imprisonment (183–98). The Confederates were guarded by both military and civilian guards and the overlap of jurisdiction provided ample opportunities for clandestine manipulation of events to favor the prisoners.

39. A Union cavalry raid on Richmond in late February and early March 1864 was interpreted by the Confederacy as designed to capture or kill members of the Confederate government and free Union prisoners of war in the Richmond area. It caused the Confederates to rethink some of their attitudes about clandestine operations against the North.

40. Thomas H. Hines Papers, University of Kentucky Library.

41. If "Col. S——" could be identified, it would tell us a good bit about how the mission to Canada was being planned. One possibility is Philip Peyton Slaughter of the VMI class of 1857, formerly colonel of the 56th Virginia Infantry Regiment. He had been seriously wounded at Chancellorsville and during the latter part of the war was employed as an assistant to Robert Ould, commissioner on exchange of prisoners of war. Another possibility is that Pierre Soule was working for Jefferson Davis with a secret service rank of colonel. After the war, Soule claimed to have done secret work for Davis and to have carried the secret service rank of brigadier general.

42. Alexander F. Robertson, *Alexander Hugh Holmes Stuart, 1807–1891* (Richmond: William Byrd Press, 1925), 206–8. Stuart apparently misremembered the nature of the money allocated to the project. Three million pounds would have involved over $14.5 million in gold. Later $1 million in gold was allocated to the project, and this was counted as being $3 million in Confederate dollars. The CS$3 million is probably the figure that Benjamin used in talking to Stuart.

43. Cleary diary entry, April 18, 1864.

44. The dates and amounts of money given to Thompson are from the Confederate States of America Secret Service Account Book, Chicago Historical Society.

45. Bennett has not been identified. A James A. Barrett was identified as the grand commander of the Order of American Knights in Missouri. Possibly Thompson meant "Barrett" instead of "Bennett," or the name might have been mistranscribed. There was also a J. F. Bullitt, the grand commander of the order in Kentucky, whose name might be confused with Bennett. Clement L. Vallandigham, former congressman and candidate for governor of Ohio, was supposed to be the supreme commander of the order in the United States. Pitman, *The Trials for Treason at Indianapolis*, 24, 325.

46. Shortly after the date of Thompson's report, John Wilkes Booth took on the mission of capturing Abraham Lincoln.

47. Rev. Stephen F. Cameron, manuscript notes for "History of the Confederate Secret Service." Cameron was an Episcopal priest who worked with the Confederates in Canada.

48. On December 3, 1864, Thompson wrote to Benjamin, "Several times I have attempted to send you communications, but I have no assurance that any one of them has been received." Given the amount of correspondence that did get through between Canada and Richmond between June and December 1864, it is possible that Thompson was blaming circumstances to excuse his failure to keep Richmond informed. OR, ser. 1, vol. 43, 2:930–36.

49. Oscar A. Kinchen, *Confederate Operations in Canada and the North* (North Quincy, Mass.: The Christopher Publishing House, 1970); Robin Winks, *Canada and the United States: the Civil War Years* (1960; reprint, Lanham, Md.: University Press of America, 1988), 278.

50. Jacob Thompson to Clement C. Clay, June 9, 1864, Cameron Manuscript, Museum of the Confederacy; Clement C. Clay to Judah Benjamin, June 17, 1864, Clement C. Clay Papers, Duke University Library; Clement C. Clay to Beverly Tucker, October 14, 1864, Clement C. Clay Papers, National Archives.

51. This is clandestine jargon to indicate somebody who acts for somebody else to protect the identity of the initiator of the action.

52. Mason Philip Smith, *Confederates Downeast* (Portland, Maine: Provincial Press, 1985), tells the story of this raid and gives good information on the participants. Unfortunately, the author accepts Jones's story, just as Holt did.

53. Files of Investigations by Levi C. Turner and Lafayette C. Baker, 1861–1866, roll 1223, file 4026, RG 110, National Archives.

54. Effie Ellsler Westin, ed., *The Stage Memories of John A. Ellsler* (Cleveland: Rowfant Club, 1950).

55. Cordial Crane to General Stanton, July 26, 1865, Letters Received by the Secretary of War, M-599, reel 3, frame 1053, RG 107.

56. Asia Booth Clark, *The Unlocked Book* (New York: Arno Press, 1977), 116–17.

57. Kimmel, *The Mad Booths of Maryland,* 168.

58. Pitman, *Trials for Treason at Indianapolis,* 97–103; J. Thompson to J. P. Benjamin, December 3, 1864, says, "The day on which the great movement was to be made become known to Mr. McDonald, candidate for Governor of Indiana, and believing that it would mar his prospects for election unless prevented, he threatened to expose all parties engaged unless the project was abandoned." OR, ser. 1, vol. 43, 2:931.

59. Headley, *Confederate Operations.*

60. An inner circle of the Order of American Knights was called the Sons of Liberty, but sometimes the name was applied to the overall organization.

61. Headley, *Confederate Operations,* 227–30.

62. Clay to Benjamin, September 12, 1864, *Southern Historical Society Papers* 7 (1879): 338–43.

63. Tidwell, *Come Retribution,* 283–88.

64. Headley, *Confederate Operations,* 231–40; Kinchen, *Operations in Canada and the North,* 104–16.

65. Tidwell, *Come Retribution,* 265, 328–29, 333–34.

66. Accompanied by P. C. Martin, the principal Confederate secret service agent in Montreal from pre-Thompson days, Booth deposited money in the Ontario Bank on

October 27, 1864, including the $300 in gold. This was brought out in the testimony of bank teller Robert Campbell at the trial of Booth's associates on May 20, 1865.

67. The ship containing the wardrobe was sunk in the St. Lawrence River, and Martin drowned. The wardrobe was recovered from the wreck in 1865, after the assassination. U.S. consul, Quebec, to secretary of state, series of reports 1864–65, Consular Despatches, RG 59.

68. Tidwell, *Come Retribution,* 328–35.

69. Special Orders No. 193, paragraph xxxi, orders Martin and Headley to report to Benjamin "for such duty as he may assign." August 16, 1864, A&IG's Office, Richmond, Confederate A&IG Special Orders, Library, Reading Room, National Archives).

70. Tidwell, *Come Retribution,* 405–8.

71. For a discussion of the nature of "Greek Fire" and its uses in the Civil War, see Arthur Sharp, "The Spirit of Christianity? Greek Fire," *Civil War Times Illustrated* 23 (September 1988): 32–37. Headley, *Confederate Operations,* 274–77.

72. Ibid., 301–7; Kinchen, *Operations in Canada and the North,* 194.

73. Kimmel, in *The Mad Booths of Maryland,* discussed this story (366n66) and Otto Eisenschiml mentioned it briefly in the text of *Why Was Lincoln Murdered,* 374–76. Beall's friends tried to scotch the story. *Confederate Veteran* 35 (September 1927): 337–39.

74. Statement of the colored troops in the service of the United States, October 31, 1863, *OR,* ser. 3, vol. 3:1115.

75. Poore, ed., *The Conspiracy Trial for the Murder of the President* 2:237–40.

76. Ibid.

77. U.S. House of Representatives, *Committee on the Assassination of Lincoln, Report No. 104,* 39th Cong., July 1866, 37.

78. Tidwell, *Come Retribution,* 418–21.

79. Hanchett, *The Lincoln Murder Conspiracies,* 77–80.

80. Ibid.; F. A. St. Lawrence, *Testimony of Sandford Conover, Dr. J. B. Merritt, and Richard Montgomery* (Toronto: Lovell and Gibson, 1865).

81. Daniels has not been identified. In view of Charles A. Dunham's occasional practice of using alias B to accuse himself of doing what he had done under alias A, Daniels's letter was compared to known samples of Dunham's handwriting, but no similarity was apparent.

82. Letters Received by the Office of the Judge Advocate General (Army), M-599, reel 3, RG 153, National Archives.

83. In the 1950s, Joseph E. Missemer of San Diego engaged in a massive research effort to document the life story of Charles A. Dunham. He had assembled several thousand typed pages of notes, including copies and transcriptions of documents, by the time of his death in 1963. The information in this paragraph and many of the following paragraphs was derived from Missemer's unpaginated notes. For example, he quotes at length from a pamphlet published in November 1856 by Caleb Mosher detailing Dunham's involvement in a swindle targeted against relatives of Mosher. Missemer Notes, U.S. National Park Service Museum at Ford's Theater, Washington, D.C.

84. Ibid.

85. This episode is covered by a number of newspaper clippings transcribed by Missemer and a letter from Dunham to Secretary of War Stanton dated February 13, 1862, ibid.

86. Dunham referred to his experiences in Richmond in several letters to editor Sidney Howard Gay intended for publication in the *New York Tribune*. It is a paradox inherent in clandestine operations that Dunham may have been recruited as a Confederate agent during this period. There is no proof of such a development, but the reader should keep the possibility in mind in judging subsequent events.

87. For example, Missemer transcribed clippings from the *Montreal Daily Transcript* and the *Montreal Gazette* of November 3, 1864, which describe Dunham's arrest. Missemer Notes.

88. Missemer quotes from the *Montreal Daily Witness* of February 15, 1865, which reported the trial. Ibid.

89. These papers are now in the Joseph Holt Collection, boxes 5 and 8, Huntington Library, Pasadena, California.

90. Poore, ed., *The Conspiracy Trial for the Murder of the President* 3:115–43.

91. Missemer notes; statement by Gen. William Henry Carroll, a retired Confederate general, as carried in the *New York Times*, July 10, 1865.

92. *New York Times*, July 10, 1865.

93. Ibid.

94. The material printed in the *Montreal Evening Telegraph* was reprinted in a broadside, a copy of which is in the Brown University Library Lincoln Collection, Providence, Rhode Island.

95. See, for example, William H. Carroll, *Proofs of the Falsity of Conover's Testimony before the Military Court at Washington City* (Montreal: M. Longmoore and Company, 1865).

96. An attempt to free the prisoners at Johnson's Island had failed in 1863 because too much leakage of information, probably from Copperheads, led to a Union protest to Canada that caused the Confederates to abandon the effort. See Tidwell, *Come Retribution*, 178–82.

97. The story of the escape from Camp Morton is in *A Thrilling Escape from Prison*, a small pamphlet written and privately printed by Tam Brooks of the 3d Confederate Cavalry Regiment, who took part in the escape. The pamphlet is in the possession of the author, who also heard Brooks tell the story. It was also reported in the *Indianapolis Daily Evening Gazette*, November 16 and 18, 1864, and in the *Indianapolis Daily Sentinel*, November 19, 1864.

98. E. G. Lee, Compiled Service Record, RG 109.

99. Sanders to the editor of the *New York Times*, February 27, 1865, printed on April 19, 1865; Sanders to Jefferson Davis, March 7, 1865, printed in *New York Herald*, July 8, 1865.

100. George Francis Train, *My Life in Many States and Foreign Lands* (New York: D. Appleton and Company, 1902). Train also published *Young America in Wall Street* and *Young America Abroad in Europe, Asia, and Australia* in 1857 and *Spread-eagleism* in 1859.

101. Thompson estimated that 60,000 Union troops had been diverted from the battlefield to guard against the Copperhead threat. Thompson to J. P. Benjamin, December 3, 1864, *OR*, ser. 1, vol. 43, 2:932.

Chapter 6: April '65

1. For personnel of the Torpedo Bureau, see entry 56, payroll 8734, box 38, RG 109.

2. Samuel G. Leitch, Compiled Service Record, RG 109.

3. William H. Snyder, ibid.

4. Rains to Secretary of War, March 27, 1865, *OR*, ser. 1, vol. 47, 3:704, 729.

5. Harney's mission is mentioned in the memoirs of several veterans of Mosby's regiment. The fullest account is in Williamson, *Mosby's Rangers*, 366–71.

6. John S. Mosby, *Mosby's War Reminiscences* (Boston: Geo. A. Jones and Company, 1887), 44.

7. Ibid.

8. Mosby, *Memoirs*, 230.

9. Mosby, *War Reminiscences*, 89.

10. Part of the signal line is described in the interrogation of a deserter from one of the stations on the line. The interrogation was dated February 4, 1865, and the deserter said that the line had been installed about two months earlier. *OR*, ser. 1, vol. 46, 2:385.

11. Charles T. O'Ferral, *Forty Years of Active Service* (New York: Neale Publishing Company, 1904) 129.

12. *OR*, ser. 1, vol. 46, 2:385.

13. Crawford, *Mosby and His Men*, 352.

14. On April 17, 1865, the 1st New York Mounted Rifles were at Jackson, North Carolina, over eighty miles south of Richmond. On April 22 they began to issue paroles at Ashland. Frederick Phisterer, *New York in the War of the Rebellion 1861 to 1865* (Albany: T. B. Lyon Company, 1912), 2:1112; 9th and 10th Virginia Cavalry Regiments, Compiled Service Records, RG 109.

15. While the Compiled Service Records in the National Archives show that paroles for Confederate soldiers were issued at Ashland on April 22, 1865, similar records show that paroles at places like Charlottesville, Louisa Court House, and Culpeper did not begin until late April or early May 1865.

16. *OR*, ser. 1, vol. 46, 3:1359. According to Michael P. Musick of the National Archives, this message was brought to the persons compiling the Official Records on February 2, 1888, in the form of a typescript by Mosby himself. It was the only record concerning the operations of Mosby's Rangers that Mosby brought in. One might suspect that Mosby was trying to influence the Muse of history by his contribution, since it fitted the conventional view of Mosby's role at the end of the war.

17. Williamson, *Mosby's Rangers*, 363; George Baylor, *Bull Run to Bull Run* (1900; reprint, Washington, D.C.: Zenger Publishing Company, 1983), 310–11.

18. Baylor, *Bull Run*, 311–16.

19. Edward Hastings Ripley, *Vermont General*, ed. Otto Eisenschiml (New York: Devin Adair Company, 1960), 306–8.

20. William H. Snyder statement, April 12, 1865, Union Provost Marshal File on Confederate Citizens (alphabetical), RG 109.

21. See Tidwell, *Come Retribution*, 418, for a longer quotation. The *Surratt Courier* of October 1988 carries a slightly garbled transcript of the entire document, "Unpublished

Atzerodt Confession Revealed Here for the First Time" (1–3). This statement was discovered a few years ago by a member of the Surratt Society of Clinton, Maryland, among the papers of William E. Doster, who had served as defense attorney for Atzerodt during the trial of Booth's associates in 1865. The statement is now in private hands.

22. Williamson, *Mosby's Rangers,* 493.

23. Crawford, *Mosby and His Men,* 344–45; Crist and Dix, eds., *The Papers of Jefferson Davis* 7:322.

24. In 1865 the Washington Monument had not been completed; the stump was only 156 feet high.

25. Quoted in Jane Chapman Whitt, *Elephants and Quaker Guns* (New York: Vantage Press, 1966), 36, 50.

26. Tidwell, *Come Retribution,* 83; Whitt, *Elephants and Quaker Guns,* 50.

27. Benjamin Franklin Cooling III and Walton H. Owen II, *Mr. Lincoln's Forts* (Shippensburg, Pa.: White Mane, 1988), 110; recollection of Rachel Lewis Keyes, 1956, mimeograph, W. T. Woodson Department of Education, "History of Fairfax County," Virginia Room, Fairfax County Library, Fairfax, Virginia.

28. Tidwell, *Come Retribution,* 316.

29. Baylor, *Bull Run,* 322–23.

30. Williamson, *Mosby's Rangers,* 373.

31. Baylor, *Bull Run,* 328.

32. Crawford, *Mosby and His Men,* 359.

33. Information on Booth's plans for the first three is firm; the only source for the fourth name is Flower, *Edwin McMasters Stanton,* 279.

34. Baylor, *Bull Run,* 324; Williamson, *Mosby's Rangers,* 486.

35. W. Gamble to Major-General Augur, April 11, 1865, *OR,* ser. 1, vol. 46, 3:715.

36. J. Barnes to Major-General Augur, April 15, 1865, ibid., 769.

37. J. H. Taylor to Major Waite, April 15, 1865, ibid., 773.

38. Application dated December 20, 1865, to the Adjutant General from seven men under Maryland provost marshal James L. McPhail for reward money for assisting in the "capture of assassin of the President of the United States." M-619, roll 458, frames 0161-0170, Letters Received by the A&IG Office, RG 109.

39. F. F. Buckley to Captain Willauer, April 16, 1865, *OR,* ser. 1, vol. 46, 3:801.

40. *New York Times,* October 22, 1863; Regina Coombs Hammett, *History of St. Mary's County* (Ridge, Md.: St. Mary's County Bicentennial Commission, 1977), 120, 128.

41. Hammett, *St. Mary's County,* 121; James H. Whyte, "The Activities of the Freedmen's Bureau in Southern Maryland 1865–1870," *Chronicles of St. Mary's* 7 (February 1959): 1–8.

42. Fitzgerald Ross, *Cities and Camps of the Confederate States,* ed. Richard Barksdale Harwell (Urbana: University of Illinois Press, 1958), 164–65. At the end of the war, Sothron went to Canada, but in 1866 he returned to St. Mary's County where he was indicted for the murder of Lieutenant White and tried and acquitted on grounds of justifiable homicide. Having been acquitted, Sothron promptly applied for restitution of the value of the produce and other property taken from The Plains during

its time in government hands. The case hung on until 1874, when it was finally denied. Book H, box 1312, RG 92, National Archives.

43. Captain Drew USA to Commodore Read USN, quoting telegram from E. M. Stanton, April 17, 1865, *ORN*, ser. 1, 5:555.

44. J. H. Taylor to Maj. J. Waite, April 12, 1865, *OR*, ser. 1, vol. 44, 3:818–19.

45. *Raleigh Standard*, April 24, 1865.

46. J. M. Waite to Bvt. Col. J. H. Taylor, April 20, 1865, *OR*, ser. 1, vol. 46, 3:870.

47. J. S. Barnes to Major-General Augur, April 20, 1865, ibid. 870; Augur to Barnes, April 20, 1865, ibid., 871.

48. John M. Waite to Bvt. Col. J. H. Taylor, April 23, 1865, ibid., 910–11.

49. Master List of Confederate Prisoners at Point Lookout, Maryland, M-598, reel 119, frame 0041, RG 109.

50. Francis Donohyon, Compiled Service Record, RG 109; 1st Virginia Reserves, ibid.

51. This information was assembled from Forty-third Battalion, Virginia Cavalry, Compiled Service Records, 109, and from the record book of the Union Provost Marshal's Office, Bowling Green (Caroline County), Virginia, in May 1865, M-598, reel 21, RG 109. Selected Records of the War Department Relating to Confederate Prisoners of War, May 1865–Nov. 1866, vol. 48, M-598, roll 21, RG 109.

52. Williamson, *Mosby's Rangers*, 375–76.

53. Robertson, ed., *Proceedings*, 24–25.

54. Cornelius Boyle, Compiled Service Record, RG 109.

55. Marsena Rudolph Patrick, *Inside Lincoln's Army*, ed. David S. Sparks (New York: Thomas Yoseloff, 1964), 496.

56. Williamson, *Mosby's Rangers*, 377–78.

57. Ibid., 378.

58. Aristides Monteiro, *War Reminiscences* (1890; reprint, Gaithersburg, Md.: Butternut Press, 1979), 204–7.

59. Williamson, *Mosby's Rangers*, 393–94.

60. Munson, *Reminiscences of a Mosby Guerrilla*, 271–73; Williamson, *Mosby's Rangers*, 397; Baylor, *Bull Run*, 341.

61. Walbrook D. Swank's *Courier for Lee & Jackson* (Shippensburg, Pa.: Burd Street Press, 1993) is the memoir of John Gill of Baltimore, who served as a courier for Gen. Fitzhugh Lee and happened to be in Mosby territory at the time Mosby dispersed his command.

62. William A. Tidwell, "Booth Crosses the Potomac: An Exercise in Historical Research," *Civil War History* 36 (December 1990): 325–33.

63. This episode is described in Tidwell, *Come Retribution*, 457–58.

64. *Richmond News Leader*, August 23, 1929.

65. W. D. Newbill, Compiled Service Record, RG 109.

66. Tidwell, *Come Retribution*, 480–89.

67. Bowie's presence at the Garrett place was recorded by F. A. Burr in the *Boston Herald*, December 11, 1881, based on an interview with William Garrett; Bowie's military record is in Compiled Service Record, RG 109; and his parole is confirmed in a record book of paroles issued at the Provost Marshal's Office, Bowling Green, Virginia, RG 109.

68. Notes including an article from the *Richmond News Leader,* May 16, 1929, Stanley Kimmel Papers, University of Tampa Library, Tampa, Florida; William B. Lightfoot, Compiled Service Record, RG 109.

69. 40th, 47th, and 55th Virginia Infantry Regiments; Forty-third Battalion, Virginia Cavalry, Compiled Service Records, RG 109.

70. Channing Smith, "The Last Time I Saw General Lee," *Confederate Veteran* 35 (September 1927): 327.

BIBLIOGRAPHY

Manuscripts and Collections

Allen Bowie Davis Papers. Manuscript. Maryland Historical Society, Baltimore.

Archives. U.S. Military Academy, West Point, New York.

Ault, William. "Eisenschiml's Question." Illinois Historical Library, Springfield.

Bowie File, Alumni Archives, Preston Library, Virginia Military Institute, Lexington.

Burt, Charlotte Coleman. "Coleman Lineage of Early America." Kentucky Historical Society, Frankfort.

Cameron, Stephen F. Manuscript Collection. Museum of the Confederacy, Richmond, Virginia.

Clay, Clement C. Manuscripts. William R. Perkins Library.

Cleary, William. Diary. University of Kentucky Library, Lexington.

Confederate States of America Secret Service Account Book. Chicago Historical Society, Chicago.

Davis, Jefferson. Papers, William R. Perkins Library, Duke University, Durham, North Carolina.

Hines, Thomas H. Papers. Manuscript Collection. University of Kentucky Library, Lexington.

Isaac Hammond Collection. Virginia State Library, Richmond.

Joseph Holt Collection. Huntington Library, Pasadena, California.

Keyes, Rachel Lewis. "History of Fairfax County." W. T. Woodson Department of Education, Virginia Room, Fairfax County Library, Fairfax, Virginia.

Kimmel, Stanley. Papers. University of Tampa Library, Tampa, Florida.

Letcher, John. Papers. Marshall Research Foundation. Virginia Military Institute, Lexington.

Lincoln Collection. Brown University Library. Providence, Rhode Island.

Mason, Charles T. Files. Manuscript Collection. Virginia Historical Society, Richmond.

Maury, Mathew Fontaine. Papers. Manuscript Collection. Library of Congress, Washington, D.C.

Military Order of the Loyal Legion of the United States (MOLLUS). U.S. Army Military History Institute, Carlisle Barracks, Pennsylvania.

Missemer, Joseph E. Notes. U.S. National Park Service Museum. Ford's Theater, Washington, D.C.

Pendleton, William N. Papers. Southern Historical Collection. University of North Carolina Library, Chapel Hill.

Register of Acts of the Confederate States of America. George Washington Flowers Memorial Collection. William R. Perkins Library, Duke University, Durham, North Carolina.

Robinson, Stuart. *The Infamous Perjuries of the "Bureau of Military Justice" Exposed.* Rare Book Collection. Library of Congress, Washington, D.C.

U.S. National Archives, Washington, D.C.

Venable, Charles V. Papers. Southern Historical Collection, University of North Carolina Library, Chapel Hill.

Winder, John H. Papers. Manuscript Department, University of North Carolina Library, Chapel Hill.

Books and Periodicals

Abzug, Robert H. "The Copperheads: Historical Approaches to Civil War Dissent in the Midwest." *Indiana Magazine of History* 66, 1 (1970): 40–55.

Armstrong, T. M. *The Biographical Encyclopedia of Kentucky.* Cincinnati: T. M. Armstrong, 1875.

Bakeless, John. *Spies of the Confederacy.* Philadelphia: Lippincott, 1970.

Baker, Lafayette C. *History of the United States Secret Service.* Philadelphia: L. C. Baker, 1867.

Balsinger, David, and Charles E. Sellier, Jr. *The Lincoln Conspiracy.* Los Angeles: Schick Sunn Classic Books, 1977.

Baylor, George. *Bull Run to Bull Run.* 1900. Washington, D.C.: Zenger Publishing Company, 1983.

Beymer, William Gilmore. *On Hazardous Service.* New York: Harper and Brothers, 1912.

Binkley, Robert C. *Realism and Nationalism, 1852–1871.* New York: Harper and Brothers, 1935.

Blakey, Arch Frederic. *General John H. Winder C.S.A.* Gainesville: University of Florida Press, 1990.

Boney, F. N. *John Letcher of Virginia.* Tuscaloosa: University of Alabama Press, 1966.

Carroll, William H. *Proofs of the Falsity of Conover's Testimony before the Military Court at Washington City.* Montreal: M. Longmoore and Company, 1865.

Chamlee, Roy Z., Jr. *Lincoln's Assassins.* Jefferson, N.C.: McFarland and Company, 1990.

Clark, Asia Booth. *The Unlocked Book.* New York: Arno Press, 1977.

Conrad, Thomas Nelson. *Confederate Spy*. New York: J. S. Ogilvie Publishing Company, 1892.

———. *Rebel Scout*. Washington, D.C.: National Publishing Company, 1904.

Cooling, Benjamin Franklin III, and Walton H. Owen II. *Mr. Lincoln's Forts*. Shippensburg, Pa.: White Mane, 1988.

Crawford, J. Marshall. *Mosby and His Men*. 1867. Gaithersburg, Md.: Olde Soldier Books, 1987.

Crist, Lynda Lasswell, and Mary Seaton Dix, eds. *The Papers of Jefferson Davis*. Vol. 5. Baton Rouge: Louisiana State University Press, 1985.

———. *The Papers of Jefferson Davis*. Vol. 7. Baton Rouge: Louisiana State University Press, 1992.

Currey, Cecil B. *Code Number 72*. Englewood Cliffs, N.J.: Prentice-Hall, 1972.

Durkin, Joseph T., S.J. *Confederate Navy Chief: Stephen R. Mallory*. Columbia: University of South Carolina Press, 1987.

Dvornik, Francis. *Origins of Intelligence Services*. New Brunswick: Rutgers University Press, 1974.

Eisenschiml, Otto. *Why Was Lincoln Murdered?* New York: Halcyon House, 1937.

———, ed. *Vermont General*. New York: The Devin-Adair Company, 1960.

Ettinger, Amos Aschback. *The Mission to Spain of Pierre Soule 1853–1855*. New Haven: Yale University Press, 1932.

Flower, Frank Abial. *Edwin McMasters Stanton*. 1905. New York: AMS Press, 1973.

Fremantle, James Arthur Lyon. *The Fremantle Diary*. Ed. Walter Lord. Boston: Little Brown and Company, 1954.

Gaddy, David Winfred. "John Williamson Palmer: Confederate Agent." *Maryland Historical Magazine* 83 (Summer 1988): 98–110.

Gentry, Mary Ann. *A History of Carroll County, Kentucky*. Madison, Ind.: Coleman Printing Company, 1984.

George, Joseph, Jr., "Black Flag Warfare: Lincoln and the Raids against Richmond and Jefferson Davis." *The Pennsylvania Magazine of History and Biography* 115 (July 1991): 291–318.

Greenhow, Rose O'Neal. *My Imprisonment and the First Year of Abolition Rule at Washington*. London: Richard Bentley, 1863.

Haines, Randall A. "The Revolutionist Charged with Complicity in Lincoln's Death." *Surratt Courier* 13 (September 1988): 5–8.

Hall, James O. "The Case of David E. George." *The Surratt Courier* 3 (March 1992): 3–5.

———. "The Dahlgren Papers." *Civil War Times Illustrated* (November 1983).

Hammett, Regina Coombs. *History of St. Mary's County*. Ridge, Md.: St. Mary's County Bicentennial Commission, 1977.

Hanchett, William. "The Historian as Gamesman: Otto Eisenschiml, 1880–1963." *Civil War History* 36 (March 1990): 5–16.

———. *The Lincoln Murder Conspiracies*. Urbana: University of Illinois Press, 1983.

———. "Lincoln's Murder: The Simple Conspiracy Theory." *Civil War Times Illustrated* 30 (November/December 1991): 28–35, 70–71.

Headley, John W. *Confederate Operations in Canada and New York*. 1906. New York: Time-Life Books, 1984.

Hudgins, Helen Hawes. *The Richard Hawes Family of Kentucky.* Franklin, Tenn.: Privately printed, 1986.

Jones, Thomas A. *J. Wilkes Booth* (Chicago: Laird and Lee, 1893).

Kahn, David. *The Code Breakers.* London: Weidenfeld and Nicolson, 1967.

Kimmel, Stanley. *The Mad Booths of Maryland.* New York: Dover, 1969.

Kinchen, Oscar A. *Confederate Operations in Canada and the North.* North Quincy, Mass.: Christopher Publishing House, 1970.

Klement, Frank L. *Dark Lanterns.* Baton Rouge: Louisiana State University Press, 1984.

Lee, Robert E. *The Wartime Papers of R. E. Lee.* Ed. Clifford Dowdey and Louis H. Manarin. New York: Bramahall House for the Virginia Civil War Commission, 1961.

Letcher, John. "Col. Richard Thomas Zarvona." *Confederate Veteran* 22 (September 1914): 418.

Levin, H. *The Lawyers and Lawmakers of Kentucky.* Chicago: Lewis Publishing Company, 1897.

Lewis, Meriwether. "The Military Orders of Daniel Ruggles: Department of Fredericksburg, April 22–June 5, 1861." *The Virginia Magazine of History and Biography* 69 (April 1961): 149–80.

Lomax, Elizabeth Lindsay. *Leaves from an Old Washington Diary.* New York: E. P. Dutton and Company, 1943.

Mackay's Montreal Directory for 1864–65. Montreal: John Lovell, 1864.

Mackey, Albert G. *Encyclopedia of Freemasonry.* Philadelphia: McClure Publishing Company, 1917.

Matthews, James M., ed. *Public Laws of the Confederate States of America Passed at First Session of Congress, 1863.* Richmond, 1863.

———. *Statutes at Large of the Provisional Government of the Confederate States of America.* Richmond, 1864.

Maury, Richard L. *A Brief Sketch of the Work of Mathew Fontaine Maury.* Richmond: Whittet and Shepperson, 1915.

Melton, H. Keith. *OSS Special Weapons and Equipment.* New York: Sterling, 1991.

Monroe, Haskell M., Jr., and James T. McIntosh, eds. *The Papers of Jefferson Davis.* Vol. 1. Baton Rouge: Louisiana State University Press, 1971.

Montague, Ludwell Lee. *Gloucester County in the Civil War.* Gloucester, Va.: DeHardit Press, 1965.

Monteiro, Aristides. *War Reminiscences.* 1890. Gaithersburg, Md.: Butternut Press, 1979.

Mosby, John S. *The Memoirs of Colonel John S. Mosby.* Ed. Charles Wells Russell. 1917. Millwood, N.Y.: Kraus, 1981.

Munson, John W. *Reminiscences of a Mosby Guerrilla.* 1906. Washington, D.C.: Zenger, 1983.

Neely, Mark, Jr., ed. "Treason in Indiana." *Lincoln Lore* no. 1632 (February 1974).

Nevins, Allan. *Ordeal of the Union.* New York: Charles Scribner's Sons, 1947.

———. *The War for the Union: The Organized War to Victory 1864–1865.* New York: Charles Scribner's Sons, 1971.

Norman, Bruce. *Secret Warfare.* New York: Sterling, 1989.

O'Ferral, Charles T. *Forty Years of Active Service.* New York: Neale Publishing Company, 1904.

Official Records of the Union and Confederate Navies in the War of the Rebellion. 30 vols. Washington, D.C.: Government Printing Office, 1894–1922.

Parker, Anna Virginia. *The Sanders Family of Grass Hills.* Madison, Ind.: Coleman Printing Company, 1966.

Patrick, Marsena Rudolph. *Inside Lincoln's Army.* Ed. David S. Sparks. New York: Thomas Yoseloff, 1964.

Phisterer, Frederick. *New York in the War of the Rebellion 1861 to 1865.* Albany: T. B. Lyon Company, 1912.

Pinkerton, Allan. *The Spy of the Rebellion.* New York: G. W. Carlton and Company, 1883.

Pitman, Ben. *The Trials for Treason at Indianapolis.* Cincinnati: Moore, Wilstach and Baldwin, 1865.

Plowden, Alison. *The Elizabethan Secret Service.* New York: St. Martin's Press, 1991.

Poore, Ben: Perley, ed. *The Conspiracy Trial for the Murder of the President.* 3 vols. 1865–66. New York: Arno Press, 1972.

Porter, Bernard. *Plots and Paranoia.* London: Unwin Hyman, 1989.

Potter, Jerry O. *The Sultana Tragedy.* Gretna, La.: Pelican, 1992.

Ramage, James S. *Rebel Raider, the Life of General John Hunt Morgan.* Lexington: University Press of Kentucky, 1986.

Ramsdell, Charles W., ed. *Laws and Joint Resolutions of the Last Session of the Confederate Congress (November 1864–March 18, 1865) Together With the Secret Acts of the Previous Congresses.* Durham, N.C.: Duke University Press, 1941.

Record of the Trial of John H. Surratt. 2 vols. Washington, D.C.: Government Printing Office, 1867.

Ripley, Edward Hastings. *Vermont General.* Ed. Otto Eisenschiml. New York: Devin Adair Company, 1960.

Robertson, Alexander F. *Alexander Hugh Holmes Stuart, 1807–1891.* Richmond: William Byrd Press, 1925.

Robertson, James I., ed. *Proceedings of the Advisory Council of the State of Virginia.* Richmond: Virginia State Library, 1977.

Robinson, William Morrison, Jr. *The Confederate Privateers.* 1928. Columbia: University of South Carolina Press, 1990.

Roman, Alfred. *The Military Operations of General Beauregard.* New York: Harper and Brothers, 1884.

Ross, Fitzgerald. *Cities and Camps of the Confederate States.* Ed. Richard Barksdale Harwell. Urbana: University of Illinois Press, 1958.

Ross, Ishbel. *Rebel Rose.* New York: Harper and Brothers, 1954.

R.O.T.C. Manual Cavalry, The. Washington, D.C.: National Service Publishing Company, 1933.

Scott, John. *Partisan Life With Col. John S. Mosby.* New York: Harper and Brothers, 1867.

Sharf, J. Thomas. *History of the Confederate States Navy.* 1887. Catasaugua, Pa.: The Fairfax Press, 1977.

Sharp, Arthur. "The Spirit of Christianity? Greek Fire." *Civil War Times Illustrated* 23 (September 1988): 32–37.

Silverstone, Paul H. *Warships of the Civil War Navies.* Annapolis: Naval Institute Press, 1989.

Smith, Channing. "The Last Time I Saw General Lee." *Confederate Veteran* 35 (September 1927): 327.

Smith, Mason Philip. *Confederates Downeast.* Portland, Maine: Provincial Press, 1985.

Southern Historical Society Papers. 51 vols. Richmond: Southern Historical Society, 1879.

St. Lawrence, F. A. *Testimony of Sandford Conover, Dr. J. B. Merritt, and Richard Montgomery.* Toronto: Lovell and Gibson, 1865.

Stuart, Meriwether. "Operation Sanders." *The Virginia Magazine of History and Biography* 81 (April 1973): 158–99.

Swank, Walbrook D. *Courier for Lee & Jackson.* Shippensburg, Pa.: Burd Street Press, 1993.

Testimony of Sandford Conover, Dr. J. B. Merritt, and Richard Montgomery, before Military Court at Washington. Toronto: Lovell and Gibson, 1865.

Thompson, Edmund R., ed. *Secret New England: Spies of the American Revolution.* Kennebunk, Maine: Association of Former Intelligence Officers, 1992.

Thornbrough, Emma Lou. *Indiana in the Civil War Era 1850–1880.* Indianapolis: Indiana Historical Bureau and Indiana Historical Society, 1965.

Tidwell, William A. "Booth Crosses the Potomac: An Exercise in Historical Research." *Civil War History* 36 (December 1990): 325–33.

Tidwell, William A., with James O. Hall and David Winfred Gaddy. *Come Retribution: The Confederate Secret Service and the Assassination of Lincoln.* Jackson: University Press of Mississippi, 1988.

Train, George Francis. *My Life in Many States and Foreign Lands.* New York: D. Appleton and Company, 1902.

Treadway, Gilbert R. *Democratic Opposition to the Lincoln Administration in Indiana.* Indianapolis: Indiana Historical Bureau, 1973.

Turner, Thomas R. *Beware the People Weeping: Public Opinion and the Assassination of President Lincoln.* Baton Rouge: Louisiana State University Press, 1982.

U.S. House of Representatives. *Committee on the Assassination of Lincoln, Report No. 104.* 39th Cong. July 1866.

Wallace, Lee A., Jr., *A Guide to Virginia Military Organizations 1861–1865.* Lynchburg, Tenn.: H. E. Howard, 1986.

War of the Rebellion, The: A Compilation of the Official Records of the Union and Confederate Armies. 128 vols. Washington, D.C.: Government Printing Office, 1880–1901.

Waters, W. Davis. "Deception in the Art of War: Gabriel Rains, Torpedo Specialist of the Confederacy." *The North Carolina Historical Review* 66 (January 1989): 25–60.

Weinert, Richard P., Jr. *The Confederate Regular Army.* Shippensburg, Pa.: White Mane, 1991.

Westin, Effie Ellsler, ed. *The Stage Memories of John A. Ellsler.* Cleveland: Rowfant Club, 1950.

Whitt, Jane Chapman. *Elephants and Quaker Guns.* New York: Vantage Press, 1966.

Whyte, James H. "The Activities of the Freedmen's Bureau in Southern Maryland 1865–1870." *Chronicles of St. Mary's* 7 (February 1959): 1–8.

Wideman, John C. *The Sinking of the USS Cairo.* Jackson: University Press of Mississippi, 1993.

Williamson, James J. *Mosby's Rangers.* 1898. New York: Time-Life Books, 1981.

Winks, Robin. *Canada and the United States: the Civil War Years.* 1960. New York: University Press of America, 1988.

Wriston, Henry Merritt. *Executive Agents in American Foreign Relations.* Gloucester, Mass.: Peter Smith, 1967.

Newspapers

Baltimore American
Boston Herald
Daily Express (Petersburg, Va.)
Indianapolis Daily Evening Gazette
Indianapolis Daily Sentinel
Montreal Daily Transcript
Montreal Daily Witness
Montreal Evening Telegraph
Montreal Gazette
New York Herald
New York Times
New York Tribune
Port Tobacco Times
Raleigh Standard
Richmond News Leader
Richmond Whig

INDEX

King George County (Va.), 71, 72, 73,
190, 229n
Kipling, Rudyard, 11
Knights of the Golden Circle, 116
Kossuth, Lajos, 122

Ladd, Dr., 20
Lake Erie, 141, 142
Land mines. See Torpedoes
Lawton, A. R., 185
Lay, George W., 42, 63, 185
Ledru-Rollin, Alexandre-Auguste, 122
Lee, Cassius F., 35, 125, 135
Lee, Edwin Grey, 18, 36, 94, 142, 156
Lee, Fitzhugh, 55, 241n
Lee, George Washington Custis:
commissioning of, 60; division under,
x, xi; father's correspondence with,
109; First Virginia Reserves and, 182;
in Washington, 59
Lee, Laura, 194
Lee, Robert E., 5, 59
—W. W. Bowie and, 69, 229n
—Boyle and, 185
—Cavalry Scouts and, 32, 54
—Grant-Sherman coordination and, xiii
—Mosby and: W. W. Bowie and, 75;
Conrad and, 70; Harney and, 169,
174; meeting of, 71, 72; J. E. B. Stuart
and, 165
—on Northern peace movement, 109–11,
115
—Rains and, 91–92
—relatives of, 35, 156
—J. Sanders and, 119
—on slave enlistment, 232n
—C. Smith and, 193–94
—spring 1865 strategy of, 7, 10
—surrender of: Baylor and, 174; The
Birth of a Nation on, 5; Burke Station
skirmish and, xii, 8; desertions prior
to, x; First Virginia Reserves and, 182;
47th Virginia Infantry Regiment and,
ix; Greenhow Group and, 75;
Johnston and, 168; Lincoln
assassination and, 1, 3, 11, 196; Mosby
troops and, 177, 184, 187; Secret Line
and, 42; Sultana sinking and, 52;

Virginia Confederates and, 191
—Virginia advisory council and, 80–81
—Washington communication lines
and, 76
Leitch, Samuel G., 161, 170, 171
Letcher, John: advisory council of, 79–81;
W. S. Barton and, 97; officers assem-
bled by, 53, 60; D. Ruggles and, 228n;
Thomas and, viii–ix, 87, 88
Letters of Marque and Reprisal, 83, 84,
85, 90–91, 231n
Libby Prison, 47
Library of Congress, 15–16, 21, 22
Lightfoot, William B., 192
Lightfoot's Battalion, 191, 192
Lincoln, Abraham: assassination of (See
under Booth, John Wilkes); Beall and,
146; Benjamin and, 28; Confederate
government policy on, 11; Dahlgren
affair and, 224n; election of, 107, 116,
123, 154–55; in group portrait, 10;
Niagara conference and, 135; political
rationale of, 77; Sanders and, 133;
Snyder and, 170–71
Lincoln administration. See Union
government
Lincoln family, 111
The Lincoln Murder Conspiracies
(Hanchett), 6–7
Liverpool Police, 122
Liverpool U.S. consul, 125, 158
Lomax, Lunsford L., 59, 60
London, 121, 122, 123, 124
Long (blockade runner), 72
Longstreet, James, 44, 91, 167
Longuemare, Emile, 37, 112, 132
Loudoun County, 74, 176
Loudoun Rangers, 170
Louisiana, 103, 104
Louisiana 3d Native Guards Regiment,
146
"Louis Napoleon" (i.e., J. Thompson), 35
Louis Napoleon (Napoleon III), 122–23
Lowden, Robert, 52
Luray, 69

McClellan, George B., 91, 141
McCulloch, Richard G., 36, 106